GENERALIZED EXPECTED UTILITY THEORY
THE RANK-DEPENDENT MODEL

GENERALIZED EXPECTED UTILITY THEORY

THE RANK-DEPENDENT MODEL

John Quiggin

Australian National University

KLUWER ACADEMIC PUBLISHERS

Boston/Dordrecht/London

Distributors for North America:
Kluwer Academic Publishers
101 Philip Drive
Assinippi Park
Norwell, Massachusetts 02061 USA

Distributors for all other countries:
Kluwer Academic Publishers Group
Distribution Centre
Post Office Box 322
3300 AH Dordrecht, THE NETHERLANDS

Library of Congress Cataloging-in-Publication Data

Quiggin, John.
Generalized expected utility theory : the rank-dependent model / John Quiggin.
p. cm.
Includes bibliographical references and index.
ISBN 0-7923-9302-3
1. Utility theory--Mathematical models. I. Title.
HB201.Q54 1993
658.4'03--dc20 92-36826
CIP

Printed on acid-free paper.

Printed in the United States of America

To Nancy

CONTENTS

PART 1

THE EXPECTED UTILITY MODEL

PART 2

THE RANK-DEPENDENT MODEL

PART 3

FURTHER PROPERTIES OF THE MODEL

PART 4

GENERALIZED EXPECTED UTILITY THEORY

Preface

Since the publication of von Neumann and Morgenstern's classic *Theory of Games and Economic Behavior* in 1944, economic analysis of choice under uncertainty has been dominated by the expected utility (EU) model. The EU model has been one of the great success stories of modern economic analysis. A wide range of phenomena that previously lay outside the domain of formal economic analysis have been successful modelled. The EU framework has been a fruitful source of new concepts and methods of analysis. Most importantly, the EU model permits the application of standard methods of comparative statics and dynamics to the analysis of choice under uncertainty.

Yet the EU model has never been without its critics. Psychologists such as Edwards and Ellsberg accumulated evidence that individual choices under uncertainty were inconsistent with the predictions of the EU model. Applied work in areas such as finance was dominated by the simpler, and apparently more tractable, mean-variance analysis popularized by Markowitz.

The most fundamental criticisms were made in the early 1950s by Allais, who focused attention on the EU independence axiom. Allais proposed a striking counterexample, the so-called 'Allais paradox', which induced even staunch advocates of EU, such as Savage, to make choices inconsistent with the independence axiom. Despite this apparent refutation of EU predictions, Allais' criticisms were not taken very seriously.

A revival of interest in these issues among economists began in the late 1970s with the publication of a number of papers presenting models based on the idea of probability weighting. The most influential was the prospect theory of Kahneman and Tversky, which permitted the analysis of behavior inconsistent with EU theory, at the price of introducing violations of dominance. Other models presented around the same time by Handa and Karmarkar also involved violations of dominance, leading to some scepticism as to the possibility of developing any normatively appealing alternative to EU.

In the 1980s, this scepticism was dispelled. A number of generalizations of EU were proposed, most of which were capable of explaining the Allais 'paradox' and other evidence inconsistent with EU, while preserving transitivity and dominance. Along with numerous specific models came the highly influential work of Machina who showed that preference functionals inconsistent with the independent axioms could be modelled in terms of local utility functions and that properties of the local utility functions such as monotonicity and risk-aversion carried over to the global preference functional.

Generalized expected utility analysis is now a flourishing sub-field of economics, with a large and active research community and the usual appurtenances, such as a biennial conference (the Foundations of Utility Research conference) and a specialist journal (the *Journal of Risk and Uncertainty*). There are now dozens of competing models and a considerable literature exploring their theoretical properties and comparing their empirical performance.

Outside this community, however, the new ideas have had only a limited impact. The EU model remains the principal tool for the analysis of choice under uncertainty. There is a widespread view that generalized models are too difficult to handle or incapable of generating sharp results. There is, then, a need to show that the new models can be used in the kinds of economic analysis for which EU has proved so powerful, and that they can yield new and interesting results.

This book is an attempt to meet this need by describing one of the most popular of the generalized models - the rank-dependent expected utility model (RDEU), also known as anticipated utility (AU), expected utility with rank-dependent preferences (EURDP), the

$\mu-\theta$ model, the dual theory of choice under uncertainty and simply as rank-dependent utility (RDU). As the profusion of names indicates, the model has been approached in many different ways by many different authors. For this reason, consideration of a single model throws light on many of the concerns that have motivated the development of generalized expect utility theories.

The popularity of the RDEU model rests on its simplicity and tractability. The model has a simple symmetrical representation in which outcomes are transformed by a von Neumann-Morgenstern utility function and (cumulative) probabilities are transformed by a weighting function. This makes it easy to derive specific functional forms. The fact that the utility function is essentially the same as that of EU theory means that ideas developed in the EU context, such as coefficients of absolute and relative risk aversion, have a direct interpretation in the RDEU framework.

The standard tools of analysis developed for EU theory may be applied, with only minor modifications, to the RDEU model. However, because RDEU admits behavior inconsistent with EU, such as simultaneous gambling and insurance, the field of potential applications is widened. The RDEU model is not so much a competitor to EU as an extension based on less restrictive assumptions.

In order to reach as wide an audience as possible, I have attempted to present the key ideas using only simple mathematical tools, at the expense of rigor and elegance if necessary. In particular, most of the main results can be understood purely in terms of discrete probability distributions.

This book draws on the work of a great many of my colleagues, too many to name individually. However, the inspiration provided by the work of Maurice Allais cannot go unmentioned. Mark Machina gave me the encouragement to persevere at a time when my efforts in this field seemed entirely fruitless. Zachary Rolnik encouraged me to write this book, and has been a supportive editor. Jock Anderson, Uzi Segal and Peter Wakker read earlier drafts of the book, and forced me to undertake the major revisions that were necessary. Without their helpful and critical comments, this would have been a far less satisfactory work. Shirley Halton read the proofs and detected numerous errors.

For all remaining errors, logical and typographical, I am entirely responsible. This book was produced and set in camera-ready form, using an Apple Macintosh IIci with Nisus word processing software and Aldus Freehand graphics.

PART 1

THE EXPECTED UTILITY MODEL

Introduction

For most of the post-war period, the economic theory of choice under uncertainty has been, in essence, the theory of expected utility. The literature on the expected utility (EU) model is vast, certainly too large to summarize here. The object of this part of the book is to set the stage for a consideration of some generalizations of EU. Chapter 1 is a general discussion of the problem of choice under uncertainty. Chapter 2 contains some background information, and presentation of the main notational conventions used in the book. Chapter 3 is a summary of those features of the EU model that are necessary to an understanding of the generalized models discussed below. The main topics are

- The axiomatic basis of EU theory
- The notion of risk aversion and comparisons of risk aversion
- The concept of stochastic dominance
- Application to economic problems involving comparative statics

In Chapter 4, the early challenges to the EU scientific research program are discussed. First, some of the evidence produced by critics of EU, notably Allais (1953), is described, along with unresolved problems in the literature, such as the Friedman–Savage (1948) problem of participation in lotteries. Then, some attempts at the development of alternative theories are described. These models foundered on the problem of stochastic dominance violations. The accumulation of evidence inconsistent with EU, combined with the fact that models designed to accommodate this evidence implied such normatively unappealing behavior as intransitivity and stochastic dominance violations, defined the central problem for the development of generalized expected utility theories.

CHAPTER 1

Uncertainty

Uncertainty pervades all aspects of life. We cannot predict the behavior of Nature, most notoriously the weather, with any certainty. From daily decisions about what clothes to wear, to critical economic decisions about savings, investment and production, this uncertainty affects us all. Probably a more important source of uncertainty is found in the unpredictable actions of other people. Not only are we confronted directly with the unpredictable behavior of other individuals, but our lives are affected by seemingly impersonal fluctuations in the behavior of markets and governments, which may ultimately be traced to the unpredictability of individual behavior. Finally, we often create our own uncertainty in games of chance, and enhance its importance by gambling for small or large stakes. Because the structure of these games is comparatively simple, games of chance have played an important rôle in the development of theories of choice under uncertainty.

1.1 The Nature of Uncertainty

Where does uncertainty come from? According to quantum mechanics, uncertainty may be inherent in Nature. Concepts of determinism, powerfully bolstered in the 18th and 19th centuries by the Newtonian model of a 'clockwork' universe, have been undermined by the discoveries of modern particle physics. In the view of theorists such as Heisenberg (1930), events at the subatomic level are fundamentally uncertain (the dissenting view, attributed to Einstein, is that "God does not play dice"). Despite the profound philosophical implications of the Heisenberg Uncertainty Principle, statistical mechanics provides a straightforward reconciliation with Newtonian determinism at the macroscopic level of everyday life. Thanks to the Law of Large Numbers, it is 'almost' certain that the average behavior of the huge number of particles making up say, an engine, will be that predicted by Newtonian mechanics.

These modern discoveries have cast doubt on the confident assertion that human behavior can ultimately be reduced to the deterministic product of chemical and physical processes. Nevertheless, there does not seem to be anything in quantum theory that precludes the development of models of human behavior as accurate as those that have been developed for, say, the orbits of the planets.

The debate over the uncertainty of human action, cast in the philosophical terms of free will and determinism, is far older than modern atomic physics. One side of this debate holds that determinism is inconsistent with human freedom of action and that the world must therefore be pervaded by uncertainty in a fundamental sense. An important modern representative of this viewpoint is Koestler (1965). At the other extreme are those, such as Skinner (1971), who see no problem in exorcising consciousness altogether from science. An intermediate viewpoint suggests that behavior may be causally determined without ceasing to be freely chosen. This viewpoint is more comfortable for practitioners of an economic mode of reasoning involving attempts to predict human behavior while stressing the notion of choice.

For economists, however, the fundamental source of uncertainty must be sought not in physical or philosophical concepts, but in human ignorance. Uncertainty relating to events that are clearly determinate (is there a pool of oil underneath this well?) can be just as important as that relating to events that may be uncertain in some fundamental sense (will the government decide to raise taxes?). In many important cases of uncertainty, some participants in a given economic setting may be uncertain with respect to a given variable, although others are fully informed. Uncertainty is a subjective state of mind rather than an objective property of the world.

To deal with uncertainty, it is necessary to examine the ways in which people collect, process and use information in decision-making. This task may be commenced by considering a number of different aspects of the phenomenon of uncertainty.

Uncertainty is essentially subjective in nature. However, it has an objective counterpart in the form of variability in the values taken by a particular variable over time and space. To the extent that uncertainty can be modelled in terms of random drawings from a population, instability or variability is a necessary condition for the existence of uncertainty. Variability is not, however, a sufficient condition for the existence of uncertainty regarding that variable in the minds of decision-makers. Take, as an example, the number of Easter eggs sold in March of a given year. This varies sharply from year to year, but the variation is largely determined by the date on which Easter falls. Thus, the value for, say, 1995, may be predicted quite well.

The concept of variability refers to the objectively observed distribution of a variable over time or perhaps space. By contrast, the term *risk* will be used to refer to subjective beliefs held by particular decision-makers concerning particular events, including individual realizations of a given random variable. It is necessary to distinguish between decisions that must be made without knowing what realization a given random variable will take and those that are made with this knowledge. People making decisions of the first type are subject to risk (as well as variability) while those making decisions of the second type are subject to variability only. Risk, rather than variability *per se*, is the major economic problem associated with uncertainty.

There is an older tradition dating back to Knight (1921), in which the term 'risk' is used for choice situations where probabilities are known, and the term 'uncertainty' is confined to situations where even probabilities are unknown. This terminology will not be followed here, Decisions under risk may be made with or without objective information on probabilities. The term *ambiguity* will be used for situations where probabilities are unknown and *uncertainty* will be used as a general term to cover risk, instability and ambiguity.

1.2 Descriptive and Normative Models

Theories of choice under uncertainty may be broadly categorized as normative and descriptive. Normative theories are not derived from any fundamental theory stating which choices are desirable or undesirable. They are merely based on the notion that preferences should in some sense be consistent across different choice problems. The simplest example of a consistency requirement which is generally (though not universally) conceded to have normative appeal is transitivity. If A is preferred to B in a pairwise choice, and B is preferred to C, A should be preferred to C. Further, given a choice from the three-object set $\{A, B, C\}$, A should be selected. Note that the requirement of transitivity says nothing about the inherent properties of the objects A, B and C or about whether it is reasonable to prefer A to B and B to C.

Normative models are typically presented in an axiomatic form. The axioms in these presentations are not merely postulates, but are intended as obviously reasonable consistency requirements. The most prominent normative theory of choice under uncertainty is the *expected utility* (EU) theory of von Neumann and Morgenstern (1944). The numerous competing normative and descriptive theories which have arisen over the years are usually defined in relation to EU theory. The dominant position of EU theory partly accounts for the central role played by axiomatic systems in the theory of choice under uncertainty, even for models which are primarily descriptive in nature.

Descriptive models are motivated by the desire to give an account of observed behavior, whether or not this is consistent with canons of rationality. Since it is difficult to isolate choices over uncertain prospects from observed market behavior, the empirical evidence on which descriptive models are based is usually derived from experiments or questionnaires. Introspection is also important as a source of evidence on preferences and particularly as a way of testing the descriptive validity of normative axioms. If I can be convinced that, in a particular problem setting, I would not follow a given normative rule, then I will not wish to propose that rule as part of a descriptive model, at least not for the problem setting in question.

The distinction between normative and descriptive models is not as clear-cut as it sometimes seems, however. For example, the need for EU theory arose because the obvious normative theory, that which prescribes maximization of *expected value* (EV) of wealth, did not appear to provide an adequate description of observed behavior (for example, people's willingness to purchase insurance), and was open to counter-arguments based on introspection (such as the St. Petersburg paradox). It is possible to mount a normative defence of EV maximization, based on the idea that EV-maximizers must eventually grow wealthy at the expense of those with more risk averse preferences. Also, EU theory admits preference patterns which could be rejected on normative grounds — for example, those displaying global risk preference. Although global risk preference may be consistent with the EU axioms, it implies (in the EU model) increasing marginal utility of consumption, and is thus inconsistent with the basic assumptions of neoclassical value theory.

On the other hand, no theory of rational choice is purely descriptive, since a theory which encompassed all observed behavior would deprive the notion of rational choice of any content. It is necessary to treat at least some observed behavior as arising from mistakes or from inappropriate representations of the choice problem. Decisions about which behavior to encompass within a model of rational choice and which to classify as experimental error must be made on grounds which are, in some sense, normative.

The models discussed in this book are primarily, but not exclusively, descriptive. The object is to account for observed behavior inconsistent with EU theory, while maintaining, as far as possible, the attractive consistency properties of that theory.

1.3 Scientific Research Programs

Expected utility theory fits neatly into Lakatos' (1970) concept of *scientific research programs.* Lakatos argues that theories must be assessed in terms of a scientific research program consisting of a *hard core* of maintained hypotheses that are not susceptible to refutation within the framework, and a *protective belt* of testable hypotheses that are adjusted in the light of new empirical evidence. Research programs are characterized by a negative heuristic that excludes hypotheses inconsistent with the core, and by a (less clearly articulated) positive heuristic that suggests the type of work that should be done to generate and test refutable hypotheses. Lakatos distinguishes between progressive and degenerating research programs. In the former, the empirical content of the theory tends to increase over time and refutations of individual predictions are met with problem shifts that yield unexpected and novel predictions. In the latter, reaction to evidence consists largely of *ad hoc* auxiliary theories that serve as immunizing strategies, protecting the theory from any possibility of refutation. However, a research program, even a degenerating one, will not be abandoned unless there is a competing research program in the field that appears to offer better prospects for progress.

For followers of the EU approach, the hard core consists of the concepts of rationality embodied in the EU axioms, with the possible addition of the postulate of risk aversion, and the negative heuristic consists of a rejection of approaches inconsistent with these concepts. The protective belt consists of hypotheses such as that of declining absolute risk aversion and empirical theories relating to such phenomena as insurance and portfolio choice. The positive heuristic involves such ideas as 'examine situations for which there is an established economic theory of behavior under certainty and see how far these results carry over to the case of uncertainty' and 'seek conditions on utility functions and probability distributions under which sharp behavioral predictions can be made.'

CHAPTER 2

Background

The object of this chapter is to present a brief history of the expected utility model, an informal outline of its basic ideas and a summary of the early debate over the independence axiom.

2.1 EU Theory — History

The EU theory of choice under uncertainty may be traced back to Bernoulli (1738, 1954). Bernoulli was the first writer to challenge the appropriateness of profit maximization as a basis for economic decisions under uncertainty. He argued (p. 24) that

> the determination of the value of an item must not be based on its price, but rather on the utility (*emolumentum*) it yields. Given a choice between a prospect yielding 20000 ducats with probability 1/2 and nothing otherwise, and one yielding 9000 ducats with certainty, a poor man would be well advised to choose the latter and a rich man the former.

In modern terms, this suggests a theory of positive but declining absolute risk aversion. Bernoulli made this more precise by asserting that "the utility resulting from any small increase in wealth will be inversely proportional to the quantity of goods previously possessed." On the basis of this assumption (implying, in modern terms, constant relative risk aversion), he derived a logarithmic utility function, illustrated its property of declining absolute risk aversion, and pointed out the advantages of diversification for a risk averse individual.

The main theoretical development in the 19th century was the adoption of explicit concepts of utility, first by Bentham and the 'Philosophic Radicals' and then by the mainstream classical and neoclassical economists. With the development of marginal utility analysis by Jevons and others, the concept of utility became indispensable to economists. Moreover, the 19th Century economists did not display any doubts about the real existence of utilities. They employed a *cardinal utility* theory in which differences in utility were comparable between individuals. The argument that, because of declining marginal utility of wealth, egalitarian income redistribution was welfare-increasing, had a considerable impact. Since such redistributive measures ran counter to the generally *laissez-faire* tenor of neoclassical economics, utility theory was regarded as something of a mixed blessing by the economics profession.

A resolution of this problem was offered by Robbins (1938) who claimed that interpersonal utility comparisons were unscientific and should be avoided[1]. This declaration was followed

[1] Robbins was not the first to criticize traditional utilitarianism in this way. Pareto's welfare theory was similarly motivated. However, Robbins' critique had more direct impact.

by a surge of interest in revealed preference theory, a means by which the troublesome concept of utility could be exorcized altogether. Although concepts of ordinal utility might still be used for convenience, the dangerous ground of cardinal utility would be strictly avoided.

Ironically, just as this approach achieved its greatest success with Samuelson's (1947) recasting of welfare economics in terms of revealed preference, the concept of cardinal utility theory was revived by von Neumann and Morgenstern in their analysis of behavior under risk, and its application to game theory. The development of Expected Utility theory by von Neumann and Morgenstern (1944) provided the basis for most subsequent analysis of economic behavior under uncertainty. The idea, as with Bernoulli, is that individuals should maximize the expectation of utility, which is a cardinal function of outcomes, normally assumed to be levels of wealth or income.

The relationship between cardinal utility and interpersonal comparisons has not been resolved. Nevertheless, the formal similarities between analysis of choice under risk, and of distribution of income across individuals, along with the almost universal assumptions of risk aversion (or, equivalently, decreasing marginal utility of wealth) cast doubt on the assertion that interpersonal comparisons of welfare must remain outside the scope of positive economics. (See Chapter 14 for further discussion of this point).

The EU approach initially faced strong competition from mean–variance analysis, exemplified by the work of Markowitz (1959) on portfolio analysis, but the logical foundations of this approach were far more dubious than those of expected utility theory. Practitioners of the mean–variance approach generally argued that, although expected utility analysis might be theoretically superior, it was of little practical use, since its formulation was so general as to prevent the derivation of sharp results. For example, Tobin (1969, p. 14) responded to the criticisms of mean–variance theory by Borch (1969) and Feldstein (1969), saying

> The [mean–variance approach] was never advertised as a complete job or the final word and I think that its critics in 1968 owe us more than demonstrations that it rests on restrictive assumptions. They need to show us how a more general and less vulnerable approach will yield the kind of comparative static results economists are interested in. This need is satisfied neither by the elegant but nearly empty existence theorems of state preference theory nor by normative prescriptions to the individual that he should consult his utility and his subjective probabilities and then maximize.

EU theorists countered with the argument that mean–variance analysis implied either that all random variables were normally distributed or that the utility function was quadratic. Given the bizarre properties of the quadratic utility function (for example, the coefficient of absolute risk aversion is everywhere increasing and marginal utility must be negative for sufficiently large wealth) and the obvious non-normality of many random variables, neither of these alternatives seemed attractive. It should be noted that these conditions only apply to mean–variance preferences that can be represented in terms of an EU preference functional. A much wider range of mean–variance preferences are consistent with the more general preference functionals described below.

This debate may be viewed, in the terminology of Lakatos (1970), as a competition between alternative scientific research programs. The resolution of the debate did not depend on critical experiments that supported the predictions of one theory and refuted those of the alternative. Rather, the crucial fact was that EU theory was a more progressive program in that it yielded new and unexpected predictions that were broadly consistent with observed data.

2.2 EU Theory — An Informal Discussion

In addition to presenting the EU function, von Neumann and Morgenstern developed an axiomatic basis for EU theory. The axioms of Expected Utility theory have been formulated in several different ways (see Fishburn 1982). However, in one form or another, the crucial axiom is the *independence axiom*. This axiom was implicit in the presentation of EU by von Neumann and Morgenstern, but its central rôle was soon recognized.

The independence axiom has been reformulated in a number of ways, most notably in Savage's (1954) *sure thing principle*. Savage argues that acceptance of the independence axiom may be justified on the same grounds as acceptance of the dominance axiom, that is, that in some sense a preferred outcome is a 'sure thing.' His argument runs as follows:

Suppose that we are considering two actions A and B and that these will have the same outcome if event E occurs, but will yield different outcomes when event E does not occur. Suppose that A is preferred to B. Now consider two acts, A' and B' such that

- A' yields the same outcome as A provided event E does not occur
- B' yields the same outcome as B provided event E does not occur
- B' and B yield the same outcome whenever E occurs.

Savage argues that, given the preference for A over B, we should also prefer A' over B'.

This argument has been criticized by many writers beginning with Allais (1953). The 'sure thing' formulation of the independence axiom depends on the choice of a particular arrangement of the possible outcomes and no obvious justification for this arrangement is given. These arguments are discussed in detail in Chapter 13.

A second, more intuitive criticism, may be developed as follows. The independence axiom implies a strict separation between the evaluation of different future states, which is rational enough in terms of an Arrow-Debreu style view of the world, but which is uncongenial to a less reductionist approach to life. This separation acts to eliminate human phenomena such as hope, fear and regret. For example, in evaluating a segment of a compound lottery in which one prize is a trip to Paris, the independence axiom forbids us to consider whether this is our only chance; that is, whether there exists another second stage lottery with prizes that would enable us to make the trip. However, many people might not wish to give up their only chance of visiting Paris (with a probability of, say, 1 per cent) in return for a given cash amount even if they would be willing to accept the same amount in return for reducing their chance from 10 per cent to 9 per cent.

Criticisms of this kind were made from the early days of utility theory. However, criticism of the axiomatic foundations of a theory is rarely very effective unless an alternative is offered. As has been observed by Lakatos (1970), a scientific research program will not be abandoned unless there is a competing program available. Since the logical foundations of mean–variance theory are far less defensible than EU theory (indeed, except for the case when mean–variance is a special case of EU, no axiomatic foundation has been proposed), mean–variance could not be a successful competitor.

2.3 Notation — The Discrete Case

The resolution of the debate between EU and mean–variance theorists was not due to a preference for theoretical elegance over practical usefulness, but rather to a gradual realization that EU theory was a more powerful basis for economic analysis than the mean–variance approach. This realization depended, to a large extent on the development of analytical tools within the EU framework that permitted the derivation of sharper, and more accurate, results than those available from the mean–variance approach. To describe these tools, it is necessary to develop some formal notation.

Theories of choice under uncertainty deal with individual preferences over a set $\mathcal{X}$ of *outcomes* and an associated set, $\mathcal{Y}$, of random variables, or *prospects*, taking values in $\mathcal{X}$. Elements of $\mathcal{Y}$ are denoted y, and elements of $\mathcal{X}$ are denoted x. In most of what follows, $\mathcal{X}$ will be assumed to be an interval of the form $[0, M]$, which may be interpreted in terms of income or wealth levels. The models presented here may also be applied to the case when $\mathcal{X}$ is a vector space and its elements are consumption bundles, but little new insight is gained from this increased generality. The outcome space is totally ordered by a preference relation, denoted by $\geq$. The associated indifference relation is denoted by $\approx$.

Discrete random variables will be represented in the form

$$\{\boldsymbol{x};\boldsymbol{p}\} = \{(x_1, x_2, \ldots x_n);(p_1, p_2, \ldots p_n)\}, \tag{2.1}$$

where p_i is the probability of outcome x_i, $\sum_{i=1}^{n} p_i = 1$, and the x_i (not necessarily distinct) are weakly ordered from worst to best, so that $x_1 \leq \ldots \leq x_n$. The elements of the outcome space $\mathcal{X}$ may themselves be regarded as prospects of the form $\{(x);(1)\}$, denoted more succinctly by δ_x and referred to as *degenerate* random variables. The *cumulative probability* of x, denoted $F(x)$, is given by $\Pr\{y \leq x\} = \sum_{x_i \leq x} p_i$.

In the case when $\mathcal{X} \subseteq \mathfrak{R}$, the *expectation* of $y = \{\boldsymbol{x};\boldsymbol{p}\}$ is denoted $\mathrm{E}[y]$, and is given by $\sum_{i=1}^{n} p_i x_i$. The notion of an expectation, or average, is, perhaps, the only statistical idea which has become part of the standard mental equipment of our society, and the best understood formal decision procedure under uncertainty is that of maximizing expected value. Most of the decision theories to be considered here are based on the notion of maximizing some modified expectation. Because of this, it is useful to examine the notion of an expectation more closely.

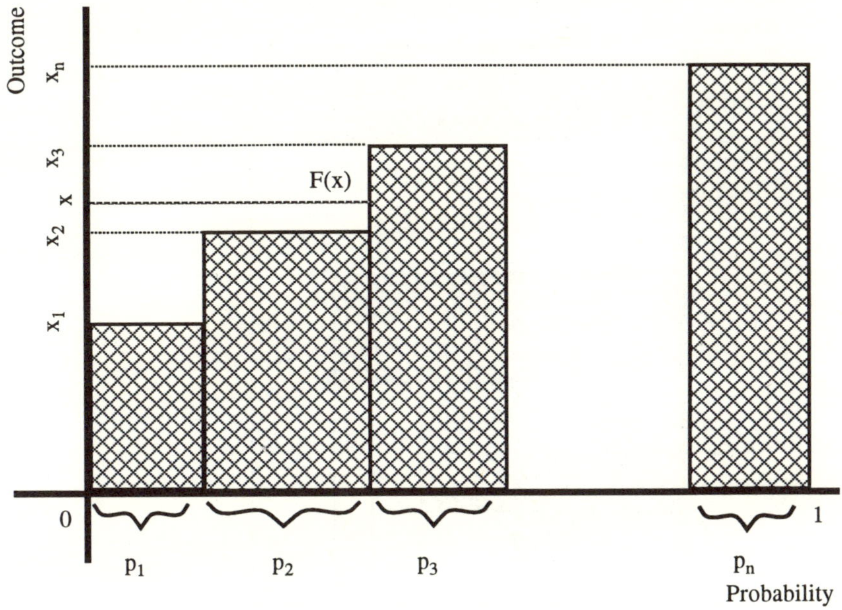

Figure 2.1: Representation of expected value

Two representations of the expectation are given in Figures 2.1 and 2.2. The first, given in Figure 2.1, corresponds to the standard representation of a random variable. The horizontal axis, ranging from zero to one, gives the probability of each event, the vertical axis gives the outcome for that event, and the shaded rectangle represents the contribution to expected value. The expectation is obtained by summing the rectangles and is the area under the graph of the step function in Figure 2.1.

The second representation, given in Figure 2.2, corresponds to the cumulative distribution function. Here the horizontal axis is the outcome space. For any element x, the distance from the horizontal axis to the shaded area is given by the cumulative probability $F(x)$. Each of the rectangles is simply a rotation of the corresponding rectangle in Figure 2.1. The expectation is now the area to the left of the step function representing the cumulative probability $F(x)$.

The expected utility model involves a modification of the expected value criterion, as represented in Figure 2.1, in which the monetary values are transformed into utilities (Figure 2.3). The rank-dependent model, to be considered below, may be regarded as involving a similar transformation applied to the representation in Figure 2.2.

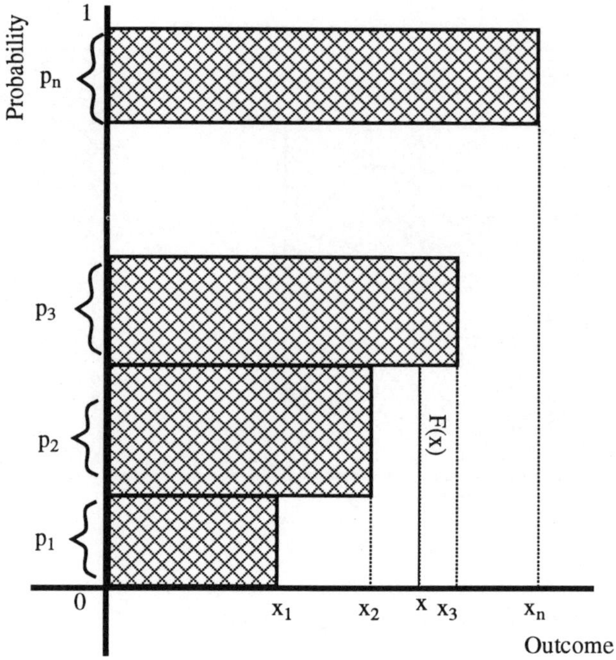

Figure 2.2: Alternative representation of expected value

Particular attention will be paid to the case when $p_i = 1/n$, $i = 1 \ldots n$. Because the x_i are not required to be distinct, most problems of interest can be expressed in this form. If n is allowed to take large values, say 100 or 1000, this formulation is sufficient to capture all the probability information we are likely to have on any practical problem. In this case, the expectation is simply given by $E[y] = (1/n) \sum_{i=1}^{n} x_i$.

For a number of models of choice under uncertainty, the distinction between discrete and continuous state spaces is crucial. The most important of these is the Prospect Theory of Kahneman and Tversky (1979). The probability weighting approach used by Kahneman and Tversky can only be defined if the set of states is finite. The possibility of extension from the discrete to the continuous case provides a test of whether a theory gives a normatively appealing account of choice under uncertainty. If a model cannot be applied to continuous probability distributions, it is unlikely to give a sensible account of problems involving a large number of low probability events.

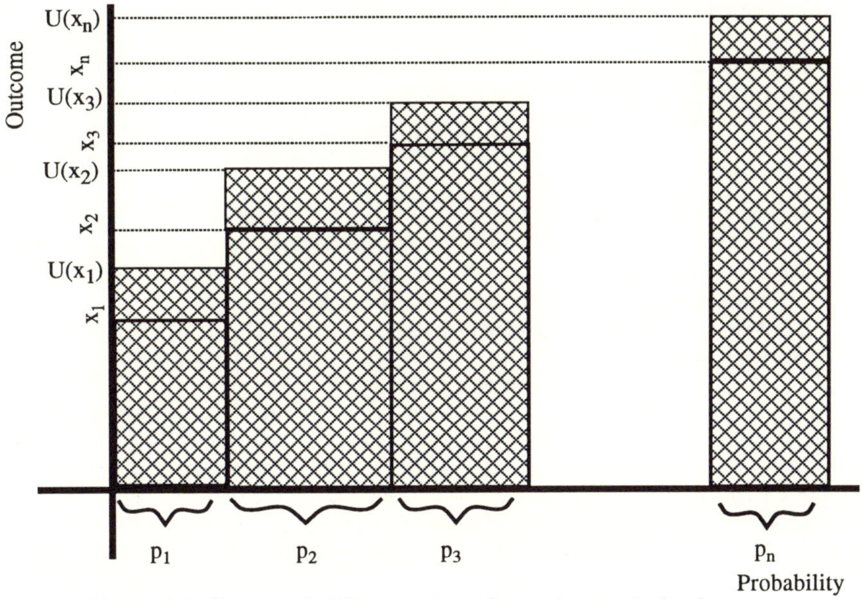

Figure 2.3: Expected utility as a transformed expected value

2.4 Notation — The General Case

For most purposes, the simple discrete representation is sufficient. However, a more general representation is desirable for two reasons. First, it permits the extension of the analysis to include the case of continuous random variables, and more general Lebesgue–Stieltjes integrable variables. Analysis in terms of the Lebesgue–Stieltjes integral is frequently more tractable than for the discrete special case. Second, it is useful in some cases, not to take prospects as primitive, but to represent choices as actions that yield different outcomes depending on the state of the world that occurs.

This more general formulation is characterized by a state space Ω, with a family S of measurable subsets and a probability measure μ. Elements of Ω, referred to as *states of the world* are denoted ω, and sets of the form $\{\omega\}$ are assumed to be measurable. A random variable y is a measurable function from Ω to $\mathcal{X}$. The space of all random variables is $\mathcal{Y}(\mathcal{X}, \Omega)$. Except where confusion is likely to result, $\mathcal{Y}(\mathcal{X}, \Omega)$ will be referred to simply as $\mathcal{Y}$.

This formulation includes the discrete representation (2.1) as a special case. In particular, in the case of n equiprobable outcomes, $\Omega = \{1, 2, \ldots N\}$, all subsets of Ω are measurable, and the measure μ is simply a counting measure $\mu(S) = \text{card}(S)/n$, where card (S) is the number of elements in S. Many results for the discrete case can be generalized simply by replacing this counting measure with an arbitrary probability measure over a space Ω. In the continuous case, it is generally useful to define $\Omega = [0, 1]$.

The space of cumulative distribution functions corresponding to $\mathcal{Y}(\mathcal{X}, \Omega)$ is denoted by $\mathcal{D}(\mathcal{X}, \Omega)$ and its elements are denoted by the letters F and G. The cumulative distribution function associated with a given random variable y is a mapping F_y: $\mathcal{X} \rightarrow \mathfrak{R}$ given by

$$F_y(x) = \Pr\{y \leq x\} = \mu\{\omega \in \Omega: y(\omega) \leq x\}. \tag{2.2}$$

When $\Omega = [0, 1]$ and the cumulative distribution function F_y is everywhere differentiable, there is an associated density function $f_y(x) = F'_y(x)$. The expectation of F_y is denoted by E[y] and the variance by σ^2_y. Where there is no danger of ambiguity, subscripts will be dropped.

In most of what follows, the analysis will be concerned only with the cumulative distribution function, and not with the actual mapping of states to consequences. If all variables having the same cumulative distribution function are treated as identical, $\mathcal{D}$ and $\mathcal{Y}$ are isomorphic. Thus, a random variable may be regarded simply as a cumulative distribution function.

This point is worth developing more formally. For simplicity, it will be assumed that $\Omega = [0, 1]$. Since all random variables having the same cumulative distribution function are regarded as identical, it is possible, for any given cumulative distribution function F, to choose a random variable y with distribution F in such a way that y preserves the natural order on Ω. More formally, for any random variable y, $\omega_1 < \omega_2 \Rightarrow y(\omega_1) \leq y(\omega_2)$. So, the states of the world in Ω are ordered from worst to best, with 0 representing the worst state and 1 representing the best.

The cumulative probability distribution of a random variable y: $\Omega \rightarrow \mathcal{X}$ may now be treated as the generalized inverse function F_y: $\mathcal{X} \rightarrow \Omega$,

$$F(x) = \sup\{y^{-1}[0, x]\}.$$

Similarly, the random variable may be treated as the generalized inverse

$$y(\omega) = \sup\{F^{-1}[0, \omega]\}.$$

A similar approach may be used to simplify the analysis when we are concerned with random variables as mappings between states and outcomes. Following Schmeidler (1989), two random variables y_1, y_2 are referred to as *comonotonic* if they yield the same ordering of the state space from best to worst; that is, if there do not exist any two states ω_1, ω_2 such that $y_1(\omega_1) < y_1(\omega_2)$ but $y_2(\omega_1) > y_2(\omega_2)$. The essential idea of comonotonicity appears to have been advanced first by Yaari (1969) who referred to comonotonic random variables as 'bets on the same event.'

If attention is restricted to a family of comonotonic random variables, the state space may be ordered from best to worst in a unique fashion (Wakker 1989a, Lemma VI). The assumption of comonotonicity is quite restrictive. However, there are many applied contexts, such as models of insurance decisions and models of the firm under uncertainty, in which it may be appropriate.

The way in which prospects have been formulated presupposes certain assumptions about risk attitudes. Most importantly, the use of cumulative distribution functions as the basis for analysis implies the assumption that people are concerned only about outcomes and not about states of the world *per se*. Another implication of the formulation relates to the *reduction of compound lotteries*. It is assumed that prospects initially expressed with outcomes that are themselves risky prospects are evaluated in terms of the ultimate probability of each outcome.

2.5 Preferences

Preferences over the space $\mathcal{Y}$ are given by a relation $\succcurlyeq$. This relation is normally assumed to be complete, reflexive and transitive. The associated equivalence relation, corresponding to the notion of indifference, is denoted ~. Whenever there is an element $x \in \mathcal{X}$ such that $y \sim \delta_x$, x is referred to as a *certainty equivalent* of y, denoted CE(y). It is normally assumed that the space $\mathcal{X}$ is sufficiently rich that every prospect has a certainty equivalent. When $\mathcal{X} = [0, M]$, the certainty equivalent is unique.

The dominant idea in the theory of choice under uncertainty is the derivation of a functional $V{:}\mathcal{Y} \rightarrow \mathfrak{R}$ that permits the ranking of any set of prospects. The functional V represents the preference ordering $\succcurlyeq$ in the sense that

$$V(y) \geq V(y') \Leftrightarrow y \succcurlyeq y'.$$

Given a choice over a set of prospects, individuals are assumed to choose so as to maximize V. In most cases, as noted above, prospects having the same cumulative distribution function are regarded as identical, so V may be regarded as a mapping $V{:}\mathcal{D} \rightarrow \mathfrak{R}$. A theory of choice under uncertainty corresponds to a family $\mathcal{V}$ of admissible functionals. For example, Expected Utility theory corresponds to those state-independent functionals that are 'linear in the probabilities.'

A crucial feature of the space $\mathcal{D}$ is that it may be regarded as a *mixture space*. This idea, already present in the work of von Neumann and Morgenstern, was developed in detail by Herstein and Milnor (1953). Fishburn (1982) employs the notion of mixture spaces extensively in his axiomatic treatment of Expected Utility. A mixture of distributions may be represented by:

$$\lambda F_1 + (1\text{-}\lambda) F_2 : x \mapsto \lambda F_1(x) + (1\text{-}\lambda) F_2(x). \tag{2.3}$$

Note that this is *not* equivalent to the natural definition for a mixture of random variables:

$$\lambda y_1 + (1\text{-}\lambda) y_2 : \omega \mapsto \lambda y_1(\omega) + (1\text{-}\lambda) y_2(\omega). \tag{2.4}$$

The mixture of distributions is a probability mixture. The mixture of random variables yields a weighted average in the outcome space. In the first case, the mixture produces a random variable which is equivalent to a two stage lottery yielding F_1 with probability λ and F_2 with probability $(1\text{-}\lambda)$. We will denote a probability mixture between two random variables by

$\lambda y_1 \oplus (1\text{-}\lambda)\, y_2$. The formal similarity of (2.3) and (2.4) has been exploited by Yaari in his development of the 'dual theory' special case of the rank-dependent expected utility model.

A variety of partial orders may be imposed on $\mathfrak{D}$ and $\mathcal{Y}$. The most natural is that of *first stochastic dominance* (Quirk and Saposnik 1962). This conditions is usually expressed in terms of cumulative distribution functions. We say that F_1 first stochastically dominates (FSD) F_2 if for all x, $F_1(x) \leq F_2(x)$. First stochastic dominance is strict if, for some x, $F_1(x) < F_2(x)$.

The first stochastic dominance condition may also be expressed in terms of random variables. For two comonotonic random variables, y_1 FSD y_2 if for all ω, $y_1(\omega) \geq y_2(\omega)$. First stochastic dominance is strict if, for ω in a set of positive measure, $y_1(\omega) > y_2(\omega)$. For comonotonic random variables, first stochastic dominance means that $\Pr\{ y_1 \geq y_2\} = 1$, that is, that y_1 is better than, or at least as good as, y_2 with probability 1. It is natural to impose the requirement that, in this case, y_1 be preferred to y_2.

The corresponding condition on distribution functions $F_1, F_2 \in \mathfrak{D}$ is $F_1(x) \leq F_2(x)\ \forall\ x$. In the absence of comonotonicity this will not imply that $\Pr\{ y_1 \geq y_2\} = 1$. However, given the assumption that preferences depend only on the cumulative distribution function, the requirement that y_1 be preferred to y_2 has the same force as in the case of comonotonicity.

CHAPTER 3

EU Theory

3.1 The EU Functional

EU theory follows the utilitarian theory of choice under certainty in deriving a real-valued functional that represents preferences in the sense that higher values of the functional correspond to increasing preference. With the notation given above, we may present a formal outline of EU theory. For any prospect $\{\boldsymbol{x};\boldsymbol{p}\}$, the *expected utility* of the prospect is defined by a functional

$$V(\{\boldsymbol{x};\boldsymbol{p}\}) = \sum_{i=1}^{n} p_i\, U(x_i) = \mathrm{E}\,[U(x)], \tag{3.1}$$

where $U\colon \mathcal{X} \to \Re$ is a *utility function.*

For the case of n equiprobable states, this is simply equivalent to summing the utilities in all states.[2] For the continuous case, we have the natural generalization.

$$V(y) = \int_{\Omega} U(x)\, dF(\omega). \tag{3.2}$$

The fact that the EU functional is a simple sum of utilities across states reflects the notion that any two equally probable states are interchangeable for the purpose of evaluating prospects. One way of looking at the generalized utility functionals examined in this book is to consider the implications of relaxing or removing this assumption.

Another way of expressing this assumption is to say expected utility functionals have the property of being 'linear in the probabilities.' Clearly (3.1) is linear in the p_i, and the integral (3.2) is linear in F. Furthermore, V is linear in the mixture space $\mathcal{D}$. That is,

$$V[\lambda F_1 + (1\text{-}\lambda)\, F_2] = \lambda V(F_1) + (1\text{-}\lambda)\, V(F_2). \tag{3.3}$$

Perhaps the most interesting implication of linearity is best expressed in terms of differences between cumulative distribution functions.

$$F_1 - F_2 = F_3 - F_4 \Rightarrow V(F_1) - V(F_2) = V(F_3) - V(F_4). \tag{3.4}$$

This property has had important implications for EU analysis. Instead of working with $\mathcal{Y}$ directly, attention has been focused on the space of distributions $\mathcal{D}$. Issues such as the definition of 'increasing risk' have been analyzed primarily in terms of conditions on cumulative distribution functions and on the difference $F_1 - F_2$ between any two cumulative distribution functions.

---

[2] Division by n does not affect the relative ranking of prospects.

This approach has proved fruitful in yielding stochastic dominance criteria, such as those of Hadar and Russell (1969). However, results for comparative static problems have generally been negative (Meyer and Ormiston 1983).

3.2 EU Axioms

Systems of axioms have played an important role in the development of EU and alternative theories. Axioms have two main interpretations. In the older interpretation, dating back to Euclid, axioms are self-evident truths about the world. Thus, the task of mathematics is to deduce less obvious truths (theorems). In the corresponding decision theoretic interpretation the EU axioms are normatively compelling rules for rational choice under uncertainty. Given a limited amount of additional information (such as preferences over a restricted class of bets) rational decisions under uncertainty can be determined.

Euclidean geometry included one axiom (the 'parallel postulate' stating that parallel lines never meet) which was not self-evident. The decision theoretic equivalent of the parallel postulate is found in the long debate (commencing with the critique of Allais 1953) of the EU independence axiom, and the many attempts to find either a normatively compelling formulation of this axiom, or a preferable alternative.

The modern mathematical interpretation of axioms began with the discovery by Gauss, Lobachevsky and others of non-Euclidean geometries, in which the Euclidean parallel postulate was violated. On this view, a system of axioms is merely an internally consistent set of rules, with no necessary reference to the real world. (However, the apparently unrealistic non-Euclidean geometry was employed in Einstein's 'curved space' model.) Axioms are not true or false, but are interesting or uninteresting depending on whether or not they have interesting implications. Thus, it is natural to consider the consequences of relaxing or modifying various axioms and to derive equivalence relationships between alternative sets of axioms. This approach has been explored most fully by Krantz et al. (1971) and Fishburn (1982).

The axioms that will be employed here have been prefigured in the discussion above. The presentation here draws on Fishburn (1982) and Yaari (1987). We begin with four axioms on the preference relation $\succcurlyeq$ that are satisfied by EU and most generalized models. These are

(EU.1) If y_1 and y_2 have the same cumulative distribution function $y_1 \sim y_2$.

(EU.2) $\succcurlyeq$ is a weak order. This means that $\succcurlyeq$ is:

- complete ;
- transitive ; and
- reflexive.

(EU.3) If y_1 FSD y_2, $y_1 \succcurlyeq y_2$.

(EU.4) The preference relation $\succcurlyeq$ is continuous[3] .

All of these axioms seem fairly plausible, although models in which they do not apply have been proposed. Three types of violations arise for (EU.1). First, models including state-dependent utility theory and regret theory have been proposed in which (EU.1) does not hold

[3] That is the set $\{y: y \succcurlyeq y^0\}$ is closed for every y^0. The use of the term "closed" presupposes a topology on Y. The most popular choice is the topology of weak convergence, associated with the L^1 norm.

because the evaluation is dependent on the particular state in which a given outcome occurs. It follows (given continuity) that (EU.3) will not hold either and that the definition of first stochastic dominance must be modified. Quiggin (1989a) describes the stochastic dominance properties of regret theory. Second, (EU.1) presupposes the existence of known probabilities. This assumption is violated in problems of ambiguity. Third, when applied to multi-stage gambles, (EU.1) is equivalent to the reduction of compound lotteries axiom. Segal (1990) has proposed a formulation of the RDEU model in which the reduction axiom does not hold. This will be discussed in Chapter 11.

A number of models have been proposed that violate transitivity, including regret theory and Fishburn's (1983) skew-symmetric bilinear model, both of which analyze pairwise choices directly. An immediate problem with models of this kind is that of extending the representation to larger choice sets. Fishburn (1988) discusses some possible options and Quiggin (1992) derives a unique extension of regret theory. The more fundamental problem, however, is why one would want to abandon transitivity. It is probably the most normatively appealing postulate for choice theory in general (the results of MacCrimmon and Larsson 1979 suggest that this view is held by ordinary people more strongly than by choice theorists). Furthermore there is little evidence of systematic violation of transitivity (the work of Tversky 1969 is discussed in Chapter 10).

The requirement of continuity is technical. The most substantial reason for rejecting continuity is offered by Kahneman and Tversky (1979) who argue that preferences are discontinuous in a neighborhood of certainty. Against this claim it may be observed, first, that perfect certainty is unattainable, and second, that it is impossible to distinguish empirically between preferences that are discontinuous and those for which indifference curves are steeply sloped.

The crucial additional axiom that identifies EU theory is the independence axiom. In the light of the discussion of $\mathfrak{D}$ as a mixture space, this may simply be stated as

(EU.5) If F, G, $H \in \mathfrak{D}$ and $F \succ G$, for any $\alpha \in [0, 1]$ the probability mixture $\alpha F + (1-\alpha)H$ is preferred to $\alpha G + (1-\alpha)H$.

In this formulation, the axiom does not have any obvious normative status. The criticisms of Allais (1953) provoked a number of attempts to reformulate the axiom in a more convincing fashion. The most important is Savage's sure thing principle, described above.

The sure thing argument is not entirely convincing. In the case of first stochastic dominance, there is a natural arrangement of the outcomes that illustrates why the dominated prospect should be rejected. This is the arrangement of the outcomes as a distribution ranging from worst to best. First stochastic dominance implies that say, the outcome at the 57th percentile of the dominating distribution will be preferred to the corresponding outcome for the dominated distribution. This natural arrangement cannot be generalized to support the 'sure thing' principle. It can, however, be used to support a weaker independence axiom and stochastic dominance rules (see Chapter 11).

3.3 Risk Aversion in EU Theory

The central behavioral concept in EU theory is that of risk aversion. Risk aversion in EU theory is unambiguously defined only for the case when $\mathcal{X} = [0, M]$, so that the expectation E[y] is well defined. Thus, the EU concept of risk aversion is a property of attitudes to wealth rather than of attitudes to risk *per se*.

An individual is *risk averse* if a certain outcome δ_x is always preferred to a risky prospect y for which $E[y] = x$. Assuming a certainty equivalent exists for each y, an equivalent characterization of risk aversion is given by the requirement that $CE(y) \leq E[y]\ \forall\ y \in \mathcal{Y}$. The extent of risk aversion may be measured by the *risk premium*, given by

$$\Delta(y) = E[y] - CE(y).$$

By Jensen's inequality, risk aversion in EU theory is equivalent to concavity of the utility function, that is, to the requirement that U'' be negative. However, the fact that the utility function is defined only up to a linear transformation means that the value of U'' alone is of little use in comparisons of risk aversion. Arrow (1965) and Pratt (1964) were the first to develop useful measures of risk aversion with the coefficients of absolute and relative risk aversion. The *coefficient of absolute risk aversion* is defined by

$$r_a(x) = -U''(x)/U'(x).$$

This coefficient is a local measure of aversion to risk. Given two individuals with different levels of r_a (at their respective current wealth levels), the individual with the higher value of r_a will always have a higher risk premium for 'sufficiently small' bets. An approximation to the risk premium for a prospect of the form $\{(x - \delta, x + \delta); (1/2, 1/2)\}$ is given by

$$\Delta(y) = 1/2\ r_a(x)\ \delta^2.$$

The coefficient of absolute risk aversion can also be used as a basis for global comparisons of risk aversion. If one individual has a higher $r_a(x)$ than another for every x, the first may be shown to be more risk averse, in the sense of having a lower certainty equivalent for any risky prospect. This is formalized in the following result

PROPOSITION 3.1: *For two individuals with utility functions U^A, U^B the following are equivalent*
(i) *U^A is a concave transformation of U^B*;
(ii) $r_a^A(x) \geq r_a^B(x)\ \forall\ x$; and
(iii) *For any y, $\Delta^A(y) \geq \Delta^B(y)$.*

Proof: Pratt (1964, Theorem 1). ■

Arrow and Pratt also proposed an alternative measure of risk aversion that is in some sense independent of wealth levels. This is the *coefficient of relative risk aversion*

$$r_r(x) = -\,xU''(x)/U'(x).$$

This coefficient measures willingness to accept bets expressed as a proportion of current wealth. A number of plausible utility functions, including the logarithmic function, display constant relative risk aversion. However, the coefficient of relative risk aversion is meaningless in problems that admit negative values of x. Examples include the theory of the firm under price uncertainty where x corresponds to the level of profits or losses.

A generalization of the concept of relative risk aversion, proposed by Zeckhauser and Keeler (1970) overcomes this restriction. The *coefficient of partial risk aversion* is given by

$$r_p(x) = -(x - x_0)\, U''(x)/U'(x),$$

where x_0 is a 'base level' chosen so that it lies below the support of all random variables under consideration. In the case of the theory of the firm, x_0 might correspond to the loss rate that would trigger bankruptcy. The coefficient of partial risk aversion measures willingness to accept bets expressed as a proportion of $x - x_o$.

It seems intuitively obvious that $r_a(x)$ will decline with x; that is, that an increase in wealth will increase an individual's willingness to accept a given bet. This hypothesis of *declining absolute risk aversion* (DARA) was mentioned above in connection with the writing of Bernoulli. It has received considerable support from empirical studies. Among the implications of DARA it is important to note the requirement that $U'''(x) > 0\ \forall\ x$.

In contrast to the widespread acceptance of DARA, there is no general consensus on the likely behavior of $r_r(x)$ and $r_p(x)$ as x increases. However, Arrow (1974) has argued that r_r will tend to increase.

3.4 Stochastic Dominance

The coefficients of risk aversion and the results of Pratt provide a basis for comparisons of risk aversion between individuals. The dual problem is that of comparing the riskiness of distributions. The development of powerful tools for the analysis of this problem constituted a decisive advance for EU theory.

The mean–variance approach to decision theory relies on a simple ranking of prospects. If one prospect has a higher mean and a lower variance than another, it must be preferred. If the first prospect has a higher mean, but also a higher variance, the ranking will depend on specific risk attitudes. It is easy to see that this is unsatisfactory. For example, it does not unequivocally suggest that one should accept a free lottery ticket, since the alternative of rejection yields a mean and variance of zero. A more general version of this point was made by Borch (1969). He showed that for any preference pair $(\mu_1, \sigma_1) \succcurlyeq (\mu_2, \sigma_2)$ with $\mu_1 \leq \mu_2$ and $\sigma_1 \neq \sigma_2$, it was possible to find random variables $y_1 \succcurlyeq y_2$ such that y_2 FSD y_1. Thus, the mean–variance approach cannot yield a consistent ranking of prospects without the imposition of additional restrictions. Sinn

(1983) and Meyer (1987) have shown that the mean-variance approach yields sensible rankings when prospects are members of a family determined by location and scale parameters. However, in this work, the mean-variance approach is not a competitor for EU theory but a convenient device for the exposition of EU results.

The development of a more acceptable approach to the problem of ranking prospects using EU theory was a major factor in its success. The crucial tool was the concept of stochastic dominance. Although various stochastic dominance concepts have been proposed, most may be interpreted in terms of a requirement that one distribution be preferred to another for all individuals with utility functions in a given class. The central concept is that of first stochastic dominance, which is defined in relation to a very general class of utility functions.

Let $\mathcal{U} = \{U : U$ is monotonically increasing with respect to the order on $X\}$. For $\mathcal{X} = [0, M]$, $\mathcal{U}$ corresponds to the class of individuals who prefer more wealth to less. For the purposes of decision theory, it may be assumed that all individuals fall into this class, since it is always possible to give away any surplus wealth.

The following proposition is due to Hadar and Russell (1969).

PROPOSITION 3.2: *Let y_1, y_2 be random variables and let F_1, F_2 be the corresponding cumulative distribution functions. Then the following conditions are equivalent*:

(i) $E[U(y_1)] \geq E[U(y_2)]\ \forall\ U \in \mathcal{U}$;

(ii) $F_1(x) \leq F_2(x)\ \forall\ x \in \mathcal{X}$; *and*

(iii) y_2 *is derived from* y_1 *by the addition of a random variable that is non-positive with probability* 1.

Proof: That (iii) $\Leftrightarrow$ (ii) and (ii) $\Rightarrow$ (i) is trivial. For the remaining implication suppose that for some x^0, $F_1(x^0) < F_2(x^0)$. Consider the utility function

$$U(x) = \begin{cases} 0 & : x < x^0 \\ 1 & : x \geq x^0 \end{cases}$$

Then, for any F,

$$\int_X U(x)\, dF(x) = F(x^0)$$

Hence, $\mathrm{E}[U(y_1)] < \mathrm{E}[U(y_2)]$, contradicting (1). The same inequality applies to any continuous utility function that approximates U sufficiently closely. ■

The definition of stochastic dominance may be generalized as follows. A distribution, y_1, stochastically dominates another, y_2, with respect to a class of utility functions, $\mathcal{U}$ if $\mathrm{E}[U(y_1)] \geq \mathrm{E}[U(y_2)]\ \forall\ U \in \mathcal{U}$. Several classes of stochastic dominance relations have been analyzed in detail. The most important is *second stochastic dominance,* defined with respect to the class of utility functions. The relevant class of utility functions is given by :

$$\mathcal{U}^2 = \{U \in \mathcal{U}^1 : U \text{ is concave}\}.$$

Given this definition, y_1 second stochastically dominates (SSD) y_2 if and only if $E[U(y_1)] \geq E[U(y_2)]\ \forall\ U \in \mathcal{U}^2$. In EU theory, $\mathcal{U}^2$ corresponds to the class of risk averse individuals. Although there is no compelling reason why all individuals should be uniformly risk averse, no other attitude makes sense in terms of EU theory (see Section 3.4).

The equivalence between the three types of definition of stochastic dominance embodied in Proposition 3.2 may be extended to the case of second stochastic dominance.

PROPOSITION 3.3 *Let y_1, y_2 be random variables and let F_1, F_2 be the corresponding cumulative distribution functions. Then the following are equivalent:*

(i) y_1 *SSD* y_2 *; and*

(ii) $\int_{t \leq x} F_1(t)\, dt \leq \int_{t \leq x} F_2(t)\, dt$

Further, if $E[y_1] = E[y_2]$, *then* (i) *and* (ii) *are equivalent to*

(iii) $y_2 =_d y_1 + y_3$ *for some* y_3 *such that* $E[y_3 \mid y_1] \equiv 0$ (*where* $=_d$ *denotes equality in distribution*).

Proof: A detailed proof is given by Rothschild and Stiglitz (1970). A sketch of a proof is as follows.

That (iii) $\Rightarrow$ (i) follows from Jensen's inequality. That (i) $\Rightarrow$ (ii) may be seen by considering functions of the form

$$U(x) = \begin{cases} x & : x < x^0 \\ x^0 & : x \geq x^0 \end{cases}$$

and following the argument of Proposition 3.1. The proof that (ii) $\Rightarrow$ (iii) is derived for the finite case when y_1 and y_2 may each take n values. Thus there are at most n^2 possible values for $y_1 - y_2$. Rothschild and Stiglitz show that it is possible to construct a probability distribution over these values in the form of a matrix, in such a way that (iii) is satisfied. ■

The first part of this result is due to Hadar and Russell. Rothschild and Stiglitz (1970) examined the case $E[y_1] = E[y_2]$, and demonstrated the equivalence of a number of possible definitions of 'increasing risk.' The basic definition is the condition that all EU risk averters prefer y_1 to y_2. The integral condition (ii) may be interpreted as saying that the density function for y_2 has more weight in the tails than that for y_1. Finally condition (iii) may be interpreted as saying that y_2 is derived from y_1 by the addition of some random noise.

It is of equal interest to note that some plausible definitions of increasing risk are not equivalent to (i)–(iii). As noted above, not all increases in variance fit into this category. There are also more restrictive definitions of an increase in risk. The first, which has proved useful in comparative static analysis, is that of a multiplicative spread about the mean. The second is the requirement that an increase in risk should lead a risk averse investor to purchase less of the risky asset in the standard one safe asset, one risky asset portfolio problem. Rothschild and Stiglitz (1971) examine this problem. Only under complex conditions on the utility function will a spread satisfying (i)–(iii) imply a reduction in purchases of the risky asset.

A less restrictive notion, corresponding to a smaller set of utility functions is that of third stochastic dominance. Consider the classes

$\mathcal{U}^3 = \{U \in \mathcal{U}^2 : U'''(x) \geq 0 \; \forall \, x\}$.

$\mathcal{U}^{3a} = \{U \in \mathcal{U}^2 : U \text{ displays DARA}\}$

The requirement that U''' be positive may be motivated by noting that this is a necessary condition for DARA.

Whitmore (1970) proves that $\mathrm{E}[U(y_1)] \geq \mathrm{E}[U(y_2)]$ for all $U \in \mathcal{U}^{3a}$ if and only if

$$\int_X \int_{t \leq x} F_1(t)\, dt\, dx \leq \int_X \int_{t \leq x} F_2(t)\, dt\, dx$$

An even closer relationship between third stochastic dominance and DARA was obtained by Bawa (1975). He showed that for distributions with the same mean, third stochastic dominance is precisely equivalent to preference by all utility functions displaying DARA.

No stochastic dominance concept yields a complete ordering on the space of random variables $\mathcal{Y}$. It is apparent, however, that the smaller is the class $\mathcal{U}$, the larger is the corresponding partial order, that is, the more pairs of distributions are ordered. This relationship is exploited in the concept of stochastic dominance with respect to a function developed by Meyer (1977a, 1977b). Meyer's analysis works in terms of the risk aversion coefficients rather than the utility functions themselves. The idea is to choose a function $r(x)$ and to consider the set of agents with a utility function more risk averse than that defined by $r(x)$. Thus

$$\mathcal{U}^r = \{U : -U''(x)/U'(x) \geq r(x) \; \forall \, x\}.$$

A refinement offered in Meyer (1977b) is to choose two functions $r_1(x)$ and $r_2(x)$, such that $r_1(x) \geq r_2(x) \; \forall \, x$ and then to consider the set of agents whose utility functions lie between r_1 and r_2. A particularly simply case arises when r_1 and r_2 are constants, which bound the level of risk aversion above and below.

This approach includes FSD and SSD as special cases. FSD corresponds to $r_1 = -\infty$, $r_2 = \infty$. SSD corresponds to $r_1 = 0$, $r_2 = \infty$. However, the approach does not appear to include the concept of third stochastic dominance.

It should also be noted that Meyer defined $r(x)$ to be the coefficient of absolute risk aversion, which makes the use of constant functions highly implausible. Typically, if the range of outcomes is unbounded, and DARA applies, the coefficient of absolute risk aversion will take all values between 0 and ∞. Thus, if any functions displaying DARA are to be included in $\mathcal{U}$, and the functions r_1 and r_2 are constant, we must have $r_1 = 0$ and $r_2 = \infty$ and $\mathcal{U}^r = \mathcal{U}^2$. But if all risk averse utility functions are included, there is no increase in generality arising from the use of the Meyer approach.

Various resolutions of this problem are possible. If the range of outcomes is bounded, functions displaying DARA may be included even though $r_1 > 0$, $r_2 < \infty$. However, the larger the outcome range, the larger the interval $[r_1, r_2]$ must be to include all reasonable utility functions for a given utility function. Another possibility is to make the functions r_1, r_2 non-constant. This would add to the complexity of the approach.

A simpler alternative is to express the functions r_1 and r_2 in terms of the coefficient of relative risk aversion. When negative values of x are possible, the coefficient of partial risk aversion, for a suitably chosen x_o, may be used. Whereas constant absolute risk aversion utility functions are implausible, functions with constant relative risk aversion seem reasonable, at least as an approximation. A wide range of plausible utility functions would satisfy the constraint that the coefficient of relative risk aversion should lie in some finite range. Empirical research, such as that reported by Newbery and Stiglitz (1981), suggests that the appropriate range is a neighborhood of 1.

The relationship between the concepts of stochastic dominance and the Arrow-Pratt analysis may be summarized by saying that stochastic dominance relates to increases in the riskiness of situations and the Arrow-Pratt analysis relates to increases in the risk aversion of individuals. This point is developed more fully by Diamond and Stiglitz (1974) who extend and integrate the increasing risk analysis of Rothschild and Stiglitz (1970, 1971) with the Arrow-Pratt analysis of the characteristics of utility functions. They show that a type of duality exists between increases in risk and in risk aversion so that results relating to one concept can be paired with similar results relating to the other.

However, this duality is not complete. The Arrow-Pratt characterization of risk aversion suffers from a major weakness, in that it yields strong results only in the case of comparisons between a risky prospect and a certain alternative. Ross (1981) examined the case of a choice between two prospects y_1 and y_2, where y_2 is riskier than y_1 in the sense of Rothschild and Stiglitz but has a higher return, that is, $y_2 = y_1 + \varepsilon$, where ε is a random variable uncorrelated with y_1, but with positive mean. It seems desirable that if a given individual prefers the less risky option, the same should be true of any other person who is more risk averse. However, as Ross showed, the Arrow-Pratt characterization does not guarantee this. Ross offered a stronger characterization of increasing risk aversion, as follows.

Let U_A and U_B be two utility functions. Then U_A is *strongly more risk averse* than U_B if and only if

$$\inf_x U_A''(x)/ U_B''(x) \geq \sup_x U_A'(x)/ U_B'(x). \tag{3.5}$$

Ross demonstrated that this requirement is strictly stronger than the Arrow-Pratt characterization, and derived stronger versions of concepts of decreasing absolute risk aversion and increasing relative risk aversion. Ross' results were strengthened by Machina and Neilson (1987) who examine the case of random initial wealth.

This section has given a summary of some of the most important features of the literature relating to stochastic dominance between prospects and comparisons of risk aversion between utility functions. A bibliography containing an extensive set of references on stochastic dominance has been provided by Bawa (1982). A more general summary of the major developments in EU theory is given by Machina (1983a).

3.5 Risk Preference in EU Theory

Analysis in EU theory has been concentrated on the case of risk averse preferences. At first sight, however, it appears that an equally convincing analysis could be applied to risk seekers, characterized by a convex utility function. The absence of a body of EU literature analyzing risk loving preferences is not due to overwhelming empirical evidence in favor of risk aversion. Rather it reflects the fact, that, within EU theory, no coherent account of risk preference is possible.

The argument against the possibility of risk preference in EU theory may be stated as follows. Suppose there are two individuals, both global risk seekers. Then they would mutually benefit from a bet in which each of them staked their entire wealth, with the odds being actuarially fair. The resolution of the bet would leave one bankrupt and the other considerably more wealthy. More generally, if there are n risk seekers, mutually desirable betting transactions among them will be available until all but one are bankrupt. Thus, we should not expect to observe global risk preference, except possibly among bankrupts and billionaires.

This argument can even be carried over to the case of a single risk seeker in a community of risk averters who face irremovable risks. The risk seeker will benefit from offering to insure the risk averters at actuarially fair rates. Even if, as seems likely, the rate struck is actuarially favorable to the risk seeker, the probability of bankruptcy will approach unity as the size of the available risk increases.

By contrast, it may be noted that in a finite community of risk averters, even perfect risk pooling cannot generally move everyone to their preferred portfolio (given a particular expected value). This is the riskless portfolio, at which point risk aversion becomes irrelevant. Only two risk seekers are required to achieve the optimal distribution of risk, for given total wealth.

A similar argument applies to people with both concave and convex segments in their utility functions. Mutually beneficial gambles will always be available to people whose present wealth lies in a concave segment of the curve. Even in a concave segment of the curve, people will tend to gamble until they reach a point at which they are risk averse, in the sense that they would refuse all risky gambles with expected outcome zero or less. This point is developed further in Chapter 4, in connection with the analysis of gambling put forward by Friedman and Savage (1948).

Risk preference is an unstable state. Because it is easy and cheap to satisfy a desire for increased risk, and difficult and costly to reduce risk, only risk aversion presents a major economic problem. Risk seekers will eliminate themselves from economic systems either by going bankrupt or by achieving a level of wealth at which they are effectively risk averse.

These arguments do not demonstrate that risk seekers are irrational. They do show, however, that, except for bankrupts and billionaires, behavior inconsistent with risk aversion cannot be explained within the EU framework by invoking the possibility of local or global risk preference.

3.6 Applications of EU Theory

The EU approach has been a progressive research program. Analytical tools such as stochastic dominance conditions and characterizations of different forms of risk aversion have been developed steadily. The extension of EU analysis to problems such as the theory of the firm has led to the generation of a number of novel and testable hypotheses. In addition, EU theory has permitted the extension of economic analysis to important problems such as insurance for which no adequate treatment was previously available. Empirical research based on the hypotheses suggested by EU analysis has been extensive and has given support to important hypotheses such as decreasing absolute risk aversion. EU theory has been applied to a wide range of problems within and outside economics and the range of applications continues to grow. Since almost all real world problems involve some degree of uncertainty, the potential scope of the theory is enormous.

The first class of applications consists of problems for which there is a well developed economic theory based on the assumption of perfect information. (For most purposes, these theories can be extended to the case of uncertainty if actors are risk neutral, either by nature or because of the availability of costless risk spreading through 'perfect' capital markets). In these applications, interest centres on the extent to which standard results of theory under certainty may be carried over to the EU framework on the assumption of risk aversion.

The classic problem has been that of allocating wealth between a safe asset with a known return and a risky asset with a higher expected return. Initial wealth is denoted by W_0, the rate of return on the safe asset by r, and the proportion of wealth allocated to the risky asset by α. The rate of return on the risky asset is a random variable θ. The maximization probiem may be written:

$$\text{Max}_\alpha \, \text{E}[U(W_0(\alpha\theta + (1-\alpha)r))]. \tag{3.6}$$

Another important application of this kind has been the theory of the firm under uncertainty. In the simplest version of this problem, that of the competitive firm under output price uncertainty, the firm must choose an output z to solve

$$\text{Max}_z \, \text{E}[\, U(pz - C(z))],$$

where p is a random price variable. This problem may be modified to deal with more complex cases including imperfect competition (Leland 1972) and uncertain output (Pope and Just 1977).

In addition to modifying the theory of individual saving and investment behavior, the application of EU theory has generated sharp debates over public investment policy. Most economists working in an efficiency framework have taken the view that the return on public investments under certainty should be the same as that for competing private investments. There has been a strong argument that this is no longer true under uncertainty. Arrow and Lind (1970) argued that, because of the very great risk spreading capacity of governments, discount rates for public investments should not include a premium for risk. Thus, assuming that private discount rates do include risk premiums, the public rate should be lower than the private one.

A second category of applications consists of problems that cannot be treated in any reasonable fashion without taking account of risk and risk aversion. An obvious category is insurance. Since the expected value of an insurance contract is normally negative for the buyer (that is, the premium must cover both expected payouts and administrative costs), no theory that does not include a concept of risk aversion can say anything useful about the demand for insurance. The general problem of insurance overlaps with the rapidly developing field of health economics, as health insurance is a major public policy issue in most Western countries. Arrow (1963) was a leading early contributor in this debate.

A third category of applications includes those motivated directly by the development of EU theory. These include attempts to estimate utility functions for individuals and groups. For example, Officer and Halter (1968) and Bond and Wonder (1980), along with many others, have sought to estimate coefficients of risk aversion using questionnaires. Just (1974, 1975), Gallagher (1978) and others have derived econometric estimates of supply response under risk. There is also an extensive practical literature on stochastic dominance, employing the ideas of higher level stochastic dominance and dominance with respect to a function developed above.

3.7 The General Control Problem

A wide range of maximization problems have been considered in the EU theory of choice under uncertainty. Many of these can be fitted into the following general framework.

$$\mathrm{Max}_{\alpha}\, \mathrm{E}[U(\phi(\theta, \alpha, W_0))], \tag{3.7}$$

where U is a von Neumann–Morgenstern utility function, α is a control variable (assumed to take positive values), θ is an economically relevant random variable with cumulative distribution function F, W_0 is initial wealth (here taken to be non-stochastic), and ϕ is a function mapping actions and realizations of θ into outcomes, normally taken to be wealth levels. The functional form (3.7) is a generalization of the control problem analyzed by Feder (1977). Two examples are the two asset (one safe asset, one risky asset) portfolio choice model and the theory of the firm under uncertainty. In the first case, α is the quantity of the risky asset, θ is the rate of return on the risky asset, and ϕ is given by

$$\phi(\theta, \alpha, W_0) = \alpha\theta + (W_0 - \alpha)\theta_0, \tag{3.8}$$

where θ_0 is the rate of return on the safe asset. For the theory of the firm under uncertainty, α is firm output, θ is output price, W_0 is net assets after fixed costs have been met, and ϕ is a profit function of the form

$$\phi(\theta, \alpha, W_0) = \alpha\theta - C(\alpha) + W_0, \tag{3.9}$$

where C is a variable cost function. The form (3.9) is a generalization of (3.8). It may be modified to cover problems such as yield uncertainty and input price uncertainty.

The first order condition for the general model (3.7) is

$$\mathrm{E}[\partial V/\partial \alpha] = 0, \tag{3.10}$$

and the second order condition is

$$D = \mathrm{E}[\partial^2 V/\partial \alpha^2] < 0 \tag{3.11}$$

If the second order condition is satisfied globally, there will exist a unique optimum. However, in many of the problems to be examined here, it is unlikely that (3.11) will hold globally. It is, therefore, useful to consider an alternative condition that guarantees the existence of a finite optimum

$$\lim_{\alpha \to \infty} \partial V/\partial \alpha \text{ exists and is less than 0.} \tag{3.12}$$

Versions of this condition have been examined for the problem of portfolio choice by Bertsekas (1974) and for the firm under uncertainty by Quiggin (1982b).

Now let λ be a parameter that affects the value of W_0. Then, differentiating (3.10) with respect to λ yields

$$E[\,\partial^2 V/\partial\alpha^2]\,\partial\alpha/\partial\lambda \; + E[\,\partial^2 V/\partial\alpha\partial W_0]\,\partial W_0/\partial\lambda = 0. \tag{3.13}$$

By (3.11),

$$\partial\alpha/\partial\lambda = -1/D\,E[\,\partial^2 V/\partial\alpha\partial W_0]\,\partial W_0/\partial\lambda.$$

Thus, $\partial\alpha/\partial\lambda$ will have the same sign as $E[\partial^2 V/\partial\alpha\partial W_0]\partial W_0/\partial\lambda$. The problem for comparative static analysis is to sign this term. This procedure of implicit differentiation is the main technical tool of the comparative static analysis undertaken in this book.

A similar procedure is used in the analysis of a change in the distribution of θ from F_1 to F_2. The distribution of θ may be represented by $\lambda F_2 + (1-\lambda)F_1$ and the change in distribution may be represented by an increase in λ from 0 to 1. We have

$$E[\,\partial^2 V/\partial\alpha^2]\,\partial\alpha/\partial\lambda \; + E[\,\partial^2 V/\partial\alpha\partial\theta\;\partial\theta/\partial\lambda] = 0.$$

This is identical to (3.13) except that, since $\partial\theta/\partial\lambda$ is stochastic, this term must be placed inside the second expectation. Once again, the problem is to sign the second term in the LHS. Numerous results of this kind have been derived in the EU literature.

Before proceeding to this task, it is necessary to derive conditions for the existence of a finite optimal value for α. It is useful to define

$$U_1 = \lim_{\alpha \to \infty} U'(x),\; U_2 = \lim_{\alpha \to -\infty} U'(x),\; \phi_\alpha^\infty = \lim_{\alpha \to \infty} \partial\phi/\partial\alpha.$$

It will be assumed that $\Pr\{\,\phi_\alpha^\infty < 0\} > 0$. This is a 'no easy money' assumption, without which, for large α, the 'risky' option yields a positive return with probability 1. Define

$$K = \lim_{\alpha \to \infty} \partial V/\partial\alpha = U_1 \int_{\phi_\alpha^\infty > 0} \phi_\alpha^\infty \, dF(\theta) \;-\; U_2 \int_{\phi_\alpha^\infty \leq 0} \phi_\alpha^\infty \, dF(\theta).$$

Then a straightforward limiting argument yields

PROPOSITION 3.4: *A finite optimum exists if $K < 0$ and not if $K > 0$.*

Proof: (Quiggin 1982b) ■

The intermediate case $K = 0$ includes the classically indeterminate case of the risk neutral firm facing constant returns to scale. Several sufficient conditions for $K < 0$ may be found. First, if $\partial^2\phi/\partial\alpha^2 < -\delta < 0$, $\Pr\{\phi_\alpha^\infty > 0\} = 0$. In the case of the theory of the firm this corresponds to a firm with a U-shaped cost curve. Second, if the utility function is bounded above, $U_1 = 0$ and $K < 0$. Third, it is sufficient that U_2 be unbounded.

To obtain sharp comparative statics results, it is necessary to impose some conditions on the function ϕ. The following assumptions are sufficiently general to cover most cases of interest

(Φ.1) $\partial\phi/\partial\theta > 0$,
(Φ.2) $\partial\phi/\partial W > 0$,
(Φ.3) $\partial^2\phi/\partial\theta\partial\alpha \geq 0$,
(Φ.4) $\partial^2\phi/\partial W\partial\alpha \geq 0$,
(Φ.5) $\partial^2\phi/\partial\theta^2 = 0$.

Assumptions (Φ.1) and (Φ.2) are natural for most of the problems under consideration here. As Diamond and Stiglitz (1974) have observed, (Φ.1) rules out short selling in portfolio problems. This is consistent with the assumption, noted above, that α is confined to positive values. Assumption (Φ.3) is natural if increases in α reflect increases in risk taking. The assumption is that the better the outcome of the risky variable, the more desirable (*ex post*) risk taking will be. (Φ.4) is a similar assumption, though in most cases, the inequality may be replaced by an equality. It states that increases in initial wealth will have a non-negative effect on the benefits of risk taking. Finally (Φ.5) states that the outcomes are linear in the risky variable. This assumption holds for the examples presented above. Moreover, in problems where it is not satisfied, (for example if the firm problem is stated in terms of uncertain demand rather than uncertain price) an appropriate monotonic transformation of the random variable can often be used to impose linearity.

It will be assumed throughout that the utility function displays decreasing absolute risk aversion. This is a sufficient but not a necessary condition for the requirement that $U''' \geq 0$.

Then the following results may be derived.

PROPOSITION 3.5:

(a) *Let F_1 be the initial distribution and F_2 the final distribution, and let θ_1 and θ_2 be the corresponding random variables. Given the assumptions above, the following are sufficient conditions for an increase in α^*.*

(i) $\theta_2 = \theta_1 + \delta$ *for some* $\delta > 0$;
(ii) $F_2 = \delta_c$, $E[F_1] \leq c$; *and*
(iii) F_1 *is derived from* F_2 *by a multiplicative spread,* $E[F_2] \geq E[F_1]$.

(b) *An increase in* W_0 *leads to an increase in* α^*.

Proof: See Appendix ■

These results are intuitively appealing in terms of the examples presented above. For the firm under uncertainty, the first part of (a) is equivalent to the law of supply. An increase in mean price will lead to an increase in output. Similarly, in the portfolio problem, this result states that an increase in the return on an asset will lead to an increase in demand for that asset.

The most economically significant intuition about increasing risk is that, if the return on an asset becomes more risky, then risk averse investors will want less of it. Similarly, an increase in price risk should lead to a reduction in output for the competitive firm with a risk averse owner.

However, Rothschild and Stiglitz (1971) have shown that the second stochastic dominance definition of increasing risk does not imply that an increase in the riskiness of an asset will lead to risk averse people buying less of it in the standard one safe asset, one risky asset portfolio problem. For general second stochastically dominating shifts, Rothschild and Stiglitz showed that a sufficient condition for the allocation to the risky asset to be reduced is that absolute risk aversion be non-increasing and that relative risk aversion be less than or equal to unity and non-increasing. The first of these conditions is uncontroversial, but the second is quite restrictive, and is not used in Proposition 3.4.

The second and third parts of (a) give conditions under which an increase in the riskiness of an activity will lead to a reduction in the resources committed to that activity. The second part is a special case of the third, though it is worth noting that the hypothesis of decreasing absolute risk aversion is not essential in this case. This result may be interpreted as saying that levels of the control variable will be lower in the presence of risk, or, conversely that risk averse agents will choose lower values of the control variable than risk neutral agents. It is important for policy purposes, since it provides the rationale for government intervention aimed at reducing risk. This rationale, put forward by Arrow and Lind (1970) among others, has been criticized, but the fundamental assumption that risk tends to reduce output has generally been taken as common ground. The third part of (a) is the most general result that has appeared in the literature, as mean-preserving spreads in the sense of Rothschild and Stiglitz (1970, 1971) do not display tractable comparative static behavior.

The result of part (b) is similarly plausible. Given the assumption of decreasing absolute risk aversion, an increase in initial wealth leads to an effective reduction in risk aversion, and hence to a less risk averse choice. The reasoning here can be used to derive results for comparisons between individuals with different levels of risk aversion, as in the work of Diamond and Stiglitz (1974).

Concluding Comments

This chapter has presented a brief overview of the key theoretical concepts associated with the EU model, and some of its most important applications. The model of production under uncertainty discussed above is central to many of the recent developments in economic theory. In various forms it is present in the literature on moral hazard, on principal-agent relationships and in the economic theory of crime and punishment. In all of these cases, the notion of risk aversion plays a critical role in the analysis. The general problem of trading off risk against expected return is ubiquitous.

Much of the remainder of the book is devoted to showing how these concepts and applications may be developed in the context of more general models of choice under uncertainty and, in particular, the RDEU model.

Appendix:

A useful Lemma is

Lemma 3.1: let f and g be real valued functions such that :

(i) g is positive and monotone decreasing; and

(ii) $\exists\ \theta^*$ such that (a) $f(\theta^*) = \int f(\theta)\, dF(\theta)$;

(b) $f(\theta) \geq f(\theta^*)$ if and only if $\theta \geq \theta^*$.

Then

$$\int f(\theta)\, g(\theta)\, dF(\theta) \leq \int f(\theta)\, dF(\theta) \int g(\theta) dF(\theta). \tag{A.1}$$

Proof: Let $g^* = g(\theta^*)$, $f^* = f(\theta^*)$. Then, since g is monotone decreasing, condition (iib) implies

$$\begin{aligned} \int g(\theta)\, (f(\theta) - f^*)\, dF(\theta) &\leq g^* \int (f(\theta) - f^*) dF(\theta), \\ &= g^* \left(\int f(\theta) dF(\theta) - f^* \int dF(\theta)\right), \\ &= 0, \text{ by condition (iia)}, \end{aligned} \tag{A.2}$$

so that

$$\int g(\theta) f(\theta) dF(\theta) \leq \int g(\theta)\, f^* dF(\theta) \tag{A.3}$$

$$= \int f(\theta) dF(\theta) \int g(\theta)\, dF(\theta). \blacksquare \tag{A.4}$$

Conditions (iia) and (iib) are always satisfied if f is monotone increasing. Thus, the lemma is a generalization of the well known fact that, if f is a monotone increasing function of some variable θ and g is a positive monotone decreasing function of θ, $E[fg] \leq E[f]\, E[g]$.

The first order condition for the general model (3.7) is

$$\partial V / \partial \alpha = E[\, \partial U / \partial \alpha] = 0, \tag{A.5}$$

or

$$E[U'(\phi(\theta, \alpha, W_0))\, \partial \phi / \partial \alpha] = 0, \tag{A.6}$$

and the second order condition is

$$D = E[\, \partial^2 V / \partial \alpha^2] < 0. \tag{A.7}$$

For the general model (3.10)

(A.8) $\partial^2 V/\partial\alpha\partial\theta = \int_X \{U''(\phi(\theta, \alpha, W_0))\partial\phi/\partial\theta\partial\phi/\partial\alpha + U'(\phi(\theta, \alpha, W_0))\partial^2\phi/\partial\theta\partial\alpha\}\, dF(\theta).$

(A.9) $\partial^2 V/\partial\alpha\partial W_0 = \int_X \{U''(\phi(\theta, \alpha, W_0))\partial\phi/\partial W\partial\phi/\partial\alpha + U'(\phi(\theta, \alpha, W_0))\partial^2\phi/\partial W\partial\alpha\}\, dF(\theta).$

$$= \partial\phi/\partial W \int_X U''(\phi(\theta, \alpha, W_0))\, \partial\phi/\partial\alpha\, dF(\theta) + \partial^2\phi/\partial W\partial\alpha \int_X U'(\phi(\theta, \alpha, W_0))\, dF(\theta).$$

It is now possible to proceed to

Proof of Proposition 3.4:

(a(i)) Implicitly differentiating (A.6) yields

(A.10) $$\partial\alpha/\partial\delta = (-1/D)\, \partial^2 V/\partial\alpha\partial\theta.$$

Hence the problem is to sign the RHS of (A.8). The second integrand is everywhere positive by (Φ.3). For the first, observe that

(A.11) $\int_X U''(\phi(\theta, \alpha, W_0))\partial\phi/\partial\theta\partial\phi/\partial\alpha\ dF(\theta) = \partial\phi/\partial\theta \int_X U''(\phi(\theta, \alpha, W_0))\partial\phi/\partial\alpha\, dF(\theta).$

Since $\partial\phi/\partial\theta$ is a positive constant by (Φ.1) and (Φ.5), the RHS may be rewritten as

$$-\ \partial\phi/\partial\theta \int_X r_a\, U'(\phi(\theta, \alpha, W_0))\partial\phi/\partial\alpha\, dF(\theta),$$

where r_a is the coefficient of absolute risk aversion. Applying Lemma 3.1 with g replaced by r_a (monotonically declining by DARA), f replaced by $U'(\phi(\theta, \alpha, W_0))\partial\phi/\partial\alpha$ and θ^* chosen so that $\partial\phi/\partial\alpha = 0$ when evaluated at $\theta = \theta^*$, we have

(A.12) $\int_X r_a\, U'(\phi(\theta, \alpha, W_0))\partial\phi/\partial\alpha\, r_a\, dF(\theta) \leq \int_X r_a \int_X U'(\phi(\theta, \alpha, W_0))\partial\phi/\partial\alpha\ dF(\theta) = 0,$

so the entire term is non-negative. Hence $\partial\alpha/\partial\delta \geq 0$.■

(a(ii)) From the first order condition (A.6), observe that U' is declining in θ. From (Φ.3), $\partial\phi/\partial\alpha$ is increasing in θ. Hence, Lemma 3.1 implies that $E[\partial\phi/\partial\alpha] \geq 0$. By (Φ.5) $\partial^2\phi/\partial\theta\partial\alpha$ is a constant, so $E[\partial\phi/\partial\alpha]$ must be equal to the $\partial\phi/\partial\alpha$ evaluated at $\theta = \mu$. The result now follows from the second order condition (A.7).■

(a(iii)) Let λ be the multiplicative spread parameter. Implicitly differentiating (A.6) with respect to λ yields

(A.13) $$\partial\alpha/\partial\lambda = \partial\alpha/\partial\delta = (-1/D)\, \partial^2 V/\partial\alpha\partial\lambda,$$

$$= -1/D\int_X \{U''(\phi(\theta,\ \alpha,\ W_0))\partial\phi/\partial\theta\ (\theta-\mu)\ \partial\phi/\partial\alpha + U'(\phi(\theta,\ \alpha,\ W_0))\partial^2\phi/\partial\theta\partial\alpha\ \partial\theta/\partial\lambda\ \}\ dF(\theta).$$

Lemma 3.1 may be used to show that the second integral is negative. By (Φ.3) and (Φ.5), $\partial^2\phi/\partial\theta\partial\alpha$ is a non-negative constant. Applying Lemma 3.1 with $g = U'$ and $f = \partial\theta/\partial\lambda$ yields the required result.

It remains to consider the first integral. Let θ^* denote the value of θ for which $\partial\phi/\partial\alpha = 0$. The integral may be partitioned as

$$\partial\phi/\partial\theta[\int_X U''(\phi(\theta,\ \alpha,\ W_0))(\theta-\ \theta^*)\partial\phi/\partial\alpha dF(\theta)\ -\ (\mu\ -\ \theta^*)\int_X U''(\phi(\theta,\ \alpha,\ W_0))\partial\phi/\partial\alpha\ dF(\theta)],$$

noting that, by (Φ.5), $\partial\phi/\partial\theta$ is a positive constant.

By definition $(\theta\ -\ \theta^*)$ and $\partial\phi/\partial\alpha$ have the same sign for all θ, so the first term is unambiguously negative. The proof of part (ii) implies that the term $(\mu\ -\ \theta^*)$ is positive, and the second integral is positive by the proof of part (i). ■

(b) Implicitly differentiating (A.6) with respect to W_0 yields

$$\partial\alpha/\partial W_0 = (-1/D)\ \partial^2 V/\partial\alpha\partial W_0.$$

By assumptions (Φ.2) and (Φ.4), it is sufficient to show that the integrals in (A.9) are positive. The positivity of the first is proved as in a(i) and the second integrand is everywhere positive.

For the first integral we may observe

$$\int_X U''(\phi(\theta,\ a,\ W_0))\ \partial\phi/\partial\alpha\ dF(\theta) = \int_X -r_a\ U'(\phi(\theta,\ a,\ W_0))\ \partial\phi/\partial\alpha\ dF(\theta),$$

where r_a is the coefficient of absolute risk aversion. Now let θ^* be the value of θ for which $\partial\phi/\partial\alpha = 0$, and let r_a^* be the corresponding value of r_a. By the DARA assumption

$$\int_X -r_a\ U'(\phi(\theta,\ a,\ W_0))\ \partial\phi/\partial\alpha\ dF(\theta) \geq r_a^* \int_X U'(\phi(\theta,\ a,\ W_0))\ \partial\phi/\partial\alpha\ dF(\theta)$$
$$= 0 \text{ by (A.6)}.$$

The second integrand is everywhere positive, so $\partial\alpha/\partial W_0 \geq 0$. ■

CHAPTER 4

The Challenge to EU Theory

There has been a steady increase in the number of 'anomalies' associated with EU theory and particularly with the independence axiom. The auxiliary hypotheses used by followers of the EU approach to explain these problems have become increasingly threadbare. The way is, therefore, open for an alternative approach.

Problems in EU theory fall into three main categories. First, there are choice problems used in experimental settings for which many subjects give responses inconsistent with the EU axioms. The most notable are the Allais problem and the common ratio effect. Second, there are observed patterns of market behavior that appear to contradict the predictions of the theory. For example, a number of other aspects of observed insurance choices are, at least arguably, inconsistent with EU theory. Third, there are problems that have emerged in the elicitation of utility functions using questionnaires. Some methods for constructing utility functions have produced thoroughly inconsistent results. Others have shown evidence of consistent bias.

Many of the most intractable problems associated with EU theory are closely related to the independence axiom, and much of the debate over EU theory has turned on this axiom. It is important to establish the weakness of this axiom on both normative and descriptive grounds and to consider possible alternatives.

Experimental tests have the advantage that subjects can be presented with a wide range of decision problems couched in terms of probabilities, thus permitting easy analysis of the results. However, there are many difficulties with experimental evidence. Although attitudes seem to be changing, economists have generally regarded experimental evidence with caution.

In addition to the well known Allais problem, a wide range of experimental violations of the EU approach have been observed. A summary of the literature is given by Machina (1983b). Attention here will be confined to a group of experimental findings that have had an important impact on the development of generalized theories of choice under uncertainty. These are the *common ratio effect* (Kahneman and Tversky 1979), *ambiguity effects* (Ellsberg 1961) and *preference reversal* (Lichtenstein and Slovic 1971, 1973).

4.1 The Allais Problem

Most of the experiments that were crucial in creating concern about the empirical validity of EU theory involved subjects' responses to hypothetical gambles. The experiments were designed on the basis of introspection suggesting that the predictions of EU theory would be violated in particular ways.

The archetype of these experiments is the well known Allais problem.[4] The Allais problem is set out as follows.

Problem 1:

Part 1: Choose between

A_1 {\$1m; 1};

and

B_1 {(0, \$1m, \$5m); (0.01, 0.89, 0.1)}.

Part 2: Choose between

A_2 {(0, \$1m); (0.89, 0.11)};

and

B_2 {(0, \$5m); (0.9, 0.1)}.

Most subjects choose A_1 and B_2, a decision inconsistent with any EU utility function. Allais' problem was chosen as a counterexample to the independence axiom. The critical feature of the paradox is the 0.01 possibility of receiving nothing in prospect B_1. Because this outcome is overweighted, choices inconsistent with EU theory are made.

The first objection to this experiment is that the sums of money involved are unrealistically large. However, similar choices have been elicited in less extreme situations. MacCrimmon and Larsson (1979) reported a series of experiments in which attempts were made to test the prevalence of Allais-type violations of the EU axioms.

MacCrimmon and Larsson considered a range of problems with three payoff parameters r, s and t, with $r > s > t$, and a probability parameter p, with $0.11 < p < 1$. The choices may then be cast in the form of choices between

$A_i \{(t,\ s);\ (1 - p_i,\ p_i)\}$;

and

$B_i \{(t,\ s,\ r);\ (1.01 - p_i,\ p_i - 0.11,\ 0.1)\}$ for $i = 1, 2$.

The Allais-type behavior is elicited by examining the choice with two different values of p. Thus, the standard Allais problem has $r =$ \$5m, $s =$ \$1m, $t = 0$, $p_1 = 1$, $p_2 = 0.11$. This problem is referred to as the common consequence problem, since changes in p affect only consequences that are common to the prospects A and B, and thus should not, according to the independence axiom, alter the preference ranking between them.

MacCrimmon and Larsson examined values of s ranging from \$1 000 000 to \$10 000 and values of p_1 and p_2 ranging from 1 to 0.11, while holding $t = 0$ and $r = 5s$. On average about one third of their subjects exhibited Allais-type violations, with the number of violations tending to decline with the size of the payoff, s, and therefore also with $r = 5s$. Their results are summarized in Figure 4.1.

[4] The Allais problem has often been referred to as the 'Allais paradox'. But it is paradoxical only if EU theory is taken to be axiomatically true.

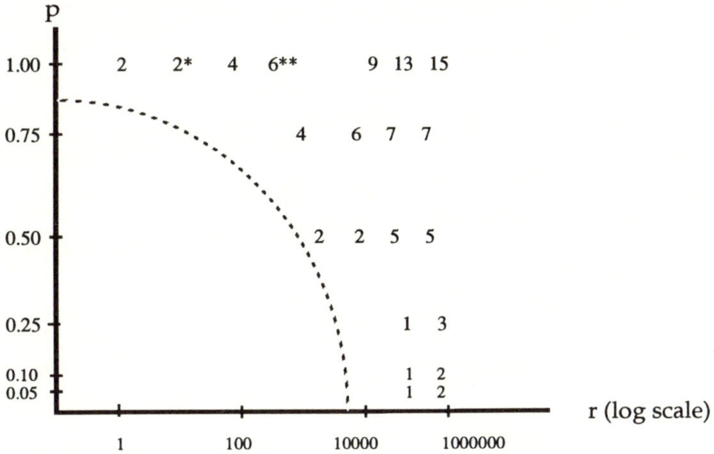

*One subject chose A on one presentation of this set, and B on the other

** Two subjects chose A on one presentation of this set and B on the other

Figure 4.1: The number of subjects, out of 19, selecting the alternative (r, p) over the alternative $(5r, 4/5p)$.

Machina (1983b) offers a diagrammatic illustration of the Allais problem that has proved useful in a number of contexts (Figures 4.2a and 4.2b)[5]. The diagram refers to prospects of the form $\{(x_1, x_2, x_3); (p_1, p_2, p_3)\}$ for fixed $x_1 < x_2 < x_3$. Since $p_2 = 1 - p_2 - p_3$, any such prospect may be represented by a point in the triangle $\{(p_1, p_3); p_1 + p_2 \le 1\}$. Preferences may be represented by indifference curves. First stochastic dominance ensures that indifference curves slope upwards to the north-east. Under EU, the independence axiom ensures that indifference curves are parallel straight lines, as in Figure 4.2a. The Allais problem may be represented with $x_1 = 0$, $x_2 = \$1\text{m}$, $x_3 = \$5\text{m}$. With the preferences as reported, B_2 is preferred to A_2. However the fact that indifference curves are parallel means that this can only happen if, also, B_1 is preferred to A_1. This is the normal pattern among the minority of subjects who conform with EU theory in the standard Allais problem.

Machina (1982) suggests the alternative hypothesis that indifference curves display 'fanning out' as in Figure 4.2b. That is, indifference curves become steeper as the probability of the good outcome x_3 rises and the probability of the bad outcome x_1 falls. This is consistent with the modal preferences in the Allais problem. However, as will be shown in Chapter 10, fanning out is not the only possible explanation.

---

[5] This diagram was first used by Marschak (1950), but its recent popularity is due to the work of Machina. It will be referred to as the unit probability triangle

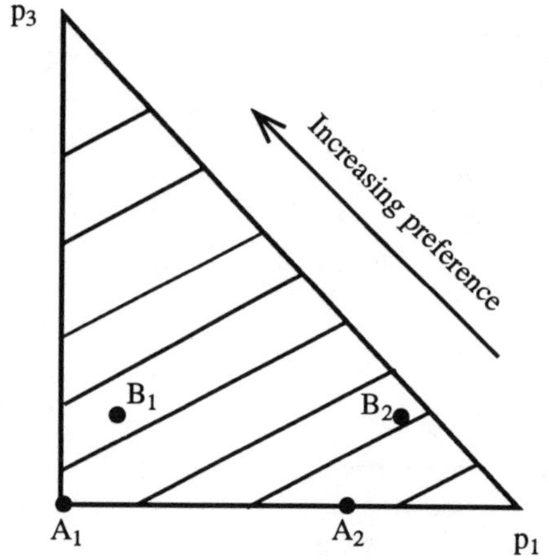

Figure 4.2a: Marschak-Machina triangle (EU preferences)

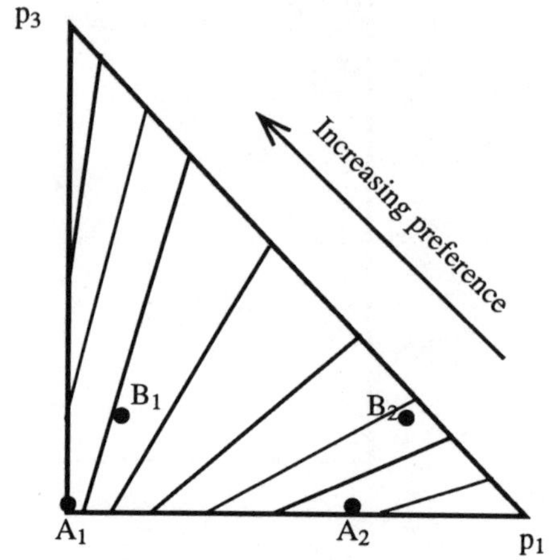

Figure 4.2b: Marschak-Machina triangle (fanning out)

4.2 The Common Ratio Effect

Although the Allais problem is the best known of the counter-examples to EU theory proposed by Allais, it is not the only one. Another well known class of problems is usually referred to as the *common ratio effect*. (The usual Allais problem is sometimes referred to as the *common consequence effect*).

The common ratio effect works best when events involving small probabilities of extreme payoffs are involved. Allais (1953) proposed a problem of the form

Problem 2:

Part 1: Choose between

A_1 {(0,\$4000);(0.2, 0.8)};

and

B_1 {\$3000, 1}.

Part 2: Choose between

A_2 {(0,\$4000);(0.8, 0.2)};

and

B_2 {(0,\$3000);(0.75, 0.25)}.

The ratio of the probabilities is the same in both cases, so according to EU theory the same outcome should be chosen each time. Kahneman and Tversky (1979) found that 80 per cent of subjects chose B_1, but only 35 per cent chose B_2. This example is open to the objection that people may simply prefer certainty when they can get it, but may otherwise choose in a manner consistent with EU.

The following example of the common ratio effect, in which there are no sure bets, is given by Kahneman and Tversky.

Problem 3:

Part 1: Choose between

A_1 {(0,\$3000);(0.1, 0.9)};

and

B_1{(0,\$6000);(0.55, 0.45)}.

Part 2: Choose between

A_2 {(0,\$3000);(0.998, 0.002)};

and

B_2 {(0,\$6000);(0.999, 0.001)}.

Once again the ratio of the probabilities is the same in both cases. Moreover, risk aversion implies that option *B* should be preferred in both cases. In fact, 86 per cent of people made this choice in the first problem, but only 27 per cent in the second problem.

MacCrimmon and Larsson (1979) generalized this problem to cover problems of choice pairs $A = \{(0, r);(1-p, p)\}$, $B = \{(0, ar);(1-bp, bp)\}$, where p varies between choice pairs. Thus in the example cited above, $r = \$3000$, $a = 2$, $b = 0.5$, $p_1 = 0.9$, $p_2 = 0.002$. MacCrimmon and Larsson fixed $a = 5$, $b = 0.8$ and allowed r to vary from \$1m to \$1 while p took on the values 1.00, 0.75, 0.25, 0.1, and 0.05. They also examined negative values for r ranging from −\$1000 to −\$1, with p taking on the values 1.00, 0.80, 0.20, and 0.04.

In general, the proportion choosing alternative A declined with p and with the absolute value of r. Overall, about 65 per cent of the subjects exhibited consistent violations of the independence axioms. Two conclusions may be drawn from the studies of the common ratio effect. The first, more firmly based, is that people presented with common ratio choices will not, in general, make choices consistent with EU theory. The second, proposed by MacCrimmon and Larsson is that the proportion choosing the higher probability will decrease with p and with the size of the payoff r. Although the data give some support to the second inference, changes in preference by one or two subjects would be enough to invalidate it.

4.3 Ambiguity

In the analysis presented above, it has been assumed that individuals are presented with a probability distribution, or that they can form well defined subjective probabilities for all relevant events. There is a good deal of evidence that this is not the case, and the distinction between risk and ambiguity is important in describing choice under uncertainty.

The best known example is the following problem posed by Ellsberg (1961).

Problem 4:

Consider an urn (Urn I) containing 50 red balls and 50 black balls, and another (Urn II) containing 100 red and black balls in unknown proportions. A ball is drawn at random from each urn. Which of the following bets do you prefer:

A_1 \$100 if a red ball is drawn from Urn I, nothing otherwise

A_2 \$100 if a red ball is drawn from Urn II, nothing otherwise

Most people choose A_1, suggesting on the standard view, that the subjective probability of a red ball from Urn II is less than 1/2. Now however, consider the bets.

B_1 \$100 if a black ball is drawn from Urn I, nothing otherwise

B_2 \$100 if a black ball is drawn from Urn II, nothing otherwise

Most people choose B_1, suggesting on the standard view, that the subjective probability of a black ball is less than 1/2, and hence that the subjective probability of a red ball is greater than 1/2. On the other hand most people are indifferent between A_1 and B_1 and between A_2 and B_2, suggesting that the subjective probability is equal to 1/2.

A second example is

Problem 5:

Consider an urn containing 30 red balls and a total of 60 black and yellow balls, the latter in unknown proportion. Which of the following bets do you prefer :

A_1 \$100 if a red ball is drawn, nil otherwise; or

A_2 \$100 if a black ball is drawn, nil otherwise.

Most people choose A_2 indicating, on the orthodox view, that the subjective probability of drawing a red ball is greater than that for a black ball. Ellsberg then offered the problem of choosing between

B_1 \$100 if a red or yellow ball is drawn, nil otherwise; and

B_2 \$100 if a black or yellow ball is drawn, nil otherwise.

Most people now choose D_2 which has the known probability 2/3, thus apparently indicating that their subjective probability for a black ball is greater than that for a red ball.

Raiffa (1961) argued that the subjective probability approach is normatively superior as a guide to rational behavior, even if it does not predict well. Raiffa pointed out an apparent inconsistency in the choices of Ellsberg's subjects. Consider the following options for Problem 4. In option 1, a fair coin is tossed and prospect A_1 is taken if heads come up, B_2 if tails come up. In option 2, heads yields A_2, and tails B_1. Dominance suggests that option 1 should be preferred. But an analysis of the prospects shows that the two options are objectively identical. Whatever the distribution of balls in Urn II, both options yield a fifty per cent chance of winning.

One explanation of the Ellsberg 'paradoxes' is related to Akerlof's (1970) 'lemons' model. Akerlof argued that the difference in price between new and almost new cars could be explained by observing that the very fact of an almost new car being offered for sale increased the likelihood that it was a 'lemon'. Similarly, the fact that a bet is offered on an uncertain event raises the possibility that the person offering the bet has information indicating that their side of the bet is favorable. Thus it is quite rational to attach a subjective probability of a black ball coming up of less than 1/3 if you are invited to bet on it, as in *C*.2, and more than 1/3 if you are invited to bet against it, as in *D*.1. If you are free to choose which outcome to bet on or can split bets as in Raiffa's example, then it is reasonable to assume the two outcomes to be equiprobable.

This point can be illustrated even more sharply by the following pair of examples:

A_1 A fair coin is tossed once. If it turns up heads you receive \$2, otherwise lose \$1; and

A_2 Same as A_1 except that the coin is biased (but you don't know in which direction).

This choice is, in formal terms, very similar to that in the urn problem, but it brings out more clearly the reason for preferring the bet at known odds, namely the fact that the person offering the bet will normally know the nature of any bias. Thus, the reactions to 'ambiguity' observed by Ellsberg can be explained in terms of the differential information sets possessed by the parties to a gamble. An alternative approach, developed in Section 10.3, treats ambiguity in terms of the RDEU model.

4.4 Preference Reversal

In its simplest presentation, preference reversal appears to be evidence, not merely against EU, but against the existence of any preference ordering over random variables. Subjects are asked to choose between two gambles. For each gamble, the amount subjects would require to give up the right to the gamble is then elicited. It would be natural to assume that the required amount would be larger for the preferred gamble, but this is not, in general, the case.

The classic experiments on preference reversal were undertaken by Lichtenstein and Slovic (1971, 1973). Their hypothesis was derived from earlier work by Slovic and Lichtenstein (1968). Lichtenstein and Slovic (1971, p. 46) concluded that

> A gamble is a multi-dimensional stimulus whose various attributes have differential effects on individual decision-making behavior ... choices and attractiveness ratings are determined primarily by a gamble's probabilities, while bids are most influenced by the amount to be won or lost.

On this basis, Lichtenstein and Slovic presented subjects with paired prospects designed to elicit preference reversals. The pairs consisted of a P-bet, yielding a modest return with a high probability, and a \$ bet yielding a large return with a low to moderate probability and a small loss with high probability. The predicted violation was that subjects would choose the P-bet, but bid more for the \$-bet.

The subjects were first asked to choose between the prospects. Values for the prospects were then elicited. Three methods were used. In two hypothetical studies, subjects were asked to state the amount they required to give up the right to the gamble or the amount they would pay to play the gamble. These may be referred to as willingness to accept (WTA) and willingness to pay (WTP) respectively. The third study used real money payments. In this study, WTA was elicited using a method proposed by Becker, de Groot and Marschak (1964). After the subject stated a price, the experimenter span a roulette wheel to select a counter-offer. If the counter-offer was greater than, or equal to the stated WTA, the experimenter would purchase the gamble and pay the amount of the counter-offer. Otherwise, the subject would play out the gamble. Subjects were given extensive arguments aimed at showing that their optimal strategy was to state their exact valuation of the bet.

Extensive and highly systematic preference reversals were found with the hypothetical WTA format. The use of real money payoffs and the Becker–de Groot–Marschak method led to only a small reduction in the number of reversals, and reversals were nearly all in the predicted direction. However, the preference reversal pattern was much weaker with the WTP format.

Subjects who exhibited preference reversal were presented with arguments against their choices. Of 11 subjects, six revised their choices as soon as the preference reversal was pointed out, three revised their choices when presented with a money pump argument and two declined to modify their choices.

Lichtenstein and Slovic's initial experiments used student subjects. In Lichtenstein and Slovic (1973) the results were replicated for gamblers in Las Vegas. An important feature of these experiments was that some bets were unattractive and subjects then stated a WTP to avoid playing the bet. In this study, systematic preference reversals were observed for both WTA and WTP statements, although the proportion of subjects choosing the $-bet was small in the case of unattractive bets. Later replications were made by Grether and Plott (1979), Reilly (1982) and Pommerehne, Schneider, and Zweifel (1982). These studies varied the amounts of money involved and the experimental conditions. All used the Becker–de Groot–Marschak method and most bets were attractive. Contrary to the expectations of at least some of the experimenters, the changed conditions did not eliminate, or even greatly reduce, the preference reversal effect.

A number of features of the preference reversal experiments are worthy of comment. First, the standard argument that respondents to the Becker–de Groot–Marschak method should reveal their exact valuation implicitly depends on the independence axiom (Karni and Safra 1987). This point is discussed further in Section 10.4.

Second, in most cases, the P-bet second stochastically dominates the $-bet. It is therefore to be expected that risk averse individuals will choose the P-bet. Also, since the P-bet is nearly a sure thing, the value of the bet is easy to estimate and is essentially independent of risk attitudes. Any biases in the valuation process will arise only in relation to the $-bet (note that even calculating the EV for this bet would be beyond the mental arithmetic capabilities of many subjects).

Third, the disparity between the WTP and WTA experiments is part of a much wider pattern in which WTA is greater than WTP (see Mitchell and Carson 1989). In studies of environmental amenity, a ratio of 5:1 is common. The heuristic would appear to be that when one is asked to sell something and is difficult to assess its value (to oneself or to the buyer) one should quote a high price and minimize the risk of selling the good for less than its true value. This would suggest a simple explanation for the reversals observed in WTA questions by Lichtenstein and Slovic (1971). Since the P-bet is easily valued, subjects are simply stating a high value for the $-bet as part of a general response pattern for WTA questions. This explanation does not cover the observation of high WTP to avoid playing unattractive $-bets in Lichtenstein and Slovic (1973). However, in this case, less than 25 per cent of responses exhibited preference reversals, as the $-bet was only rarely chosen.

4.5 Gambling

Since no theory appears able to encompass all of the behavioral patterns observed in empirical settings, the crucial issue for EU theory is its ability to predict behavior in market settings. One of the first major problems to emerge in EU theory derived from observed behavior in markets involving uncertainty such as those for insurance and gambling. Most people take out insurance against adverse events such as motor vehicle accidents. A large proportion also gamble, for example by buying lottery tickets. In both cases, the odds offered are actuarially unfair, so that both gambling and insurance are inconsistent with the maximization of expected value.

There is a well developed analysis of insurance purchases under EU. However, EU theory has little to say about gambling. This is a serious limitation. Gambling, as well as being the inspiration for the development of probability theory, is an economically significant aspect of uncertainty. Yet gambling is inconsistent with EU theory unless the very plausible hypothesis of risk aversion is abandoned, and the coexistence of gambling and insurance purchase is very difficult to fit into the EU framework.

Some types of gambling can be explained easily enough. For example, some betting on horse races may reflect divergent beliefs about the outcome. This is reflected in the large amounts of effort devoted to collecting and analyzing information about the quality of horses, jockeys and tracks. On the other hand, there are a large number of racetrack bettors who collect no information at all, and bet on a random basis.

Some types of gambling may be regarded as entertainment activities rather than as financial decisions. For instance, given the virtual certainty of losing on slot machines in the medium to long run, it seems reasonable to assume that this activity is undertaken largely for entertainment. Similar explanations may be advanced for participation in various time-consuming gambling games such as bingo.

In respect of lottery tickets, however, the only plausible reason for betting is the chance of winning a large amount of money. The predominance of this motive is confirmed by psychological studies (Walker 1984). The purchase of lottery tickets by people who are generally risk averse constitutes a significant problem for EU theory, which is very difficult to explain without resorting to the content-decreasing measure of excluding gambling from the realm of rational behavior.

At least some elements of racetrack betting would appear to fall into the same category. A series of studies from Griffith (1949) to Ali (1977) has shown that bettors are willing to pay a higher margin for long-priced horses. That is, the expected loss from consistently backing long-priced horses is quite large (similar to the loss involved in buying lottery tickets) and the expected loss for short-priced horses is very small (about 2 cents for every dollar invested). Some studies have suggested that a strategy of routinely backing horses at odds on would lead to small positive profits, though this seems unlikely.

Friedman and Savage (1948) attempted to explain the coexistence of gambling and insurance using the concept of an S-shaped utility function. The idea is that people will be risk averse with respect to changes in wealth within a neighborhood of their current wealth level but may be risk seeking with respect to prospects that may take them into a higher social class. Thus, the utility function may be regarded as concave for low income levels and convex for some higher incomes. Friedman and Savage introduced a third concave segment, at still higher income levels, as a response to the observation that lotteries typically have multiple prizes whereas convexity throughout the upper range would imply that a lottery with a single large prize would be preferred. (Figure 4.3).

The main problem with the Friedman–Savage model, and most of its successors, is that it predicts too much gambling. Mutually beneficial gambles will always be available to people whose present wealth lies in a concave segment of the curve. Even in a concave segment of the curve, people will tend to gamble until they reach a point at which they are risk averse in the sense that they would refuse all risky gambles with expected outcome zero or less. This condition may be expressed by saying that at a stable outcome x_0, the utility function 'looks concave', in the sense that for any x_1, x_2 such that $x_0 = \lambda x_1 + (1 - \lambda)x_2$,

$$U(x_0) > \lambda U(x_1) + (1 - \lambda)U(x_2). \tag{4.1}$$

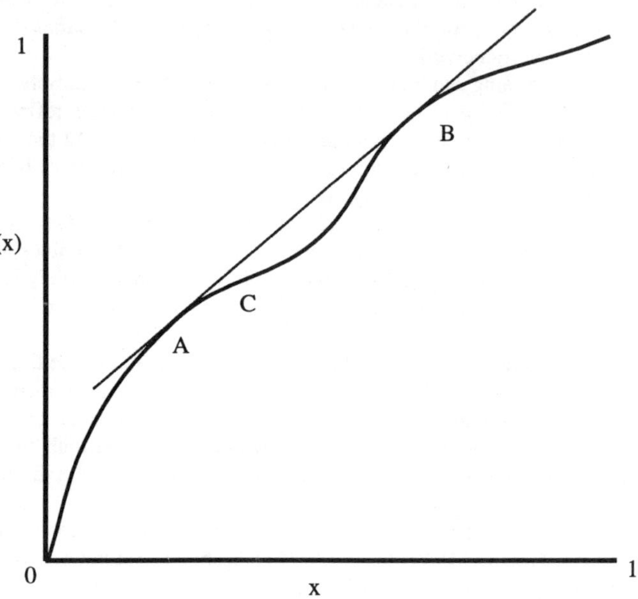

Figure 4.3: The Friedman-Savage utility function

Friedman and Savage indicate at least partial awareness of this point but they do not appear to realize that their model implies gambling behavior radically different from that observed in practice. Whereas most people only buy one or a few lottery tickets at a time, the model implies that people should gamble continuously until their wealth falls below point A, or they win a prize that takes wealth above point B, at which point they should stop altogether.

Observed gambling patterns can only be explained if the utility function shifts so as to keep the individual permanently at a point like C.

This may be shown as follows. Let the individual's wealth before any lottery tickets are purchased be denoted x_0. (It may be assumed for convenience that x_0 is a known constant. Provided the range of possible outcomes is small, the introduction of some uncertainty into the initial position will not affect the argument. Now let n be the number of tickets, x^* the lottery prize, δ the cost of a ticket and k the number of tickets purchased.

Then the decision problem is

$$\text{Max}_k\,(k/n)U(x_0 - k\delta + x^*) + (1 - (k/n))U(x_0 - k\delta). \tag{4.2}$$

The first order condition is

$$[U(x_0 - k\delta + x^*) - U(x_0 - k\delta)]/n + \delta[kU'(x_0 - k\delta + x)/n + (1 - k/n)U'(x_0 - k\delta)] = 0 \tag{4.3}$$

It is reasonable to assume that k is small in relation to n and, thus, to approximate (4.3) by

$$(1/n)[U(x_0 - k\delta + x) - U(x_0 - k\delta)] - \delta U'(x_0 - k\delta) = 0,$$

or

$$(U(x_0 - k\delta + x^*) - U(x_0 - k\delta))/U'(x_0 - k\delta) = n\delta. \tag{4.4}$$

If U is convex over the relevant range, (4.4) will have a solution for positive k whenever the lottery is fair, that is, whenever $x^* = n\delta$, and also for any lottery where the operator's profit is sufficiently small. The crucial feature of the problem, however, is that initial wealth is irrelevant. All that matters is $x_0 - k\delta$, the residual wealth after the purchase of lottery tickets.

This feature of the Friedman–Savage model implies pathological gambling behavior. An increase in wealth will be spent exclusively on lottery tickets until a point like A is reached. Conversely, a reduction in wealth will affect only expenditure on lottery tickets until this is reduced to zero. If A represents a subsistence level, below which reductions in wealth have drastic consequences, the model represents addicts who gamble themselves into destitution.

4.6 Insurance

Even in the absence of simultaneous gambling, a number of aspects of observed insurance decisions appear to be contrary to the predictions of EU theory. However, because of the complexity of insurance decisions, it is rarely possible to obtain clear-cut results from observations of market behavior alone, and it is usually necessary to rely on a mixture of market and experimental evidence.

Perhaps the most surprising claim to come out of studies of insurance decisions is the claim that people prefer insurance against high probability, low loss events to insurance against low probability, high loss events when the expected losses and premiums are equal. This claim was advanced by Slovic et al. (1977), and followed the earlier results of Edwards (1962).

A more solidly confirmed piece of evidence on insurance behavior is the widespread reluctance to accept contracts involving excess clauses and deductibles, when full insurance is available, even at actuarially unfair prices. A final piece of evidence relates to the bundling of insurance options. EU theory predicts that the price people are willing to pay for insurance against any of three mutually exclusive risks should be equal to the sum of the prices they are willing to pay for any one. By contrast, Slovic et al. (1977) found it was easier to sell a package consisting of insurance against a high probability low loss event and a low probability high loss event, than to sell either separately. The type of event insured against appears to be crucial here.

In summary, although many of the apparent violations of EU theory in empirical choices can be explained (e.g. by reference to information problems and context effects), they are sufficiently widespread to suggest that an alternative theory capable of explaining them would be useful. At the very least, it would be desirable to have a theory of rational choice of which EU was a subset, and which embodied plausible representations of some of the non-EU behavior patterns that have been suggested. In this way, instead of setting up problems in which violations of EU might or might not be observed, it would be possible to estimate a consistent set of preferences and test the restrictions implied by EU theory.

4.7 Construction of Utility Functions

A final category of violations of EU theory arises from attempts to estimate utility functions. This evidence is particularly important because it arises from attempts to apply EU theory rather than, as in the case of the Allais problem, from attempts to refute it. Thus, there has been a conscious attempt to avoid postulating extreme or unrealistic circumstances.

The first approach used to estimate the utility function, pioneered by von Neumann and Morgenstern themselves, was based on the *standard reference contract.* Here the outcomes x_1 and x_2 of a risky prospect are held constant. For any x_3, such that $x_1 \; P \; x_3 \; P \; x_2$, the questioner elicits the probability p such that x_3 is the certainty equivalent of $\{(x_1, x_2); (p, 1\text{-}p)\}$. The utility function is then constructed on the basis that

$$U(x_3) = pU(x_1) + (1\text{-}p)U(x_2), \tag{4.5}$$

given some arbitrary initial choice such as $U(x_1) = 0$, $U(x_2) = 1$. This method has generally performed poorly (Dillon 1971). It is apparent that it depends crucially on the assumption that preferences are 'linear in the probabilities.' If any form of probability weighting occurs, this method leads to inconsistent results.

As a result of these difficulties, a number of writers have advocated the use of fixed probabilities with variable outcomes (Davidson, Suppes and Siegel 1957, Anderson, Dillon and Hardaker 1977). One approach of this kind, known as the *equally likely risky outcomes* (ELRO) method, is to fix p and x_1 and then, for each x_2, elicit $x_3 = (x_1, x_2; p, 1\text{-}p)$. It is possible to apply equation (4.5) recursively to generate a utility function for a set of outcomes. An appropriate functional form may then be fitted to the resulting curve. This procedure has proved more satisfactory than the standard reference contract approach, in that it yields internally consistent estimates of the utility function. However, changes in the probability p lead to changes in the estimated utility function (Karmarkar 1974, McCord and de Neufville 1983).

Once again, this is consistent with probability weighting.

One of the most successful methods of eliciting utility functions has been the *equally likely certainty equivalent* (ELCE) approach of Anderson, Dillon and Hardaker (1977) based on fixed 50-50 odds. In this approach, the utility function is estimated on the basis of choices between prospects all of which are of the form $\{x_1, x_2 ; 1/2, 1/2\}$. This method has encountered fewer problems than any of the others described above. In summary, the evidence from attempts to construct utility functions suggests the existence of some form of probability weighting that is sufficiently important to make the derivation of the expectation of utility unreliable as a guide to preferences whenever prospects involving different probabilities are compared. The evidence also suggests that probability weighting is most significant for small probabilities and least significant when both outcomes are equiprobable. However, an alternative possible explanation for the success of the ELCE approach is that probability weighting for a given probability pair (p, 1-p) may be different when the preferred outcome arises with probability p than when it arises with probability 1-p. More recently, Miyamoto (1988) has proposed a more general method of eliciting EU preferences that is independent of probability transformations.

4.8 Probability Weighting

A major feature of most of the violations that have been observed is the apparent overweighting of low probability events with extreme consequences. This has also been observed directly in many psychological experiments aimed at eliciting subjective probabilities used in decisions, such as those of Edwards (1953, 1954). This has been a major point of departure for the alternatives to EU theory that are examined in subsequent chapters.

A widespread response to the violations of EU theory has been the use of models in which probabilities are replaced by decision weights. This notion was canvassed by Allais (1953), but not completely formalized. It subsequently appeared in a number of forms in the psychological literature on uncertainty. Empirical studies such as those of Mosteller and Nogee (1951) and Ali (1977) suggested that the decision weight associated with a given event was related to the objective probability by an S-shaped function.

The simplest approach to the problem, adopted by writers in the psychological literature such as Edwards (1953, 1954) and in the economics literature by Handa (1977), has been to replace the EU functional $\sum_{i=1}^{n} p_i U(x_i)$ with a subjective expected value function of the form

$$V = \sum_{i=1}^{n} \phi(p_i)\, x_i,$$

where ϕ is a continuous probability weighting function mapping the unit interval onto itself.

Handa presented an axiomatized theory, called the certainty equivalent, or CE, theory. This approach seemed to hold out the possibility of explaining many of the observed anomalies in EU theory. Unfortunately, it necessarily involves violations of dominance, except in the special case $\phi(p) = p$, $\forall\, p$, which implies maximization of expected value.

The problem may be seen from the following example. Suppose $\phi(1/3) < 1/3$. Then, for sufficiently small ε_1, ε_2, ε_3, a prospect of the form $\{(x-\varepsilon_1, x-\varepsilon_2, x-\varepsilon_3) ; (1/3, 1/3, 1/3)\}$ will be preferred to δ_x, even though the latter prospect dominates the former (indeed, it yields a better outcome with probability 1). It is straightforward to show that, given a sufficiently rich set of prospects, violations of dominance can only be avoided by setting $\phi(p) = p, \forall p$. (See Fishburn 1978 for a detailed proof.)

One obvious generalization of Handa's approach would be obtained by reintroducing a utility function, yielding a subjective expected utility functional $\sum_{i=1}^{n} \phi(p_i)U(x_i)$. Functionals of this kind were examined by Edwards (1962). Unfortunately, the same problems arise. If violations of dominance are excluded, the model is equivalent to EU.

4.9 Prospect Theory and Subjectively Weighted Utility

The subjective expected utility functional form $\sum_{i=1}^{n} \phi(p_i)U(x_i)$ has also been adopted by Kahneman and Tversky (1979), but their *prospect theory* approach involved a number of other features prompted by psychological analysis of decision problems. The most significant was the claim that "the carriers of value or utility are changes of wealth, rather than final asset positions that include current wealth" (Kahneman and Tversky 1979, p. 273). This claim is supported by reference to a number of experimental choice problems, notably those on risk seeking in the domain of losses. With the x_i interpreted as changes from current income, Kahneman and Tversky incorporate risk seeking in the domain of losses into their analysis, by making U convex for negative values.

Strictly interpreted, the abandonment of final wealth as the argument for the utility function would exclude the plausible and empirically well supported postulate of decreasing absolute risk aversion. Kahneman and Tversky accept the reality of decreasing absolute risk aversion, but argue that it is fairly unimportant and that their approach generally provides a satisfactory approximation.

Examples of the kind described in the previous section indicate that prospect theory is subject to violations of dominance. There are a number of possible responses to this problem. Kahneman and Tversky adopted the assumption that dominated prospects were 'edited out'. This assumption eliminated the problem of dominance violations at the price of introducing systematic intransitivities and discontinuities into the resulting preference pattern.

A second noteworthy feature of the Prospect Theory model is that it cannot easily be applied to continuous probability distributions, in which no outcome has positive measure. Moreover, different means of approximating a given continuous probability distribution by discrete prospects lead to radically different evaluations.

First, consider an arbitrary continuously distributed random variable y with cumulative distribution function $F(s) = \Pr\{x \leq s\}$. An obvious approximation arises by dividing the outcome space into n equiprobable events with value x_j, where $x_j = F^{-1}(j/n)$. Thus, the approximate prospect is of the form

$$y = \{(x_1, x_2, \ldots x_n); (1/n, 1/n, \ldots 1/n)\}$$

Thus,

$$V(y) = \sum_{i=1}^{n} \phi(1/n)\, v(x_i))$$

The property of overweighting of small probabilities described above suggests that this formulation is likely to involve supercertainty, with weights adding to more than unity. This implies that people will prefer uncertain prospects to certain ones, provided that the relevant random variables are continuously distributed and the spread of outcomes is not too large.

A rather different result is obtained if the outcome space is partitioned into equal intervals, rather than equiprobable events. Suppose that $\mathcal{X}$ is a sub-interval of the real line, of the form $[0, M]$. Then a continuous random variable could be approximated by a prospect of the form $\{(x_1, x_2, \ldots x_n); (p_1, p_2 \ldots p_n)\}$ where $x_i = i/M$ and $p_i = F(x_i) - F(x_{i-1})$. Given a single-peaked distribution, p_i will be smallest for values of i near 1 and n and largest for intermediate values of i. This means that the outlying events are more likely to be overweighted relative to their true probability. As n becomes large, even the intermediate events will have a fairly small probability and the supercertainty effect noted above will emerge.

Thus, two major problems emerge with the treatment of continuous distributions in Prospect Theory. First, assuming that such distributions are evaluated by means of discrete approximations, the evaluation will depend crucially on arbitrary choices about the manner of approximation. Second, if continuous distributions are approximated by discrete distributions with large values of n, Prospect Theory predicts a supercertainty effect. This is at variance with the majority of available evidence, which suggests that people usually prefer certain events to uncertain ones with the same expected value.

These problems may be traced to the use of the function ϕ to transform the probabilities of individual events. Since ϕ is non-linear, the evaluation of a prospect depends crucially on the partition of the set of states of the world into events. In the case of continuous distributions, this cannot be done, and any approximation reflects an arbitrary decision. However, the problem also arises when there are large numbers of discrete outcomes. It is necessary to decide whether two fairly similar outcomes should be treated as parts of the same event or as two separate events. The converse of this is that any two events with the same probability are treated in an identical manner. By contrast, the reasoning used to justify overweighting of small probabilities relies on the implicit assumption that low probability events are extreme events.

One obvious problem with the approaches described above was that the probability weights $\phi(p_i)$ generally did not sum to unity, thus ensuring that when two events with closely similar outcomes 'merged' there was a discontinuous jump in the value of the function. Karmarkar (1978) attempted to eliminate this problem by replacing the $\phi(p_i)$ with normalized weights of the form

$$\phi^*(p_i) = \phi(p_i) / \sum_{i=1}^{n} \phi(p_j).$$

Karmarkar imposed the additional condition that

$$\phi(p) = p^{\alpha} \quad 0 < \alpha \leq 1,$$

This approach is denoted *subjectively weighted utility* (SWU). In Karmarkar (1979), it was shown that the SWU approach could explain the Allais problem, and it may also be used to explain the common ratio effect and other problems. Examples of the kind used in Section 4.2

will not generate violations of dominance. Nonetheless, such violations of dominance do arise, as the following example from Quiggin (1985) shows.

The condition $\alpha < 1$ implies that, for any $p_i > 1/2$

$$\phi(p_i) < 2\phi(p_i/2). \tag{4.6}$$

Let

$$L = \{(0, x);(1/4, 3/4)\},$$

be a lottery with free tickets and a prize x awarded with probability 3/4. Now suppose that the lottery is operated in two states and the government of state 1 decides to tax the winners. However, instead of imposing a uniform tax, the government injects a further element of gambling. Fifty per cent of winners, selected at random, are levied a tax of δ_1, while the other fifty per cent are levied a tax of δ_2. Investors thus have a choice of two lotteries, L_1 = L and

$$L_2 = \{(0,\ x\text{-}\delta_1,\ x\text{-}\delta_2);\ (1/4,\ 3/8,\ 3/8)\}.$$

L_1 dominates L_2. On the other hand, from (4.6), provided δ_1 and δ_2 are small enough, L_2 will be preferred to L_1 by individuals with SWU preferences.

PART 2

THE RANK-DEPENDENT MODEL

Introduction

The main focus of this book is on the rank-dependent expected utility (RDEU) model, first proposed by Quiggin (1982a). RDEU is a generalization of EU that preserves the standard properties of continuity, transitivity and first stochastic dominance. The main features of the RDEU model, including its functional form and the history of its independent presentation by a number of authors, are explored in Chapter 5. It is argued that RDEU is the only natural generalization of EU that can incorporate notions such as probability weighting.

The ideas of risk aversion and risk preference are developed, and contrasted with those applicable to EU theory, in Chapter 6. Related ideas such as risk premiums and comparisons of risk aversion are also considered. The main theoretical novelty is the development of a notion of increasing risk more restrictive, but also more tractable, than that of Rothschild and Stiglitz. This 'monotone spread' concept is shown to have a natural relationship with an appealing concept of risk aversion for the RDEU model.

Chapter 7 contains a large class of comparative static results for the RDEU model. Since the existence of a large body of comparative static results is central to the appeal of the EU model, the fact that most of these results can be extended, and in many cases generalized for the RDEU case is very important. The central tool is a Correspondence Principle, exploiting the fact that RDEU may be interpreted as EU taken with respect to a transformed random variable.

One of the most important extensions is to the case of preferences which are not globally risk averse. In Chapter 8, the RDEU model is applied to the Friedman–Savage problem and an optimal prize structure for lotteries is derived.

CHAPTER 5

Rank-dependent Expected Utility – An Outline

The preceding chapters have described the developments that led to a demand for theories of choice which combined the power of EU with the ability to account for empirical behavior inconsistent with the EU model. In the 1980s, this demand was met with a profusion of new models. Fishburn (1988) discusses at least a dozen. There are perhaps twenty more models that either have been produced since Fishburn's survey or fell outside the scope of his enquiry. As is inevitable in such a crowded field, the majority of the new models have received little attention following their initial publication.

Undoubtedly the most influential work in the field has been that of Machina (see Chapter 12). However, Machina's concern was not so much to present a specific model as to consider the general behavior of preferences in the absence of independence, and to present general hypotheses (most notably that of 'fanning out') that might explain the observed violations or EU predictions. Machina did present for illustrative purposes, an example of a functional form, that of preferences 'quadratic in the probabilities', but this form has received little subsequent attention.

Among the specific functional forms that have been presented, few have stimulated as much interest as the rank-dependent expected utility (RDEU) model. There are a number of reasons for this. First, the model, presented in 1982 under the name 'anticipated utility', was in the field relatively early. Second, its independent discovery by a number of different writers encouraged a widespread dissemination of the basic ideas. Third, and not independently of the preceding points, the model represents in many ways, a natural generalization of EU theory. Finally, RDEU has particularly tractable properties for economic analysis.

The RDEU model may be viewed in a number of different ways. First, it may be regarded as an extension of the probability weighting approach to the case of multiple outcomes. Following the violations of dominance exhibited by the functional forms proposed by Handa (1977) and Kahneman and Tversky (1979), and the failure of Karmarkar's (1978, 1979) normalization to rectify the problem, it was widely assumed that no approach based on probability weights could avoid violations of dominance. The RDEU model offers the only extension of two-outcome probability weights consistent with first stochastic dominance.

Second, RDEU may be interpreted as offering an alternative notion of risk aversion and risk preference that depends only on the existence of risk and not on the nature of the outcome space. Allais' (1988) approach, in which the cardinal utility of wealth is assumed to be known under certainty, and risk aversion refers to risk in utilities, embodies this idea.

A third interpretation of the RDEU model is based on a modification of Savage's sure thing argument. The notion here is that it is natural to code prospects in a rank-ordered fashion, and that sure thing arguments can be applied only to states which are both equally probable and equally ranked. This gives rise to the notion of ordinal independence (Segal 1989, Green and

Jullien 1988) and, in combination with separability assumptions, (Quiggin 1989b) yields the RDEU model.

Finally, consideration of the formal properties of EU leads naturally to Yaari's (1987) dual model in which the utility function is assumed to be linear, so that risk attitudes are captured entirely by the utilities.

The object of this chapter is to present an outline of the RDEU model and the main ideas motivating it. I have adopted a historical approach, seeking to outline the different ways in which the model was independently discovered. The various approaches to the discovery of the model throw light on different aspects of the model and its structure.

5.1 The Development of RDEU Theory

The general notion of a weighting function depending on the entire vector of probabilities rather than on the probabilities of individual events was first proposed by Allais (1953). Allais did not, at that time, suggest a functional form or a set of axioms, and the idea remained undeveloped for another 25 years.

The functional form of RDEU theory was first proposed in an undergraduate thesis (Quiggin 1979) as a response to the violations of dominance present in the model of Handa (1977). The crucial idea was that the overweighting of small probabilities proposed by Handa and others should be applied only to low probability extreme outcomes, and not to low probability intermediate outcomes. This idea led immediately to the rank-dependent model, and to the requirement that the entire probability distribution, rather than individual probabilities, should be transformed. An application to data on the risk attitudes of Australian farmers was published as Quiggin (1981) and the first published version of the full model, including a set of axioms, appeared in Quiggin (1982a).

This work attracted little attention for some years. As a result, the functional form associated with the rank-dependent model was independently rediscovered on several separate occasions, with quite different motivating arguments. Thus, the model represents an interesting example of the theory of multiple discoveries, put forward by Merton (1973) and discussed in an economic context by Stigler (1982).

First, there was the 'dual model' of Yaari (1984, 1987), developed further by Roell (1987). The motivation here was mainly axiomatic. Yaari exploited a number of formal symmetries between EU and a special case of RDEU in which the utility function is linear. The linearity of the utility function implied that, in the dual model, risk attitudes are entirely divorced from declining marginal utility of wealth.

A second rediscovery, also based on the notion of risk aversion as a phenomenon distinct from declining marginal utility of wealth, was made by Allais (1987, 1988) whose work had provided the starting point for the whole field. Most advocates of the EU approach have treated cardinal utility as a convenient instrument for modelling uncertain choice that permits risk aversion to be described in terms of decreasing marginal utility of wealth. By contrast, Allais has always insisted on the psychological reality of cardinal utility. It is the desire to incorporate an explicit cardinal utility function that led Allais to his formulation of RDEU.

Another closely related development is the work of Schmeidler (1989) and Gilboa (1987), based on the notion of non-additive measures or capacities, originally developed in the work of

Choquet (1953–4). The problem here is taken to be one of ambiguity, in that the probabilities of the different states are unknown.

In addition to these developments in the theory of choice under uncertainty, the RDEU functional form (usually with a linear utility function as in the work of Yaari) has been applied to problems of social choice and income distribution, with distributions of welfare across individuals taking the place of random variables over states. Examples include Weymark (1981) and Ebert (1988).

5.2 The RDEU Model

The development of the rank-dependent expected utility (RDEU) or anticipated utility[6] (AU) model was motivated by the probability weighting models discussed in Chapter 4. Like earlier models, RDEU is based on a probability weighting function q: $[0, 1] \rightarrow [0, 1]$. However, the weighting function is applied, not to the probabilities of individual events, but to the cumulative distribution function.

The RDEU functional is given by

$$V(\{\boldsymbol{x};\boldsymbol{p}\}) = \sum_{i=1}^{n} U(x_i)\, h_i(\boldsymbol{p}), \tag{5.1}$$

where

$$\begin{aligned} h_i(\boldsymbol{p}) &= q(\sum_{j=1}^{i} p_j) - q(\sum_{j=1}^{i-1} p_j), \\ &= q(F(x_i)) - q(F(x_{i-1})). \end{aligned} \tag{5.2}$$

In comparing functional forms, it is sometimes useful to consider the function

$$q^*(p) = 1 - q(1-p).$$

For the two outcome case, the weighting vector is

$$h(\boldsymbol{p}) = (q(p_1), q^*(p_2)).$$

That is, q defines the weight on the worse outcome and q^* defines the weight on the better outcome. The weighting function is said to be *symmetric* when $q(p) = q^*(p)\ \forall p$.

Expression of the weighting function in terms of q^* is particularly useful when we are considering bets that offer a positive payoff x with probability p and nothing otherwise. Using the natural normalization $U(0) = 0$, the anticipated utility of the prospect may be expressed simply as $V\{(0, x); (p, 1\text{-}p)\} = q^*(p)U(x)$.

---

[6] The term 'anticipated utility' reflected the idea that the weighting function is integrated to yield an anticipated value of $U(x)$, which may be different from the mathematical expectation. However this terminology would be equally applicable to a number of other models. It has, therefore, been dropped, in favor of the more descriptive term 'rank-dependent expected utility'.

Because q is applied to the cumulative distribution function, the weight $h_i(\boldsymbol{p})$ depends on all the elements of $\boldsymbol{p}$ and not merely on p_i. This means that it is possible for two events with the same objective probability to have different weights. This feature distinguishes RDEU theory from other theories based on decision weights, such as those of Handa (1977) and Kahneman and Tversky (1979), which may be shown to raise problems with violations of dominance. Intuitively, the idea is that, although events with low probabilities and extreme outcomes may be given a weight significantly higher than their objective probability, events with the same probability and intermediate outcomes need not be treated in the same way.

Another feature of the earlier probability weighting models is that they could not be applied to the case of continuous (or mixed continuous and discrete) probability distributions. For continuous distributions, the probability of any point outcome is zero, and weighting models based on individual probabilities cannot be used. By contrast, the RDEU model has a natural generalization. Let $F \in \mathfrak{D}$, and let $H = q^\circ F$ denote the composition of q with F. Then

$$V(F) = \int_X U(x)\, dH(x) = \int_\Omega U(y(\omega))\, q'(\omega)\, d\omega. \tag{5.3}$$

When F is differentiable and hence has an associated density function f, we may write

$$V(F) = \int_X U(x)\, q'(F(x))\, f(x)\, dx. \tag{5.4}$$

Some features of the RDEU model may be observed immediately. First, since it is based on a single preference functional, preferences must display transitivity. Second, as long as U and q are monotonically increasing, preferences preserve first stochastic dominance. This is immediately apparent for discrete prospects of the form $y = \{\boldsymbol{x};\ \boldsymbol{p}\}$, $y' = \{\boldsymbol{x}';\boldsymbol{p}\}$ that share the same vector of probabilities $\boldsymbol{p}$. For y first stochastically dominates y' if and only if $x_i \geq x_i'\ \forall\ i$. The monotonicity of U assures that $U(x_i) \geq U(x_i')\ \forall\ i$, and the monotonicity of q assures that all of the h_i are positive. By partitioning the state space appropriately, any two discrete prospects can be compared in this fashion. For example if one prospect has n distinct outcomes and another has m distinct outcomes, both can be rewritten, using at most nm states, so as to share the same vector of probabilities. Since any distribution may be written as the limit of discrete distributions, first stochastic dominance is preserved for arbitrary distributions.

The issue of continuity is a little more complex. Assume that U and q are continuous. Whenever the x_i are distinct, V is continuous with respect to changes in the x_i. Continuity is similarly apparent when one of the p_i increases and another decreases. The more problematic case arises when the x_i are non–distinct, so that a change in the values of the x_i can lead to a change in the rankings of the outcomes and hence in the weights h_i. However, appropriate re–labelling ensures that all sufficiently small changes will leave the ordering of the x_i undisturbed, so that V is continuous in a neighborhood of any $\{\boldsymbol{x};\boldsymbol{p}\}$ and hence continuous everywhere.

5.3 The Transformation Function

Just as in EU theory, the utility function in RDEU is normally taken to be concave or linear. There is less consensus concerning the appropriate shape for the probability transformation function q. Quiggin (1982a, 1987) proposed an S–shaped function such as that illustrated in Figure 5.1. This is characterized by overweighting of extreme low probability outcomes. It is natural to consider the hypothesis of symmetry as a special case of this functional form. The S–shaped functional form was also popular in the earlier literature on probability weights. Most of the evidence was based on two–outcome prospects, where the RDEU model (with a symmetric weighting function q) agrees with a probability weight model. The phenomenon of overweighting, which was observed for both low probability large positive outcomes and low probability large negative outcomes naturally yielded this functional form in the simple probability weighting framework. Moreover, if violations of dominance are to be avoided for the two outcome case, it is necessary that the weighting function ϕ have the property $\phi(p) + \phi(1-p) = 1 \ \forall \ p$.

Other writers, notably Chew, Karni and Safra (1987) and Segal (1987a) have analyzed the case of a concave function (Figure 5.2). This means that, for any two equiprobable outcomes, the worse receives a higher weight than the better. This property is akin to risk aversion, and may be shown to yield a natural (but not the only) extension of the notion of risk aversion to the EU model.

A weaker notion of risk aversion is associated with the more general class of functions satisfying $q(p) \geq p \ \forall \ p$, as in Figure 5.3. That is, in any two–outcome prospect, the worse outcome is overweighted, and the better one is underweighted. The relationship between this notions of risk aversion and that associated with concavity will be discussed in Chapter 6.

Finally, some empirical studies have found support for the globally convex functional form illustrated in Figure 5.4. In most cases, these studies have not compared this form with the more intuitively appealing hypothesis of overweighting, illustrated by Figure 5.1. As will be argued below, the results of Allais-type problems support 5.1 as against 5.4.

A number of specific functional forms for q, exhibiting the patterns described above, may be considered. The simplest are functions of the form $q(p) = p^{\gamma}$. For $0 < \gamma < 1$, q is concave. For $\gamma > 1$, q is convex. The case $\gamma = 1$ corresponds to EU. Karmarkar (1978, 1979) proposed the functional form $q(p) = p^{\gamma}/(p^{\gamma} + (1\text{-}p)^{\gamma})$, yielding an S-shaped transformation function for $0 < \gamma < 1$. This function is symmetric, so that $q(p) = q^*(p)$ and, in particular, $q(1/2) = 1/2$, as in Quiggin (1982a). To remove the requirement of symmetry, Tversky and Kahneman (1990) proposed the modified form $q(p) = p^{\gamma}/(p^{\gamma} + (1\text{-}p)^{\gamma})^{1/\gamma}$. The transformation is S-shaped whenever $0 < \gamma < 1$, but it is symmetric only for the EU case $\gamma = 1$.

The various conditions on the transformation function may also be illustrated using Machina's unit probability triangle approach. Concave (convex) transformation functions imply broadly concave (convex) indifference curves, as in Figures 5.5(a) and 5.5(b). The pattern for the S-shaped transformation function (Figure 5.5 (c)) is more complex. In the lower right-hand corner, where the probability of the good outcome is near zero, it is overweighted and indifference curves are convex. Conversely, in the upper left hand corner, indifference curves are concave.

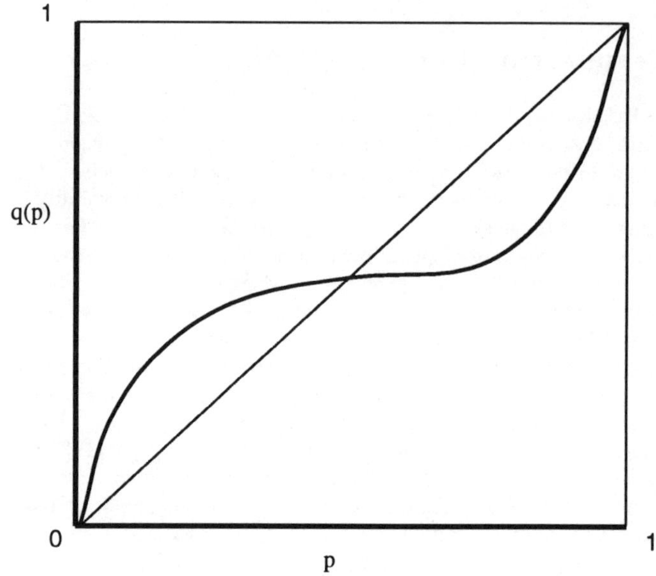

Figure 5.1: RDEU probability weighting function
Overweighting of small probabilities

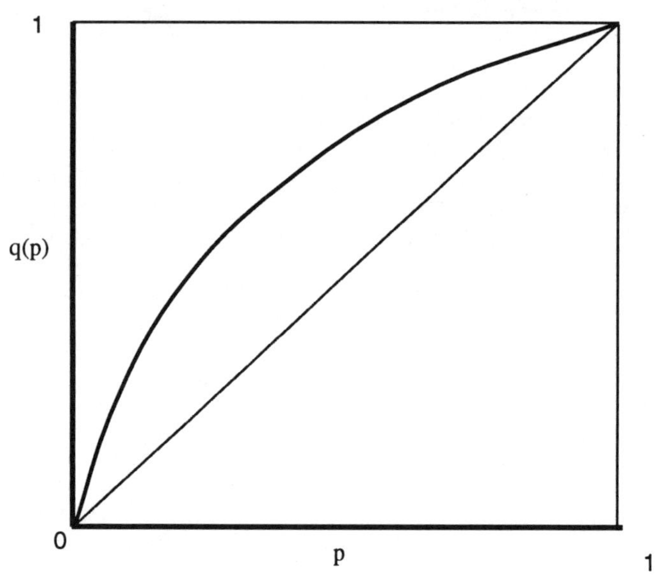

Figure 5.2: RDEU probability weighting function
Concave function (preserves SSD)

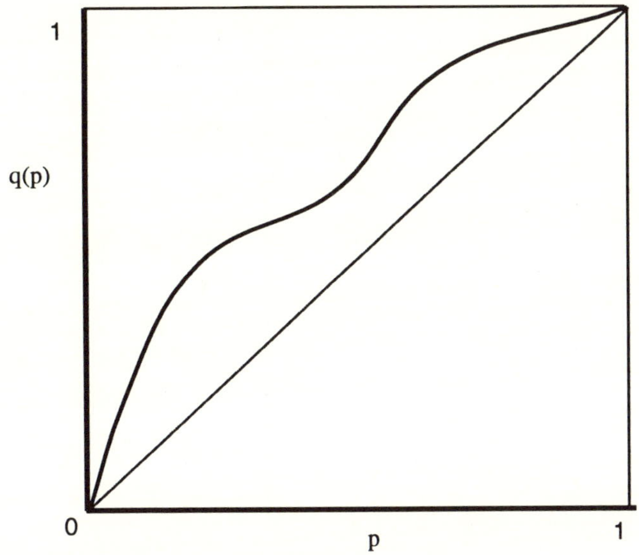

Figure 5.3: RDEU probability weighting function
$q(p) \geq p$ (risk averse)

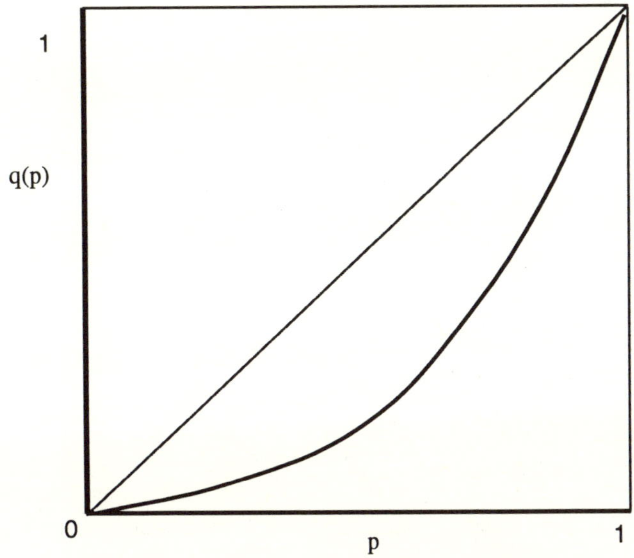

Figure 5.4: RDEU probability weighting function
Convex function (risk seeking)

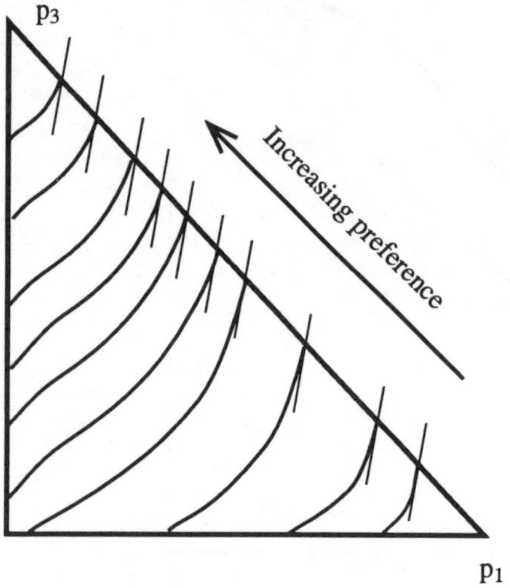

Figure 5.5a: Marschak-Machina triangle
(RDEU with concave *q*)

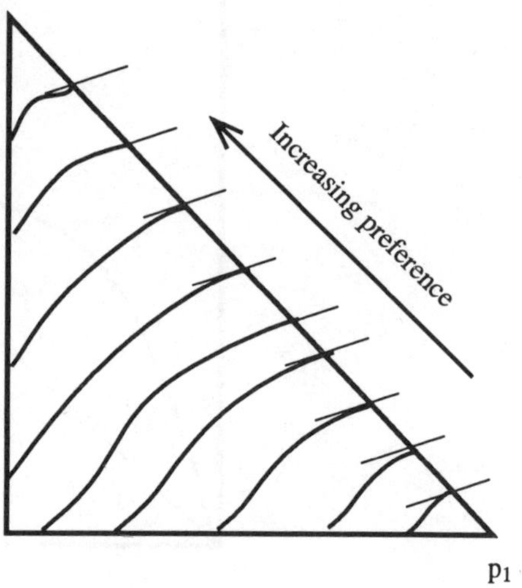

Figure 5.5b: Marschak-Machina triangle
(RDEU with convex *q*)

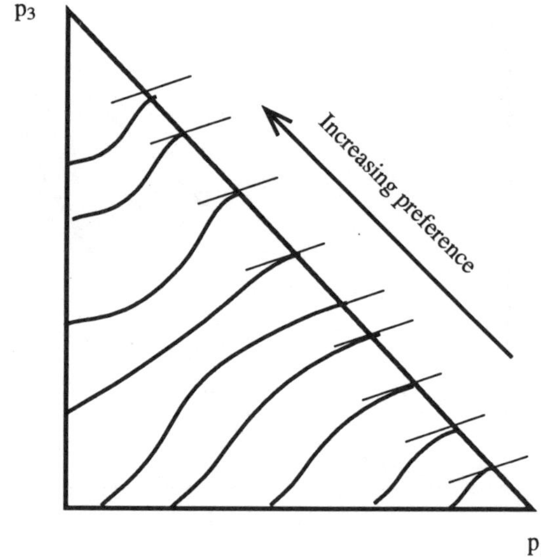

Figure 5.5(c): Marschak-Machina triangle
(RDEU with S-shaped *q*)

One interesting feature of the indifference curves in the unit probability triangle is that the tangents at the hypotenuse are all parallel. This result is independent of the choice of functional form. It arises because prospects along the hypotenuse are of the form $\{(x_1, x_3); (p, 1\text{-}p)\}$. The associated indifference curve consists of prospects $y = \{(x_1, x_2, x_3); (p_1, p_2, p_3)\}$ such that

$$V(y) = q(p)\ U(x_1) + q^*(p)U(x_3)$$

For a given small change in $\boldsymbol{p}$, we have

$$dV = q'(p)\ (U(x_1)dp_1 + U(x_2)dp_2 + U(x_3)dp_3) = 0$$

Using the convenient normalization $U(x_2) = 0$, the slope of the tangent at the hypotenuse is simply $U(x_1)/U(x_3)$.

5.4 RDEU — Probability Weighting Interpretation

In Chapter 4, evidence was presented to suggest that probability weighting was present when the predictions of EU theory were violated. Attempts to model this phenomenon by transforming probabilities were unsuccessful. Quiggin (1982a) suggested that the basic problem with these approaches was the fact that all events with the same probability were weighted equally. The evidence of overweighting related specifically to outlying, low probability, events.

For example, the Allais problem turns crucially on one low probability outlying event – the 1 per cent chance of receiving nothing in the high payoff bet. It is this event that generates risk averse choices in the first part of the problem. Similarly, in the Friedman–Savage paradox, it is crucial that the outcomes of winning a lottery or suffering an insurable loss are extreme events.

A natural way of formalizing this insight is given by the representation of random variables as acts mapping states of the world into outcomes. Suppose that the state space is partitioned in such a way that all states are equally probable. The simple probability weighting models discussed in Chapter 4 do not yield any useful insights into problems with this structure. In these models, all states must be overweighted (or underweighted) in precisely the same way. Further, unless the weight is equal to the objective probability, violations of dominance are inevitable.

The solution offered by the rank-dependent approach is to arrange the states of the world so that the outcomes they yield are ordered from worst to best, then to give each state a weight that depends on its ranking as well as its probability. To explain the Friedman–Savage and Allais problems, the crucial idea is that the events at the upper and lower tails of the distribution should be overweighted, while those in the center should be underweighted.

The following example illustrates further the notion that equally probable events should not necessarily receive the same weight. Suppose an individual's normal wage income is uniformly distributed over a range from \$20 000.01 to \$21 000.00. There is also a 1/100 000 chance that the person will win a contest for which the prize is a job paying \$1m a year. The probability of receiving any specified income in the relevant range \$20 000.01 to \$21 000.00 (*e.g.* \$21 439.72) is also 1/100 000. Nevertheless, it seems reasonable that the extreme outcome

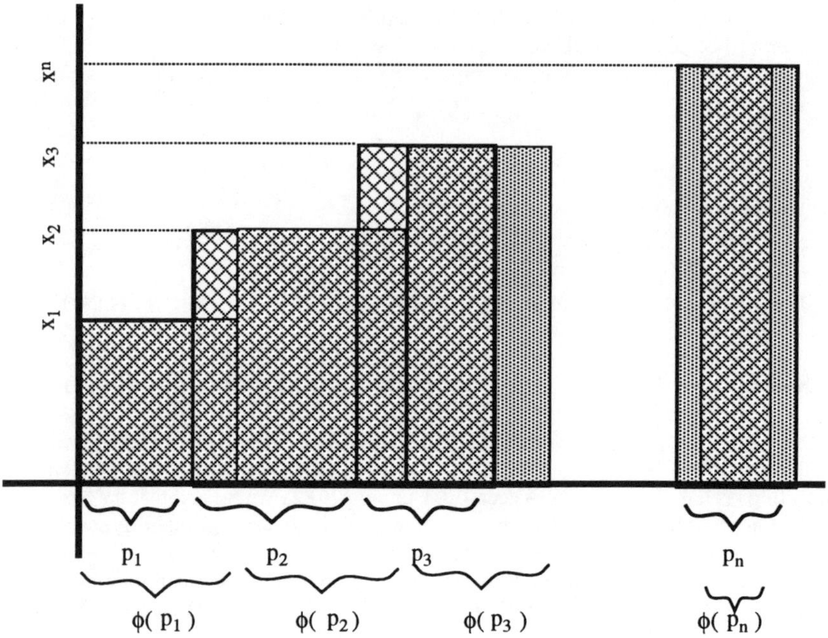

Figure 5.6: Probability weighting — transforms of individual probabilities

will not be weighted in the same way as an intermediate outcome such as $21 439.72. There are a number of ways in which the notion that extreme outcomes should receive more weight might be formalized. The simplest, explored here is to weight the outcomes in a manner which depends on their ranking in the probability distribution under consideration.

The difference between transforming individual probabilities and transforming the probability distribution may be illustrated using a diagrammatic representation.[7] The standard approach to probability weighting involves transforming the bases of the rectangles in Figure 2.1, which correspond to the probabilities of individual events, leading to a representation like that in Figure 5.6. The RDEU approach, illustrated in Figure 5.7, begins with the alternative representation of expected value given in Figure 2.2, and involves transforming the vertical distance from each point to the origin, just as in the case of the transformation used to obtain the EU model from Figure 2.1. The base of each of the rectangles now becomes the distance between the transformed points.

---

[7] The idea here is closely associated with the measure representation approach of Segal (1989), discussed further in Chapter 12. The exposition follows Wakker (1989b).

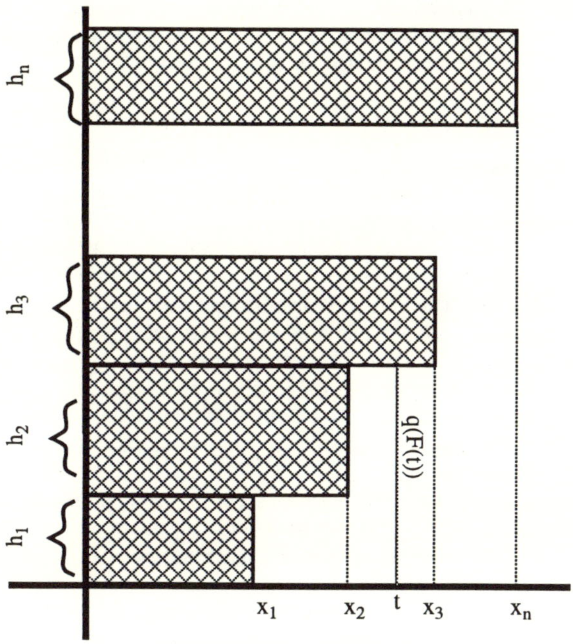

Figure 5.7: RDEU probability weighting (case of linear utility function)

$$h_i = q(F(x_i)) - q(F(x_{i-1}))$$

5.5 The Dual Approach

One of the most influential presentations of an RDEU model has been the 'dual model' of Yaari (1984, 1987), developed further by Roell (1987). The motivation here was mainly axiomatic. Yaari's axiomatic analysis will be considered in Chapter 11. The approach may be described fairly simply.

Yaari observed that $\mathcal{Y}$ is a mixture space in two ways. It contains probability mixtures of the form

$$\lambda F_1 + (1-\lambda)F_2 : x \mapsto \lambda F_1(x) + (1-\lambda)\, F_2(x), \tag{5.5}$$

and outcome mixtures such that

$$\lambda y_1 + (1-\lambda) y_2 : \omega \mapsto \lambda y_1(\omega) + (1-\lambda)\, y_2(\omega). \tag{5.6}$$

EU theory requires that preferences should have the property of linearity in probability mixtures. Yaari applied this requirement to outcome mixtures instead. To obtain the most appealing 'dual' representation of preferences, Yaari worked with the *decumulative distribution function* $G(x) = (1\text{-}F(x))$. He therefore obtained the functional form

$$V(G) = \int_X q^*(G(x))\, dx = \int_X x\, dq^*(G(x)). \qquad (5.7)$$

This form is linear in the outcomes and non-linear in the probabilities, and is a special case of (5.3).[8]

The property of linearity in the outcomes means that Yaari's model is unlikely to be a fully satisfactory description of individual choice under uncertainty. In particular, it is inconsistent with decreasing absolute risk aversion, since it implies that risk attitudes are unaffected by changes in x. Yaari's model displays both constant absolute risk aversion and constant relative risk aversion. This combination is not possible in EU theory and seems implausible in practice.

On the other hand, Yaari's model may be useful in analyzing risk averse (or risk seeking) behavior in cases where there is no reason to suppose that preferences are characterized by a von Neumann–Morgenstern utility function. One example, suggested by Yaari, is the profit (or loss) of a corporate firm with many shareholders. Another is risk of loss of life due, for example, to nuclear power accidents.

Nonetheless, the main interest of (5.7) arises from its status as a tractable polar case, enhanced by the availability of Yaari's dual interpretation. The absence of complicating effects arising from the concavity of the utility function means that many results can be derived easily in the linear utility case, then extended to the general case.

An example is Yaari's analysis of portfolio choice. Consider the simple one risky asset, one safe asset model, where the return on the safe asset is set to zero and the expected return on the risky asset is positive. Under EU theory, all agents, no matter how risk averse, will allocate some portion of their wealth to the risky asset. This is because agents are effectively risk neutral in a neighborhood of certainty. As the rate of return on the risky asset rises, the amount allocated to it increases, until, for sufficiently attractive risky assets, the whole of wealth is allocated to the risky asset.

By contrast, in Yaari's model, the agent allocates wealth in an all-or-nothing fashion. The evaluation of the prospect arising from allocating a proportion λ of wealth to the risky asset is given by

$$V(\lambda) = \int \lambda r W\, dq(F(r)) = \lambda W \int r\, dq(F(r)).$$

This is maximized by setting $\lambda = 0$ whenever $\int r\, dq(F(r)) < 0$ and $\lambda = 1$ whenever $\int r dq(F(r)) > 0$. This result is interesting in a number of ways. The integral $\int r\, dq(F(r))$ may be regarded as the expectation of the transformed variable $\tilde{r}$ with cumulative distribution function $q^\circ F$. Agents in Yaari's model act as expected value maximizers with respect to this transformed distribution. More generally, it will be found useful to consider RDEU as maximization of expected utility with respect to a transformed distribution.

[8] It should be noted that all of Yaari's results are expressed in terms of q^* (denoted in Yaari's paper by f) so that a statement such as "f is convex" should be interpreted, in the notation of this book as "q is concave."

Yaari's result that agents may reject bets at actuarially favorable odds even when the amounts involved are very small also carries over to the general case. It is the basis of Segal and Spivak's (1990) notion of first order risk aversion, considered in the following chapter. This aspect of the model appears realistic, but the notion of plunging does not. As Yaari observes (1987, p. 110)

> Under expected utility, a risk averse investor will always put *some* resources into a risky security, provided its expected rate of return is positive. I am prepared to suggest that both positions — "never stay put" in expected utility theory and "stay put until plunging becomes justified" in the dual theory – are extreme. Real investment behavior probably lies somewhere in between. (emphasis in original)

As will be shown below, the general RDEU model accords with the happy medium suggested by Yaari.

Similarly tractable results are found for the standard comparative static problem. An increase in risk aversion inhibits plunging and, for risk averse investors, an increase in the riskiness of the asset inhibits plunging. More general versions of this result are obtained for the unrestricted RDEU model in Chapter 7.

Another interesting feature of Yaari's analysis is the notion of *dual paradoxes*. As Yaari (p. 106) observes, examples can be found where "one would expect to observe behavior which is inconsistent with the dual theory while being consistent with expected utility theory." The common ratio problem in EU theory may be seen as the dual of the constant relative risk aversion property of Yaari's model. Although constant relative risk aversion is a plausible assumption, it is likely that most individuals would violate it under some circumstances. This is consistent with EU but not with Yaari's model.

The general RDEU model incorporates both EU and the dual model as special cases. It is, therefore, capable of accommodating the behavior found in dual paradoxes as well as that found in the usual EU paradoxes. However, consideration of the properties of the dual model may suggest possible counterexamples for RDEU theory. In particular when risks are very small, probability attitudes become the primary source of risk aversion and behavior under RDEU is approximated by the dual model. This point is discussed further in Section 6.3.

Another class of paradoxes discussed by Yaari relate to income distribution. Newbery (1970) shows that there does not exist a von Neumann–Morgenstern utility function whose expected value ranks distributions in the same order as their Gini coefficients. Yaari observes that the Gini coefficient may be derived from the dual model when $q^*(p) = p^2$. On the other hand, the dual model is inconsistent with measures of equality derived from EU theory such as those of Atkinson (1970). The general relationship between RDEU theory and measures of income equality is discussed in Section 14.1.

5.6 The Allais Model

One of the most important anomalies leading to the development of generalizations of EU has been the Allais 'paradox'. This has variously been viewed as a puzzle to be solved, as an example of fallacious reasoning or simply as an amusing oddity. For Allais himself, however, the 'paradox' represented an illustration of a fundamental property of a theory of risk competing with EU theory. The central tenets of this theory were

(i) The reality of cardinal utility, independent of any considerations of risk

(ii) The existence of risk attitudes concerning the variability of cardinal utility

(iii) Universal preference for security in a neighborhood of certainty

Allais presented these hypotheses as early as 1952, but did not, at that time, develop or axiomatize them. When, in the middle 1980s, he produced a formal model incorporating his ideas, it turned out to be identical to the RDEU model.

Allais (1988) proposes the *principle of cardinal isovariation*; that is, the requirement that adding an equal increment δ to cardinal utility in every state of the world should increase the value of the preference functional by exactly δ. It is easy to see that the RDEU functional given by (5.1) and (5.2) has this property. It may also be shown that the RDEU functional is unique in this respect. Given the linearity hypothesis, we require a functional form of the class

$$V\{\boldsymbol{x};\boldsymbol{p}\} = \sum_{i=1}^{n} h_i(\boldsymbol{p})\, x_i \, . \tag{5.8}$$

This class of functionals was in fact proposed by Allais (1953) but not developed further at that time. Quiggin (1982a) showed that the RDEU functional is the only member of this class consistent with continuity and first stochastic dominance (see Section 5.8).

Allais (1987) derives the equivalent formulation

$$V(\boldsymbol{x};\boldsymbol{p}) = U(x_1)+q^*(\sum_{i=2}^{n} p_i)\,(U(x_2)-U(x_1)) + q^*(\sum_{i=3}^{n} p_i)\,(U(x_3)-U(x_2)) \;\ldots + \; q^*(p_n)(U(x_n)-U(x_{n-1}))$$

and proposes functional forms for q similar to those illustrated in Figures 5.1 and 5.2 .[9]

The RDEU model satisfies Allais' postulate that risk attitudes arise independently of the marginal utility of wealth. Further, provided $q(p) > p$ for small p, there is a preference for security in a neighborhood of certainty. This property is satisfied by all of the functional forms that have been proposed in the literature. The most controversial aspects of Allais' theory relate to the notion of cardinal utility.

Most advocates of the EU approach have treated cardinal utility as a convenient instrument for modelling uncertain choice that permits risk aversion to be described in terms of decreasing marginal utility of wealth. By contrast, Allais has always insisted on the psychological reality of cardinal utility, at least in the sense of an interval scale. For example, Allais (1988) asks respondents to a survey to compare the utility gains or losses from changes in wealth at different starting points. This is meaningful only if utility can be measured on an interval scale. A useful discussion of the early debate between Allais and the followers of von Neumann and Morgenstern is given by Fishburn (1989).

---

[9] Fig 1 in Allais (1987) should be interpreted as the graph of q^*.

A number of issues arise in considering Allais' position. The first relates to Allais' insistence on the psychological reality of cardinal utility. This implies that utility of wealth should be measurable, even in the absence of uncertainty, on some form of interval scale. Allais accepts this implication wholeheartedly. A corollary of Allais' position, which caused considerable confusion early in the debate, is the view that risk attitudes must be expressed in relation to distributions of cardinal utility. For example, Allais (1953) suggests that risk averse people will be concerned with variability in cardinal utility. Most EU theorists at the time interpreted Allais' arguments as a simple mistake, resulting from a failure to comprehend that risk aversion was captured in the concavity of the utility function.

Most early advocates of EU, writing just after Samuelson (1947) had completed the ordinalist recasting of welfare economics, rejected Allais' viewpoint outright. Savage (1954) warned against confusing the von Neumann–Morgenstern utility function with "the now almost obsolete notion of utility in riskless situations." Arrow (1951) described cardinal utility under certainty as "a meaningless concept" and Luce and Raiffa (1957) described Allais' viewpoint as a fallacy. (For further discussion of the early debate on this point see Fishburn 1989 and Wakker 1991a).

None of this seems very convincing. The ordinalist revolution, associated most closely with the work of Samuelson, rested on the demonstration, that, *in the absence of uncertainty*, no inferences concerning cardinal utility could be made from observed choices over consumption bundles. This does not seem to provide a basis for declaring that the concept is meaningless. In the positivist philosophy of science associated with ordinalism, a statement such as 'marginal utility is diminishing in wealth' is meaningless if it has no consequences that are, at least in principle, observable. It is an illegitimate extension of this approach to claim that, because no consequences of the statement can be observed in a given context, the statement becomes meaningless in that context.[10] Uncertainty provides a context in which statements about cardinal utility have observable consequences.

Although few writers are willing, like Allais, to take the notion of cardinal utility to its logical conclusion, the idea remains in the background of most discussions of EU theory. Introspective arguments for the concavity of the utility function are implicitly based on decreasing marginal utility of wealth. By contrast, introspection about willingness to pay to avoid (or accept) risk does not yield strong intuitions in favor of global risk aversion.

A further difficulty with the denial of cardinal utility is that certainty is taken to be the standard case, so that the theory of choice under uncertainty is a special topic requiring logically separate tools. In fact, certainty is simply a theoretical ideal state, which is never attained.

Another interesting set of issues arise from the observation that utility functions, identical in form with those of von Neumann–Morgenstern are found in the context of intertemporal choice. The same functional forms are found to be useful and the interpretations given to their parameters are strikingly similar. This is particularly true of the constant relative risk aversion class of functions with the coefficient of relative risk aversion being interpreted as a measure of aversion to intertemporal variations in income or consumption. The most natural basis for such an aversion is diminishing marginal utility of wealth. Bailey, Olson and Wonnacott (1980) make this identification explicit, though they are criticized for doing so by Drèze (1982).

Similar parallels arise in the normative theory of social choice. The most notable is

---

[10] For example, the concepts associated with the theory of optics do not become meaningless in a cave.

Harsanyi's (1955) derivation of utilitarianism from individual Expected Utility maximizing behavior. More generally, any analysis of variation across states of the world has a natural interpretation in terms of allocations of consumption across individuals, and most plausible models involve diminishing marginal utility. This brings us back to our starting point, since the desire to eliminate 'unscientific' interpersonal comparisons of welfare was one of the main motivations for the development of the New Welfare economics.

Finally, von Neumann and Morgenstern themselves were primarily concerned with the development of solution concepts for game theory. As Wakker (1991a, p. 10) observes

> The same cardinal function that provides an expectation representing individuals' preferences over randomized outcomes is also used to provide the unit of exchange between players. The applicability of risky utility functions as means of exchange between players is as disputable as their applicability to welfare theory, or to any other case of decision making under certainty.

In summary, Allais' basic positions in his controversy with the 'American school' appear to have been vindicated. These are the claims that cardinal utility is a concept with validity independent of the context of choice under uncertainty, and that risk aversion is not identical with concavity of the utility function. The methodological basis for the rejection of cardinal utility does not stand up to close scrutiny. More important, the empirical hypothesis that risk averse behavior can be explained purely by concavity of the utility function has been contradicted by empirical observations commencing with the counterexamples proposed by Allais.

5.7 RDEU and Ambiguity

A number of independent discoveries of the RDEU model have been described in the preceding sections. Another closely related development is the work of Schmeidler (1989)[11] and Gilboa (1987). Unlike the models presented by Quiggin, Yaari and Segal, where objective probabilities are taken as given, the work of Schmeidler and Gilboa is concerned with the case of ambiguity[12] and is motivated to a significant extent by the work of Ellsberg. The central idea is that of non-additive probabilities. Schmeidler begins by considering the class of problems where there are *n* possible states and the information about all of the states is symmetric. An example would be a case where we know there are 100 balls in an urn, numbered from 1 to 100. The balls are *not* identical in size, but we have no information on which balls are large (hence more likely to be drawn) and which are small. The *Principle of Insufficient Reason*, going back at least to Laplace, suggests that in such a case the probability of any ball being drawn is the same as that of any other, and all the probabilities should be set equal to 1/100. Schmeidler accepts the first part of the Principle, but not the second. It is easy to see that if probabilities are equal and additive, they must all be 1/100, since the sum over all probabilities must be 1. However, this argument does not follow if probabilities are non-additive.

Schmeidler follows Anscombe and Aumann (1963) in distinguishing between lotteries

[11] Schmeidler's work on this topic commenced in 1982 and preceded that of Gilboa, despite its later publication.

[12] Schmeidler and Gilboa follow the usage of Knight in distinguishing uncertainty (=ambiguity) and risk.

with objective probabilities ('roulette lotteries') and those with only subjective probabilities ('horse lotteries'). Schmeidler's construction involves a two-stage lottery, in which the first stage is a subjective probability 'horse lottery' with prizes that are in turn objective probability 'roulette lotteries'. Gilboa shows that the approach may be developed without any reference to objective probabilities.

The formal analysis is based on the theory of capacities (non-additive measures), originally developed in the work of Choquet (1953–4). A capacity is a function μ on a σ-field of subsets of some space Ω. A capacity is monotonic with respect to set inclusion, so that $\Omega_1 \subseteq \Omega_2 \Rightarrow \mu(\Omega_1) \leq \mu(\Omega_2)$. For disjoint subsets Ω_1, Ω_2 this implies

$$\text{(a) } \mu(\Omega_1 \cup \Omega_2) \geq \mu(\Omega_1),\ \mu(\Omega_2),$$

but not necessarily

$$\text{(b) } \mu(\Omega_1 \cup \Omega_2) = \mu(\Omega_1) + \mu(\Omega_2).$$

as is the case with additive measures. Attention will be confined here to the case of non-additive probabilities, characterized by the requirement that $\mu(\Omega) = 1$.

For a measurable function φ: $\Omega \to [0, M]$, the Choquet integral is defined by

$$\int \varphi \, d\mu = \int_0^M \mu(\omega \in \Omega\text{: } \varphi(\omega) \geq \tau) \, d\tau.$$

Given a utility function U:[0, M], Schmeidler and Gilboa suggest taking the expectation of U with respect to the non-additive measure μ, yielding the Choquet expected utility functional $\int U^\circ \varphi \, d\mu$.

The model is simplest for a finite set of possible states of the world $S_1 \ldots S_n$. Assume without loss of generality that, for a given prospect, the states are numbered so that $x_1 \leq \ldots \leq x_n$. Then the utility of the prospect is given by

$$V(x) = U(x_1)\,\mu(S_1) + \sum_{i=2}^{n} (U(x_i) - U(x_{i-1}))\,\mu(\bigcup_{j=1}^{i} S_j).$$

Hence

$$V(x) = U(x_1)\,\mu(S_1) + \sum_{i=2}^{n} U(x_i)\,(\mu(\bigcup_{j=1}^{i} S_j) - \mu(\bigcup_{j=1}^{i-1} S_j)). \tag{5.9}$$

To make a direct comparison between two different prospects in this approach, it is necessary to assume that they are comonotonic, that is, they yield the same ordering of the state space from best to worst (Section 2.4).

Consider now the case where P is a probability measure and q:[0, 1] $\to$ [0, 1] is a monotonic transformation function, and let $\mu = q^\circ P$. Except that the representation (5.9) is expressed in terms of a measure rather than a transformation of probabilities, it is the same as that of the RDEU model (5.2). Equation (5.9) may be interpreted by regarding the non-additive measure μ as a weighting function. The weight on state i is the difference between the total weight of all the states up to and including i and the total weight of all the states worse than i.

Whereas in expected utility theory, the weight on state i is simply $\mu(S_i)$, in the non-additive models the weight depends on the ranking of state i. Non-additive models not derived from transformation functions are possible. However, Wakker (1990a) shows that, provided first stochastic dominance is satisfied, Choquet expected utility is equivalent to RDEU.

The major difference between the Schmeidler–Gilboa model and the usual approach to RDEU is one of interpretation. The standard presentation of RDEU is based on the assumption of known objective probabilities that are transformed to yield non-additive decision weights. By contrast, in the Schmeidler–Gilboa model, probabilities are initially unknown, and the decision weights are interpreted as non-additive subjective probabilities. Schmeidler argues that RDEU preferences are not normatively reasonable when objective probabilities are given. He states

> It may seem conceptually inconsistent to postulate a decision maker who, while computing anticipated utility, assigns weight $f(p)$ to an event known to him to be of probability p, $p \neq f(p)$. ... The use of the terms "anticipation" and "weight" instead of "expectation" and "probability" does not resolve, in my opinion, the inconsistencies.

As Schmeidler observes, this is ultimately a question of opinion (or perhaps taste). Nevertheless, several responses may be made. First, in practice, few decision-makers actually compute anything. Viewed as a descriptive theory, RDEU is an attempt to model the choices that are observed, not a description of the choice process. From a normative standpoint, there does not seem to be a great difference between deriving two subjective probabilities of 5 per cent but declining to add them up, as in Schmeidler's work, and taking two events with an objective probability of 5 per cent but regarding them as not equivalent to one event with a probability of 10 per cent, as in the usual RDEU models.

5.8 RDEU as a Natural Extension

Allais (1986, *p* 275) discussing the independent work of Quiggin, Yaari and Segal observes

> It is *very significant* that, starting from entirely different premisses, all three authors have been led to a *mathematical formulation* that is analogous to my own. (emphasis in original)

Multiple discoveries such as those of RDEU are surprisingly common in science (Merton 1973). The classic example in economics is the independent development of marginal utility theory by Jevons, Walras and Menger (see Stigler 1982 for further discussion).

The fact that the same model has resulted from such different starting points indicates that it is, in some sense, a natural extension of the EU model. In fact, the form given by (5.1) and (5.2) is the only possible generalization of EU theory that is separable in $\boldsymbol{x}$ and $\boldsymbol{p}$ (except for the rank ordering which is implicit in our notation) and in which the requirements of first stochastic dominance, transitivity and continuity are satisfied.

This notion may be formalized by considering the simplest case of probability weighting arising when there are only two outcomes. The prospect is therefore of the form $\{(x_1, x_2);(p, 1-p)\}$

and we have

$$h_1(p,\ 1-p) = q(p),$$

$$h_2(p,\ 1-p) = 1 - q(p).$$

If q is symmetric, so that $q(1-p) = 1-q(p)$, this is exactly equivalent to the earlier probability weighting models. The problem is how to extend the function h by selecting weights for the case of three or more outcomes, preserving continuity, transitivity and first stochastic dominance. The following argument shows that the definition proposed in (5.2) is the only feasible extension.

Consider the two prospects

$$y_1 = \{(x_1,\ x_2);\ (p_1,\ 1-p_1)\};$$

and

$$y_2 = \{\boldsymbol{x};\boldsymbol{p}\} = \{(x_1,\ x_3,\ x_2);\ (p_2,\ p_1-p_2,\ 1-p_1)\},$$

with $x_1 < x_3 < x_2$.[13]

By continuity, as $U(x_3)$ approaches $U(x_1), V(y_2)$ must approach $V(y_1)$. At the limit, $x_1 = x_3$, $y_1 = y_3$ and

$$q(p_1)U(x_1) + (1 - q(p_1))U(x_2) = (h_1(\boldsymbol{p}) + h_2(\boldsymbol{p}))U(x_1) + h_3(\boldsymbol{p})\ U(x_3). \qquad (5.10)$$

Since x_1 and x_2 are chosen arbitrarily, and the separation property implies that $h(\boldsymbol{p})$ is independent of x, (5.10) can only be satisfied if

$$h_1(\boldsymbol{p}) + h_2(\boldsymbol{p}) = q(p_1), \text{ and}$$

$$h_3(\boldsymbol{p}) = 1-q(p_1).$$

Conversely, by allowing x_3 to approach x_2, it may be shown that

$$h_1(\boldsymbol{p}) = q(p_2),$$

and hence

$$h(\boldsymbol{p}) = (q(p_2),\ q(p_1) - q(p_2),\ 1 - q(p_1)).$$

More generally, for $\boldsymbol{p} = (p_1,\ p_2,\ p_3)$, this implies

[13] In most presentations of probability weighting models prior to the RDEU model, the outcomes were assumed to be distinct. The notation used in this book does not impose this assumption. However, in order to illustrate the role of continuity, it will be useful to suppose, for the purposes of this section that the x_i are distinct.

$$h(\boldsymbol{p}) = (q(p_1),\ q(p_1+p_2) - q(p_1),\ 1 - q(p_1+p_2)).$$

The argument can now be extended by induction to show that, for general $\boldsymbol{p}$

$$h_i(\boldsymbol{p}) = q(\sum_{j=1}^{i} p_j) - q(\sum_{j=1}^{i-1} p_j), \text{ as in (5.2).}$$

This argument demonstrates that RDEU is the natural extension of the probability weighting models discussed in Chapter 4. The separable nature of the model may also be seen to yield the properties exploited by Yaari and Allais in their independent derivation of the model. As will be argued in Chapters 6 and 7, it also provides the basis for a natural extension of most of the EU analysis of choice under uncertainty to preferences that violate the independence axiom.

Concluding Comments

Many of the new models of choice under uncertainty have encapsulated a single intuitive insight into reasons why people might violate the EU axioms. The relative success of the RDEU model may be accounted for by the fact, illustrated by its independent discovery from widely different starting points, that it is capable of representing many different intuitions. As will be shown in Chapter 10, this flexibility permits the RDEU model to account for most of the observed violations of EU predictions.

Although the RDEU model has been a relative success, neither it nor any other generalized model has made substantial progress in displacing EU as the main tool for economic analysis of behavior under uncertainty. In my view, the critical problem has been that the literature on generalizations of EU has been concerned primarily with the properties of preferences. By contrast, economic analysis is concerned with choice, and how choices change in relation to changing prices, technology and information. Until generalized models are applied to these topics they will remain in the borderland between economics, psychology and philosophy.

There are three main ways to approach the task of applying generalized models, such as RDEU, to problems of economic interest. First, conditions may be established under which results derived using EU theory may be carried over to a more general framework. This has the benefit of showing that these results are not dependent on the special assumptions of EU theory. It will be shown in Chapters 6 and 7 that the majority of the standard EU results on preferences and comparative statics may be extended to the RDEU model. The second way of applying generalized utility theories is to flag cases where results from EU theory may not carry across. These will normally be results that depend critically on the independence axiom or on more technical properties of EU theory, such as second order risk aversion, discussed in Chapter 6. The third area of application is the extension of analysis into areas that cannot be treated using EU theory. The most important of these is that of behavior characterized by a mixture of risk preference and risk aversion, as in the problem of simultaneous gambling and insurance discussed by Friedman and Savage. This problem is addressed in Chapter 8.

CHAPTER 6

Risk Aversion in RDEU Theory

The concept of risk aversion plays a central role in EU theory. The power of the Arrow–Pratt analysis of risk aversion and of the corresponding interpretation of increasing risk in terms of stochastic dominance contributed in large measure to the success of EU theory in replacing the mean–variance approach in both theoretical and applied study of problems relating to risk. One requirement for more general theories of choice under risk to be acceptable as a replacement for EU theory is the existence of appropriate concepts of increases in risk and in risk aversion.

The basic concept of risk aversion is fairly straightforward. People are risk averse if they always prefer an outcome received with certainty to a risky prospect with the same expected value. Risk aversion may, therefore, be regarded as a partial ordering on the space $\mathcal{Y}$. In EU theory, risk aversion corresponds to a simple condition on the utility function. It is a straightforward consequence of Jensen's inequality that risk aversion will hold if and only if U is concave.[14] Conversely, a given random variable, y, will be preferred to another, y', by all risk averse EU maximizers if and only if y second stochastically dominates y'.

Risk aversion alone is therefore sufficient to impose a good deal of structure on preferences. Any person with risk averse EU preferences will always prefer a random prospect to one that it second stochastically dominates. Conversely, EU preferences are risk averse if they always preserve second stochastic dominance.

As noted by Machina (1984), this equivalence does not hold in more general theories. The crucial issue at this point is that there are two potential definitions of risk aversion for generalized utility theories. The obvious choice is the original definition – preference for certain prospects over risky ones. In fact, however, attention in the literature has been concentrated almost exclusively on the second definition – that of preserving second stochastic dominance.

This focus has arisen largely because of the dominant position of the generalized smooth preferences model of Machina (1982). In this model (discussed in Chapter 12), the second stochastic dominance properties of EU theory may easily be generalized, but the more basic definition is intractable. The interpretation of Machina's model in terms of local utility functions leads naturally to the definition of risk aversion in terms of concavity of the local utility functions and hence of the preservation of second stochastic dominance.

The RDEU model suggests a different approach. RDEU theory may be viewed as embodying a fundamental distinction between attitudes to outcomes and attitudes to probabilities. It is apparent, then, that risk aversion in the RDEU sense must combine two different concepts.

---

[14]Jensen's inequality states that the mean of a concave (convex) function over a set of real numbers is less than (greater than) the value of the function evaluated at the mean. This property, though not its application to the theory of choice under uncertainty, played an important role in the development of the theory of concave and convex functions, See Hardy, Littlewood and Polya (1952).

First, there is outcome risk aversion, associated with the idea that the marginal utility of wealth is declining. This is the standard notion of risk aversion from EU theory defined by concavity of the utility function. Second, there are attitudes specific to probability preferences.[15] An obvious ground for risk aversion in probability weighting arises for people characterized by pessimism, that is, those who adopt a set of decision weights that yields an expected value for a transformed risky prospect lower than the mathematical expectation. This yields a natural generalization of the basic definition of risk aversion to the RDEU model. An alternative, more restrictive, characterization of pessimism leads to a generalization of the definition of risk aversion in terms of second stochastic dominance.

6.1 The Correspondence Principle

Application of the RDEU model is greatly simplified by the existence of a simple correspondence between RDEU and EU. RDEU theory may be regarded as the EU model applied to the 'transformed' random variable $\tilde{y}$ having probability distribution $\{\boldsymbol{x};\ h(\boldsymbol{p})\}$. It is apparent that if any property of the original distribution random variables y_0, y_1 is carried over to the transformed random variable $\tilde{y}_0$, $\tilde{y}_1$, any EU result depending on that property will also be carried over. In particular, if y_0 first stochastically dominates y_1, $\tilde{y}_0$ first stochastically dominates $\tilde{y}_1$. Hence RDEU theory respects first stochastic dominance, a result that was proved by direct methods in Section 5.2.[16]

This idea may be developed further with some formal definitions. First, a general relation R, such as first or second stochastic dominance, may be written $y_0\ R\ y_1$. Any relation may be represented as a set of ordered pairs $\{(y_0, y_1): y_0\ R\ y_1\}$. A transformation q maps any pair of random variables (y_0, y_1) into a pair $(\tilde{y}_0, \tilde{y}_1)$. The transformation q is said to *preserve* R if $y_0\ R\ y_1 \Rightarrow \tilde{y}_0\ \mathrm{R}\ \tilde{y}_1$. For any R, denote by $Q^*(R)$ the class of functions $q \in \mathcal{Q}$ that preserve R. A utility function U will be said to *respect* a relation R if $\mathrm{EU}(y_0) \geq \mathrm{EU}(y_1)$ whenever $y_0\ R\ y_1$, and the class of utility functions respecting a given R will be denoted $U^*(R)$. This yields

Correspondence Principle for Stochastic Dominance: Let R be a relation on $\mathcal{Y}$. Then for RDEU preferences V, with $U \in U^*(R)$ and $q \in Q^*(R)$, $V(y_0) \geq V(y_1)$ whenever $y_0\ R\ y_1$.

Before considering applications to risk aversion, the principle will be illustrated by two examples of first order stochastic dominance relations R on $\mathcal{Y}$ and the corresponding classes of transformations $Q^*(R)$.

Example 1: Let $R = \{\ (y_0, y_1) : y_0$ first stochastically dominates $y_1\}$.
Then $Q^*(R) = \mathcal{Q}$.

[15]It is arguable that the term 'risk aversion' is more properly applied to preferences over probabilities than to preferences over outcomes.

[16] By contrast, the earlier probability weighting models of Handa and Kahneman and Tversky not only permit, but require, violations of first stochastic dominance. Kahneman and Tversky invoke the notion of 'editing' to eliminate violations of first stochastic dominance from their model.

That is, any monotonically increasing transformation function q preserves the relationship of first stochastic dominance. First stochastic dominance is defined by the requirement that $F_0(x) \le F_1(x)\ \forall\ x$. The condition $q^{\circ}F_0(x) \le q^{\circ}F_1(x)\ \forall\ x$ will be satisfied for all such F_0, F_1 if and only if q is (weakly) monotone increasing. The fact that RDEU preserves first stochastic dominance was proved by Quiggin (1982a).

A particularly useful special case of first stochastic dominance, preserved by all RDEU transformations, corresponds to a rightward translation of the entire cumulative distribution function.

Example 2: Let $R = \{ (y_0, y_1) : \exists\ \delta > 0, y_0 = y_1 + \delta \}$.
Then $Q^*(R) = \mathcal{Q}$.

In this case, it is not even necessary that q should be monotone increasing. For if $y_0 = y_1 + \delta$, the corresponding equality $\tilde{y}_0 = \tilde{y}_1 + \delta$ will hold for any q: $[0, 1] \to [0, 1]$.

6.2 Pessimism and RDEU Risk Aversion

It was observed in the introduction that risk aversion in the RDEU model must encompass two distinct phenomena — attitudes to the marginal utility of wealth and attitudes to probabilities *per se*. Most attention will be focused on attitudes to probabilities. However, some brief observations on the utility function are in order.

RDEU is normally associated with a concave utility function, as in EU theory. Indeed the plausibility of the concavity assumption, which is equivalent to declining marginal utility of wealth, is enhanced by the fact that risk seeking behavior can be modelled in terms of probability attitudes, without the use of convex segments in the utility function, as in the work of Friedman and Savage (1948). The possibility of modelling risk seeking with diminishing marginal utility of wealth seems more attractive than the converse possibility, observed by Yaari (1987), of modelling risk aversion without diminishing marginal utility. Risk seeking is discussed further in Section 6.7 and Chapter 8.

A number of writers, notably Yaari (1987), confine attention to the case when U is linear. In the analysis of individual choice, this case is, as Yaari himself notes, primarily of pedagogical interest. However, as Yaari argues, risk averse behavior by corporations may be modelled with a linear utility function. Since corporations have a large number of shareholders, standard risk spreading arguments in the EU literature suggest that they should act in a risk neutral fashion, provided their profits are uncorrelated with national income as a whole. Even in the absence of a perfect capital market, the existence of a large group of shareholders, few of whom derive their entire income from their stockholding, means that there is no obvious basis for maximizing the expected value of a particular non-linear utility function over wealth.

Given the assumption that U is at least weakly concave, attention will be confined primarily to the transformation function. A transformation function may be described as *pessimistic* with respect to a random variable y if $\int y\ dq(F_y) \le \int y\ dF_y = E[y]$. A transformation function will be described simply as pessimistic if it is pessimistic with respect to all random variables. Converse definitions apply for *optimism*. It is possible to characterize transformations with these properties.

LEMMA 6.1: *An individual is pessimistic if and only if $q(p) \geq p \ \forall \ p$, and optimistic if and only if $q(p) \leq p \ \forall \ p$.*

Proof: If $q(p) \geq p \ \forall \ p$, y FSD $\tilde{y} \ \ \forall \ y$. Hence, $\int y \, dq(F_y) \leq \int y \, dF_y$ as required.

Conversely, if for some $p, q(p) > p$, then, for $x_1 < x_2$, $\{(x_1, x_2); (p, 1-p)\}$ is a counterexample to the pessimism condition. The proof for optimism is identical. ■

This result is well known and appears to have been first derived by Yaari (1984, 1987) for the special case of linear U and independently rediscovered by Quiggin (1986) and Segal (1987b). For linear U, RDEU preference functionals will be risk averse in this sense if and only if the transformation function q lies everywhere above the 45 degree line as in Figure 5.3.

An attractive interpretation of this result may be obtained using the correspondence principle presented in Section 6.1. The correspondence principle may be used to derive the appropriate extensions to RDEU theory of both concepts of risk aversion. The classes of transformations corresponding to the basic definition of risk aversion and the second stochastic dominance definition may be characterized by the relations on the space of distributions that they preserve.

LEMMA 6.2: *Let* $R = \{ (F_1, F_2) : F_1 = \delta_c, E[F_2] \leq c \}$.
Then $Q^*(R) = \{q \in \mathcal{Q}: q(p) \geq p \ \forall \ p\}$.

Proof: By Lemma 6.1, for $q \in Q^*$, $F_1, F_2 \in R$, $E[q^\circ F_2] \leq E[F_2] \leq c = E[F_1] = E[q^\circ F_1]$.

Conversely for $q \notin Q^*$, $\exists \ F$, $E[q^\circ F] \leq E[F] = E[\ \delta_{q^\circ F}] = E[q^\circ \ \delta_{q^\circ F}]$.

That is, the pessimistic transformation functions are precisely those that preserve the relation that characterizes the standard definition of risk aversion. The next result exploits the Correspondence Principle to give a characterization of RDEU preferences that preserve risk aversion in this sense.

PROPOSITION 6.1: *The following conditions on a weighting function q are equivalent*

(i) *For any random variable y and concave outcome utility function U,*

$$V(y) = \int_\Omega U(x) \, dq(F_y(x)) \leq V(E[y]) = U(E[y]) \text{ ; and}$$

(ii) $q(p) \geq p \ \forall \ p$.

Proof: Sufficiency follows from Lemma 6.2 and the Correspondence Principle
Necessity follows from Lemma 6.1. ■

An RDEU preference functional with concave U and $q(p) \geq p \ \forall \ p$ will be described as *RDEU risk averse*. A difficulty with this definition is that it is expressed in terms of the functional form, rather than directly in terms of preferences. A characterization of risk aversion in terms of preferences is given in Chapter 11.4.

If the condition that U be concave is dropped, the conditions for risk aversion become more complex. Essentially the requirement is that the transformation function should be 'pessimistic enough' to outweigh the convexity of the utility function. This is not possible for some utility functions, notably the power functions. Cohen and Chateauneuf (1991) derive a weaker set of necessary conditions. Setting the outcome space to [0, 1], and normalizing to $U(0) = 0$, $U(1) = 1$, they show if U is not concave, risk aversion requires

(i) $q(p) \geq p \; \forall \; p$

(ii) $U(p) \geq q^*(p) \; \forall \; p$

(iii) $\exists \; k \geq 1, \; U'(x) \leq k \; (U(x) - U(y))/(x-y) \; \forall \; x \leq y$

A sufficient condition for risk aversion is given by (iii) combined with the requirement that $q^*(p) \leq pk$. A dual result shows that an individual with a concave utility function may be globally risk seeking if the transformation function is sufficiently optimistic. Given the plausibility of diminishing marginal utility and the evident examples of risk seeking, this latter result is, perhaps, the more empirically significant.

We turn now to the definition of risk aversion as preservation of second stochastic dominance. The corresponding result is

LEMMA 6.3: *Let* $R = \{(F_0, F_1) : F_0$ *second stochastically dominates* $F_1\}$
Then $Q^*(R) = \{q \in \mathcal{Q}: q$ *concave*$\}$.

Proof: It is sufficient to prove the result for the case when y_1 is derived from y_0 by a simple spread and $\mathrm{E}[y_1] \leq \mathrm{E}[y_0]$. Thus, there exists ω^* such that $y_1(\omega) \leq y_0(\omega)$ if and only if $\omega \leq \omega^*$ and

$$\int_0^{\omega^*} y_0(\omega) - y_1(\omega) \, d\omega \geq \int_{\omega^*}^1 y_1(\omega) - y_0(\omega) \, d\omega$$

The transformation q preserves the spread relation if and only if

$$\int_0^{\omega^*} (y_0(\omega) - y_1(\omega)) \, q'(\omega) \, d\omega \geq \int_{\omega^*}^1 (y_1(\omega) - y_0(\omega)) \, q'(\omega) \, d\omega$$

Concavity implies

$$\int_0^{\omega^*} (y_0(\omega) - y_1(\omega)) \, q'(\omega) \, d\omega \geq q'(\omega^*) \int_0^{\omega^*} y_0(\omega) - y_1(\omega) d\omega \geq q'(\omega^*) \int_{\omega^*}^1 y_1(\omega) - y_0(\omega) \, d\omega$$

$$\geq \int_{\omega^*}^1 (y_1(\omega) - y_0(\omega)) \, q'(\omega) \, d\omega$$

For the converse, suppose $q'(p)$ is increasing over some range. Consider discrete prospects consisting of n equiprobable outcomes, and assume that U is linear. In this case the weight on the i–th outcome may be referred to as h_i. It is possible to find an appropriate q such that, for some i, $h_i > h_{i-1}$. Now consider a prospect y_0, such that $w_i = w_{i-1}$. A shift to a prospect y_1, involving increasing w_i by δ and decreasing w_{i-1} by the same amount has the property that F_0 SSD F_1. However, $V(y_1) - V(y_0) = \delta(h_{i-1} - h_i) + o(\delta) > 0$ for small δ. ■

It follows that an RDEU preference functional will preserve second stochastic dominance if and only U and q are concave, as in Figure 5.2. This result was first proved by Chew, Karni and Safra (1987), using results of Machina (1982). A direct proof for the special case of linear U is given by Yaari (1987). An RDEU functional with concave U and q will be described as *SSD risk averse.*

Concavity of the transformation function q implies a strong form of pessimism, which may best be illustrated for the discrete case. Consider a discrete random variable y = $\{\boldsymbol{x};\boldsymbol{p}\}$ and the transformed random variable $\tilde{y} = \{\boldsymbol{x};\ \boldsymbol{h}(\boldsymbol{p})\}$. For each i, the extent to which the i-th outcome is overweighted (or underweighted) may be measured by the ratio $h_i(\boldsymbol{p})/p_i$. If q is concave, $h_i(\boldsymbol{p})/p_i$ is decreasing in i. That is, the worst outcome is overweighted most, and the best outcome underweighted most. More generally, for any two outcomes, the better of the two is weighted less heavily than the worse.

To show that the distinction between the conditions in Lemmas 6.2 and 6.3 is not vacuous, it is necessary to exhibit an RDEU functional V, satisfying the conditions of Lemma 6.2, and random variables y_1 and y_2, such that y_1 SSD y_2, but $V(y_1) < V(y_2)$. The counterexample in Lemma 6.3 satisfies this condition. Thus, the class of RDEU functionals preserving second stochastic dominance is strictly smaller than those that are risk averse in the classical sense of preferring certainty to risk.

The original presentation of the model in Quiggin (1982a) did not allow for the possibility of globally concave q because of the restriction that $q(1/2) = 1/2$. However, the following related result was proved:

LEMMA 6.4: *Let* $R = \{(F_0, F_1)$: F_0 *second stochastically dominates* F_1, F_0 *and* F_1 *are symmetric distributions*$\}$
Then $q \in Q^*(R)$ *if* q *is symmetric (that is,* $q(p) = 1 - q(1-p)$*) and* q *is concave on* $[0, 1/2]$.

Some particularly interesting results may be obtained for S–shaped functions satisfying the symmetry condition of Lemma 6.4, as illustrated in Figure 5.1. Individuals with concave utility functions and weighting functions satisfying this condition display risk averse behavior towards random variables with symmetric distributions. For more general random variables, this preference functional displays neither global risk aversion nor global risk seeking, but overweighting of low probability extreme events. Broadly speaking, people with this type of preferences are risk averse towards negatively skewed variables, but may be risk seeking for positively skewed variables.

6.3 First and Second Order Risk Aversion

One of the most striking results in EU theory is that full insurance is always sub-optimal whenever rates are actuarially unfair and the utility function is smooth. Because the utility function U is smooth, it is possible to obtain a linear first order approximation in a neighborhood of any x. The slope of the linear approximation is given by $U'(x)$. The existence of this linear approximation means that, except for second order effects, EU preferences are risk neutral in a neighborhood of certainty. The point may be seen by considering random variables of the form $y_k = \{(x\text{-}k\delta,\ x+k\delta);\ (1/2,\ 1/2)\}$, where δ is a positive constant and $k > 0$ is a scaling factor.

Taking a Taylor series expansion around x, we have

$$U(x \pm k\delta) = U(x) \pm k\delta U'(x) + (k\delta)^2/2\ U''(x)$$

so that

$$E[U(y_k)] = U(x) - o(k\delta) \tag{6.1}$$

where $o(\bullet)$ denotes a positive function that takes the value zero at zero and is of higher order than its argument.

An actuarially fair insurance policy would yield the outcome x with certainty, and would always be preferred to the risky variable y_k. An actuarially unfair insurance policy will yield a return $x - \alpha k\delta$, where α is the insurer's margin, expressed as a proportion of the insurance payout. For sufficiently small values of k, the second order term $o(k\delta)$ in (6.1) must be smaller than $\alpha k\delta$, and the individual will choose not to insure against the risk. Because of this result, Segal and Spivak (1990) say that EU theory is characterized by second order risk aversion.

Consider now the case of an RDEU-maximizer with a linear utility function and a strictly pessimistic transformation function. The utility function may be set so that $U(x) = x$. We have

$$\begin{aligned} V(y_k) &= q(1/2)\,(x-k\delta) + (1 - q(1/2))\,(x+k\delta) \\ &= x - (2q(1/2) - 1)\,k\delta \end{aligned}$$

Since $q(1/2) > 1/2$, $(2q(1/2) - 1)$ is a positive constant . If $(2q(1/2) - 1) > \alpha$, the insurance contract will be preferred for every value of k. If $(2q(1/2) - 1) < \alpha$, insurance will be rejected for every value of k. Since $(2q(1/2) - 1)\ k\delta$ is $O(k\delta)$, Segal and Spivak say that the linear RDEU model is characterized by first order risk aversion.

The analysis presented above extends from the case of 50-50 bets to that of general random variables of the form $x + k\theta$. The Taylor approximation for EU becomes

$$E[U(y_k)] = U(x) + k^2\, var(\theta) \tag{6.2}$$

and k^2 var(θ) is $o(k)$.

For a general RDEU preference functional (U, q), the linear approximation at x is simply the functional with linear utility and transformation function q. So, full insurance will be purchased whenever $(2q(1/2) - 1) > \alpha$. However, insurance may be purchased for sufficiently large k, even when $(2q(1/2) - 1) < \alpha$. That is, even if first order risk aversion is too weak to induce the purchase of insurance, second order risk aversion may lead to a preference for insurance when k^2 var(θ) is sufficiently large, and the first order linear approximation is inappropriate.

A number of other applications of the notion of first order risk aversion are possible. One of the most interesting relates to the notion of precautionary saving. The main ideas can be expressed in a two-period framework (Segal, Spivak and Zeira 1988) provide an analysis of the n period case). Consider the problem of a consumer with known first period income $y_1 = \delta_y$ and random second period income y_2 such that $E[y_2] = \bar{y}$. The consumer's problem is to choose first period consumption c_1 to maximize

$$V = U(c_1) + E[U(c_2)]$$

subject to
$$c_2 = y_2 + \bar{y} - c_1$$

The consumer displays precautionary saving if $c_1 < \bar{y}$, or, equivalently, if $E[c_2] > c_1$. Under EU, risk aversion is not sufficient for precautionary saving. The consumer will display precautionary saving under decreasing absolute risk aversion, but not under increasing absolute risk aversion. This may be seen by applying Jensen's inequality to the first order condition

$$U'(c_1) = E[U'(c_2)]$$

Now consider an RDEU maximizer with linear utility, as in the Yaari model. Provided the individual is pessimistic, the first order condition will be satisfied with $E[c_2] > c_1$. (The argument is essentially identical to Lemma 6.2.) Using the notion of first order risk aversion, Segal, Spivak and Zeira extend the result to the case of general RDEU preferences. They observe that, provided uncertainty is bounded, probability attitudes will be dominant and an RDEU risk averse individual will display precautionary saving.

These results refer to the basic notions of risk and risk aversion. Segal, Spivak and Zeira show that they cannot be extended to the case when the individual is SSD risk averse and y_2 is related to y_1 by a mean-preserving spread in the sense of Rothschild and Stiglitz. However, it is easily shown that the results may be extended to the case of monotone spreads, defined in Section 6.5.

6.4 Risk Premiums and Coefficients of Risk Aversion

The basic concept of risk aversion may also be expressed in terms of the risk premium. This is the difference between the expectation of a random variable and its certainty equivalent. It is natural, in the light of the discussion above, to partition the RDEU risk premium into two components, one reflecting pessimism and the other reflecting outcome risk aversion. The simplest way of doing this, proposed by Hilton (1988), is to set the pessimism premium for a random variable y equal to the difference between the mean of y and the mean of the transformed variable having cumulative distribution function $q(F_y)$, and then to set the outcome premium equal to the EU risk premium for the transformed variable. The respective premia are represented by the terms in curly brackets on the RHS of the following equation

$$\Delta = E[y] - CE(y) = \{\int x\, dF_y - \int x\, dq(F_y)\} + \{\int x\, dq(F_y) - U^{-1}(\int U(x)\, dq(F_y))\} \qquad (6.3)$$

The pessimism premium for a given random variable y, given by the first term on the RHS of (6.3), will be denoted $\Delta_q(y)$. The outcome risk premium, given by the second term, will be denoted $\Delta_U(y)$. From (6.3), $\Delta_q(y)$ is positive for all y if and only if $q(p) \geq p\ \forall\ p$ and that

$\Delta_U(y)$ is positive for all y if and only if U is concave. The combined risk premium is positive whenever preferences are RDEU risk averse.This approach requires knowledge of the RDEU preference functional. A partition in terms of preferences alone is given in Section 11.4.

An important feature of the pessimism premium is that it is linear with respect to multiplicative spreads about the mean. This may be observed by considering a variable of the form $\delta_c + k\varepsilon$, where $E[\varepsilon] = 0$. Denote by ε^* the transformed variable obtained by composing q with the cumulative distribution function of ε. For $k > 0$,

$$\Delta_q = k\,(E[\varepsilon] - E[\varepsilon^*]),$$

so that Δ_q/k is a constant for positive k. Also, the pessimism premium is independent of changes in base wealth, that is, $\Delta_q(y) = \Delta_q(y + W_0)$, $\forall\ W_0$.

The partition of the RDEU risk premium may be used to provide a formal approach to the notions of first and second order risk aversion. For a random variable of the form $\delta_c + k\varepsilon$, define $\partial\Delta/\partial k|_0^+$ as the limit of $\partial\Delta/\partial k$ as k approaches zero from above. The argument above shows that $\partial\Delta_q/\partial k$ is a positive constant for all positive k, and hence so is $\partial\Delta_q/\partial k|_0^+$. By contrast, $\Delta_U(y)$ is non–linear in k and is $o(k)$ for small k. That is, as $k \to 0$, so does $\Delta_U(y)/k$, so that $\partial\Delta_U/\partial k|_0^+ = 0$. This reflects an important property of EU theory, which may be referred to as *risk neutrality in a neighborhood of certainty*, Segal and Spivak (1990) define first order risk aversion by the requirement that $\partial\Delta/\partial k|_0^+$ is positive, and second order risk aversion by the condition that Δ is positive, but $o(k)$, so that $\partial\Delta/\partial k|_0^+ = 0$. Thus, EU preferences with concave U display second order risk aversion. RDEU preferences display first order risk aversion provided $q(p) \geq p$, $\forall\ p$.

For sufficiently small k, the risk premium is dominated by Δ_q. More generally, behavior towards sufficiently small risks will be determined entirely by the nature of the probability transformation function. This implies that the condition $q(p) \geq p\ \forall\ p$ is necessary for global risk aversion, whether or not U is concave (compare Section 6.3).

A measure related to the pessimism premium may be defined in terms of probabilities rather than prospects. The *probability weighting coefficient* may be defined as

$$\rho(p) = (1\text{-}p)q(p)/pq^*(1-p) \qquad (6.4)$$

Given a bet of the form $\{(x_1, x_2);(p, 1-p)\}$, this coefficient expresses the ratio between the objective odds on the more favored event, and the odds implied by the decision weights. The probability weighting coefficient may be regarded as a measure of optimism or pessimism. For an optimist, $\rho(p) \leq 1\ \forall p \in [0,1]$, and, for a pessimist, $\rho(p) \geq 1\ \forall p \in [0,1]$. Hence, an individual is RDEU risk averse if and only if the probability weighting coefficient is greater than unity for all p and the Arrow-Pratt coefficient of risk aversion $-U''(x)/U'(x)$ is positive $\forall x$.

For SSD risk aversion, the necessary and sufficient conditions are that both U and q be concave. Thus we may define a coefficient of risk aversion $-q''(p)/q'(p)$ analogous to the Arrow-Pratt coefficient. An individual will be SSD-risk averse if and only if $-q''(p)/q'(p) \geq 0\ \forall\ p$ and $-U''(x)/U'(x) \geq 0\ \forall\ x$.

The separation between the probabilistic risk premium and the outcome risk premium presented here is dependent on knowledge of the preference functional. In Section 11.4, it will be shown that a direct behavioral characterization of probabilistic risk aversion and declining marginal utility is possible for individuals with RDEU preferences.

6.5 An Alternative Definition of Increasing Risk

Many kinds of answers have been offered to the question: When is a random variable y_1 'more risky' than another random variable y_0 with the same expected value? It is natural to consider this question by first considering the difference between certainty and risk; that is, between a given outcome received with certainty and a risky prospect having expected value equal to that certain outcome. Any interpretation of the term 'more risky' may be regarded as abstracting some crucial feature of this contrast between certain and risky events and using it as a basis for comparison between risky prospects.

The most commonly used statistical concept of risk is the variance, along with related measures such as standard deviation and coefficient of variation. Mean–variance analysis of choice under risk was initially a strong competitor with the EU research program, and remains important in some applied areas such as the theory of finance.

The most commonly used concept of increasing risk in the EU literature has been the notion of second stochastic dominance (Hadar and Russell 1969). One distribution y_0 second stochastically dominates another y_1, if all risk averters prefer y_0 to y_1. Risk averters are defined as those who always prefer a certain outcome to a risky prospect with the same expected value. In expected utility (EU) theory, this group consists of all those with concave utility functions.

As was shown in Lemma 6.3, second stochastic dominance is preserved by all RDEU preference functionals for which both U and q are concave. However, unlike the situation in EU theory, preservation of second stochastic dominance is not equivalent to preference for certainty over risk. As was shown in Lemma 6.2, this condition is satisfied for all RDEU risk averse individuals (those with concave U and $q(p) \geq p$).

This difficulty arises with a number of generalized theories of choice under uncertainty. In these models, risk aversion, in the sense of preference for a given outcome received with certainty and a risky prospect having expected value equal to that certain outcome does not imply aversion to increasing risk in the sense of stochastic dominance. The dominant tendency in the literature, as in the work of Machina, Chew, Karni and Safra (1987) and Green and Jullien (1988) has been to redefine risk aversion in order to preserve the equivalence with aversion to second stochastically dominated distributions.

However, second stochastic dominance cannot be regarded as a natural stochastic dominance concept in these models, since its appeal is derived from its properties in EU theory. It seems reasonable to derive a notion of stochastic dominance appropriate to the class of RDEU functionals with U concave and q pessimistic.

Examination of the example given above suggests that the required property is that y_1 should be derived from y_0 by a *monotone spread.* Suppose that λ is a spread parameter such that as λ increases all of the outcomes move 'further away' from some central point, so that the distance between the outcomes for any two states increases. Then an increase in λ may be referred to as a monotone spread (Quiggin 1986, 1991b, see also Meyer and Ormiston 1989 who use the term 'deterministic transformation.')

More formally, recalling that the states $\omega \in \Omega$ are ordered from worst to best, we may say that y_1 is derived from y_0 by a mean–preserving monotone spread if

- $E[y_1] = E[y_0]$
- $y_1(\omega) - y_0(\omega)$ is a monotone non-decreasing function of ω

This class includes multiplicative spreads about the mean, such as increases in the variance of the normal distribution. Moreover, all monotone spreads satisfy the single crossing property. However, unlike the simple spread relationship, the monotone spread relationship is transitive; that is, the result of any combination of monotone spreads is also a monotone spread. The relationship therefore imposes a partial ordering on $\mathfrak{D}$. This is clearly a desirable property for a notion of increasing risk. Another property of monotone spreads that makes them particularly appropriate to the RDEU framework is that, if F_0 is related to F_1 by a monotone spread, the same condition applies to $q°F_0$ and $q°F_1$.

The following example shows that the class of monotone spreads is strictly smaller than the class of simple mean–preserving spreads. Suppose there are four states of the world, each with probability 1/4, and let $y_0 = \{(x_1, x_2, x_3, x_4); (1/4, 1/4, 1/4, 1/4)\}$ For small ε, let $y_1 = \{(x_1, x_2 - \varepsilon, x_3 + \varepsilon, x_4)(1/4, 1/4, 1/4, 1/4)\}$. Then y_1 is derived from y_0 by a simple mean–preserving spread. This is not a monotone spread, however, since the change in state 4 is less than the change in state 3, and the change in state 2 is (algebraically) less than the change in state 1.

The monotone spread concept is equivalent to the requirement that the riskier random variable, regarded as a mapping from Ω to X is equivalent to a concave transform of the original one. Thus, there is a natural duality between an increase in risk aversion (a concave transformation of the utility function) and a monotone spread (a concave transformation of the random variable). Also, it is apparent that, if y_1 is derived from y_0 by a monotone spread, it is possible to write $y_1 = y_1 + \psi$, where ψ is a random variable comonotonic with y_1. The converse will be proved below. The crucial property of monotone spreads is

PROPOSITION 6.2: *Let y_0, y_1 be random variables related by a mean-preserving monotone spread. Then for all RDEU risk averse functionals V, $V(y_0) \geq V(y_1)$.*

Proof: For $\lambda \in [0, 1]$, let $y_\lambda = \lambda y_1 + (1 - \lambda)y_0$

$$\partial V/\partial\lambda = \int_\Omega U'(y_\lambda(\omega))(y_1(\omega) - y_0(\omega))\, q(\omega)d\omega. \tag{6.5}$$

Since U' is monotone decreasing in ω by concavity and the ordering of Ω, and $(y_1(\omega) - y_0(\omega))$ is monotone increasing in ω by the monotone spread property

$$\partial V/\partial\lambda \leq \int_\Omega U'(y_\lambda(\omega))\, dq(F(\omega)) \int_\Omega (y_1(\omega) - y_0(\omega))\, q(\omega)d\omega,$$

Since $y_1(\omega) - y_0(\omega)$ is an increasing function from Ω to $\Re$ it is an element of Y. Hence, by Proposition 6.1,

$$\int_\Omega (y_1(\omega) - y_0(\omega))\, q(\omega) d\omega \le \int_\Omega (y_1(\omega) - y_0(\omega))\, d\omega = 0,$$

since $\mathrm{E}[y_1] - \mathrm{E}[y_2] = 0$. Thus, $\partial V/\partial\lambda \le 0$, as required. ■

The converse will be proved in Proposition 6.3 in the next section. This result may be restated in terms of the Correspondence Principle.

Example 3: Let $R = \{(y_0, y_1): y_1$ is derived from y_0 by a monotone spread, $\mathrm{E}[y_1] \le \mathrm{E}[y_0]\}$
Then $Q^*(R) = \{q \in \mathcal{Q}: q(p) \ge p \;\forall\; p\}$.

Proof: All transformation functions preserve the monotone spread relation, so it is only necessary to prove that $\mathrm{E}[\tilde{y}_1] \le \mathrm{E}[\tilde{y}_0]$ if and only if $q(p) \ge p \;\forall\; p$. Consider the associated random variable $\tilde{y}_1 - \tilde{y}_0$. This preserves the ordering on Ω by virtue of the monotone spread relation. Hence $\mathrm{E}[\tilde{y}_1] - \mathrm{E}[\tilde{y}_0] \le \mathrm{E}[y_2] - \mathrm{E}[y_0] \le 0, \;\forall\; y_0 \,R\, y_1 \Leftrightarrow q(p) \ge p \;\forall\; p$. ■

6.6 The Rothschild–Stiglitz Theory of Increasing Risk

A particularly influential treatment of the question of increasing risk is that of Rothschild and Stiglitz (1970, 1971). They show that, when y_0 and y_1 have the same mean, four types of intuitively plausible definitions are equivalent. First, they derive the equivalence between the requirement that all risk averters prefer y_0 to y_1 and an integral condition, a special case of the second stochastic dominance condition derived by Hadar and Russell. Rothschild and Stiglitz interpret this condition as meaning that 'y_1 has more weight in the tails than y_0.' Both of these conditions may be regarded as abstracting natural statistical features of the difference between certain outcomes and risky prospects.

The third condition is based on the derivation of y_1 from y_0 by the addition of 'noise', that is, by the addition of another source of risk. In the analysis of Rothschild and Stiglitz it is assumed that this source of risk is independent of the original risky variable y_0. The fourth condition is that y_1 should be derived from y_0 as the limit of a sequence of simple mean–preserving spreads. A simple mean-preserving spread is one for which the cumulative distribution functions intersect only once, satisfying the *single crossing property*:

$$\exists\; \theta^* \text{ such that } \theta \le \theta^* \Leftrightarrow F_0(\theta) \le F_1(\theta).$$

More precisely, Rothschild and Stiglitz prove that, for any two random variables y_0, y_1, such that $\mathrm{E}[y_0] = \mathrm{E}[y_1]$ the following are equivalent:

- y_0 second stochastically dominates y_1;
- $V(y_0) \ge V(y_1)$ for any EU risk averter; and
- y_1 is equal in distribution to $y_0 + y_3$ for some y_3 such that $\mathrm{E}[y_3 \mid y_0] = 0$.
- y_1 is derived from y_0 as the limit of a sequence of simple mean–preserving spreads.

It is now possible to consider monotone spreads as an alternative notion of 'increasing risk', in the sense of Rothschild and Stiglitz. As with the Rothcschild-Stiglitz notion of increasing risk, the definition of monotone spreads may be expressed in several equivalent ways including the idea that all RDEU risk averters are made worse off by an increase in risk, that a riskier distribution shifts weight from the center of the distribution to the tails, and that an increase in risk may be defined as arising from the addition of one risky variable to another.

Because the monotone spread concept represents a more restrictive notion of increasing risk, it yields an expansion of the class of preference functionals for which stochastic dominance applies. In particular, all RDEU risk averse individuals, and not merely those with concave weighting functions, are averse to mean–preserving monotone spreads.

The monotone spread concept is an alternative, and more restrictive, interpretation of the notion that the riskier variable should have more weight in the tails. This may be seen from the result that the riskier cumulative distribution function is equivalent to a concave transform of the original one. By contrast, the second stochastic dominance approach requires that the integral of the riskier cumulative distribution function should lie above the integral of the original one. There is a duality here with the alternative conditions on the probability weighting function q. The second stochastic dominance approach is associated with concave q. The monotone spreads definition requires that q should lie above the identity function.

Finally, the alternative notion of increasing risk may be interpreted in terms of random variables by saying that the riskier variable is derived by adding an additional random variable that is comonotonic with the original one. The requirement that additional risk be comonotonic is more restrictive than the condition imposed by Rothschild and Stiglitz. However, there is an argument to suggest that it is a more natural way to think of increasing risk. Individuals with EU preferences facing an initial risky distribution y will be 'almost' indifferent regarding the addition of 'sufficiently small' quantities of uncorrelated noise, whereas they will be made worse off by the addition of any additional risk comonotonic with y.

The equivalences may be formally stated as follows:

PROPOSITION 6.3: *Let y_0, y_1 be random variables with equal means and cumulative distribution functions F_0 and F_1 respectively. Then the following conditions are equivalent.*
(i) *For all RDEU risk averse functionals V, $V(y_0) \geq V(y_1)$;*
(ii) *y_1 is equal in distribution to $y_0 + \psi$, where $E[\psi] = 0$, and ψ is comonotonic with y_0; and*
(iii) *y_1 is derived from y_0 by a monotone spread.*

Proof: (ii) $\Rightarrow$ (iii)

By the definition of a monotone spread, $y_1(\omega) - y_0(\omega)$ is an increasing function from Ω to $\Re$, hence a random variable and $E[y_1(\omega) - y_0(\omega)] = 0$

(iii)$\Rightarrow$(i)

This is proved in Proposition 6.2.

(i) $\Rightarrow$(ii)

Define $\psi(\omega) = y_1(\omega) - y_0(\omega)$. It is clear that $E[\psi] = 0$, and it remains to be proved that ψ is comonotonic with y_0. For any sets Ω_1, Ω_2 of nonzero measure, if y_0 is greater on Ω_1 than on Ω_2, Ω_2 cannot lie above Ω_1. For if this were the case, it would be possible to define subintervals I_1, I_2 of Ω_1, Ω_2 respectively having equal measure and q satisfying $q(p) \geq p \; \forall \; p$, such that

$$q'(t) = \begin{cases} 2 & p \in I_1 \\ 0 & p \in I_2 \\ 1 & \text{otherwise} \end{cases}$$

For linear U, this implies

$$V(y_1) - V(y_0) = \int_\Omega \psi(\omega)\, q(\omega)\, d\omega,$$
$$= \int_\Omega \psi(\omega)\, d\omega + \int_{I_1} \psi(\omega)\, d\omega - \int_{I_2} \psi(\omega)\, d\omega\,.$$

The first term on the RHS is zero since the two distributions have equal expectations. Since I_1 and I_2 have equal measure, and ψ is greater on I_2 than on I_1, the sum of the remaining terms must be positive, contradicting (i).

Hence, except possibly for a set of zero measure, ψ must have the required property. This implies that it is possible to define $\psi^\rho =_d \psi = y_1 - y_0$ such that

$$y_0(\omega_1) \geq y_0(\omega_2) \Leftrightarrow \psi^\rho(\omega_1) \geq \psi^\rho(\omega_2).\blacksquare$$

6.7 Risk Seeking Behavior

Given the strong emphasis of EU theory on concepts of risk aversion, it might be supposed that risk aversion in some form would be a standard assumption for RDEU theory. However, one of the major concerns of a number of utility theorists has been to explain behavior inconsistent with the standard assumptions of risk aversion. Such behavior is observed in experimental settings (eg Kahneman and Tversky 1979) and in market choices such as simultaneous gambling and purchase of insurance. The discussion in Chapters 3 and 4 showed that attempts by Friedman and Savage (1948) and others to solve these problems in an EU context cannot be regarded as successful.

The main requirement for a solution of the problem in an RDEU framework is that the function q should display optimism, at least with respect to some random variables. The most plausible solutions are based on 'overweighting' concepts, which involve optimism with respect to some random variables and pessimism with respect to others. However, it is worth considering the case of global optimism. No less an authority than Adam Smith has lent his support to the view that this type of attitude is predominant, stating (1776, p. 164, pp. 124–5 in 1976 edition)

> The chance of gain is by every man more or less overvalued and the chance of loss is by most men undervalued and by scarce any man who is in tolerable health and spirits valued more than it is worth.

Assuming that U is concave, the choices of an optimist facing uncertainty will reflect a balance between two conflicting forces. Optimism encourages risk taking but decreasing marginal utility discourages it. Since the effects of probability weighting are independent of the scale of the bet, optimism will tend to predominate when bets are small (that is, when all the outcomes are near the current wealth level). Outcome risk aversion will tend to predominate when bets are large. For example, an optimist faced with the opportunity to participate in an actuarially fair bet will always wish to put some money on, (since EU analysis shows that behavior approaches risk neutrality as distributions collapse towards the mean). However, as the stake increases outcome risk aversion will start to play a role. Thus, with small stakes, small winning probabilities and large prizes, there will be a trade-off between optimism and outcome risk-aversion. Appropriate conditions on U and q (such as boundedness of U and ρ) will ensure that a finite optimum exists (some results of this kind are given in Section 7.3 and Chapter 8).

It is important to note that the correspondence principle derived in Section 6.1 may be used to extend some results for risk averse expected utility maximizers to the class of optimists with concave utility functions, even though these are not globally risk averse. For example, all monotone increasing transformation functions preserve first stochastic dominance, so any result on the response of a risk averse EU maximizer to a first stochastically dominating shift in the distribution will apply equally to the class of optimists with concave utility functions. Similarly, all transformation functions preserve the effect of a translation of the cumulative distribution function to the right, associated with an increase in initial wealth.

RDEU theory presents the possibility of a comparative static analysis in the absence of risk aversion. As was shown in Chapter 3, the EU analysis of risk seeking behavior yields corner solutions with implausible comparative static properties.

Concluding Comments

The main object of this chapter has been to extend the EU analysis of risk aversion to the RDEU case. Instead of a unique extension, however, there turn out to be two possible extensions. The first, based on the natural notion of risk aversion, leads to the pessimism condition and to the notion of monotone spreads. The second, based on the notion of second stochastic dominance leads to the requirement that q, as well as U, should be concave. The first form of risk aversion involves a more restrictive criterion for comparison between distributions, but imposes less restrictive conditions on preferences.

The choice between the two approaches to risk aversion is primarily one of analytical convenience. When changes in risk arise from transformations in the distribution, it will usually be possible to apply a monotone spread analysis. As will be shown in Chapter 7, this approach is more powerful and tractable, even in the EU context. However, when changes in risk arise from the addition of multiple independent sources of uncertainty, it is necessary to use the tools of second stochastic dominance.

The discussion of risk premiums and first and second order risk supports Allais' claim that people have attitudes to risk *per se*, independent of the marginal utility of wealth. The results presented here, notably those of Segal and Spivak, suggest that it is these probability attitudes that should be referred to as risk aversion (or preference). Attitudes to the marginal utility of wealth should be distinguished by some other name. However, this would run against well established usage. For this reason the terms RDEU risk averse and SSD risk averse will be used to refer to properties of global preferences and not of the probability transformation q.

CHAPTER 7

Comparative Statics for RDEU Theory

As has already been observed, generalized choice theories may be applied in three different ways: to show that results previously derived under the hypothesis of EU maximization apply in a more general setting; to indicate where EU results may not apply; and to analyze problems that lie outside the scope of EU theory. This chapter is primarily devoted to the first of these problems.

The main object is to show that the standard EU analysis of the comparative statics of choice under uncertainty carries over, under plausible conditions, to the RDEU model. In fact, somewhat more than this is achieved. First, it is shown that a number of results do not depend on risk aversion in the general case. This is a significant extension, since there will not, in general, exist an interior optimum in the EU case for preferences that are not risk averse. Second, the notion of monotone spreads is found to yield strong results for the comparative risk aversion problem analyzed by Ross (1981).

The chapter begins with a generalization of the comparative static results derived in Chapter 3 to incorporate the notion of monotone spreads. This is followed by a discussion of extension methods and the presentation of a Correspondence Principle for comparative statics, which is used to derive an extension of the main class of results to the RDEU case. The notion of monotone spreads is applied to the problem of comparative risk aversion for EU theory. Finally, two concepts of comparative risk aversion for RDEU theory are analyzed and compared. Most of these results were first published in Quiggin (1991a, 1991b).

7.1 Comparative Static Problems

EU theory has proved a powerful tool for the analysis of choice under uncertainty. Problems that have been investigated using the EU model include portfolio choice (Diamond and Stiglitz 1974), savings decisions (Sandmo 1970), labor supply (Newbery and Stiglitz 1981) and the theory of the firm (Sandmo 1971, Coes 1977). The existence of a number of observed violations of the predictions of EU theory, described in Chapter 4, combined with the theoretical criticism directed against the independence axiom, must cast some doubt on the empirical relevance of these results.

Until recently, however, economists wishing to analyze problems such as the behavior of the firm under uncertainty have had little alternative but to persevere with the use of EU theory as the basis of analysis. The early alternative models of behavior such as those of Handa (1977) and Kahneman and Tversky (1979) involved problems such as violations of (statewise) dominance and transitivity.

The problem is changed radically by the availability of models, such as RDEU, that can account for the empirical evidence that contradicts EU theory, while retaining the desirable properties of transitivity and dominance. However, this increase in scope is of little use if generalized models are unable to generate sharp comparative static results of the type that have made EU theory such a powerful tool of analysis. To repeat Tobin's (1969, p. 14) challenge to EU theorists critical of the implausible restrictions imposed by mean–variance theory

> its critics owe us more than demonstrations that it rests on restrictive assumptions. They need to show us how a more general and less vulnerable approach will yield the kind of comparative static results economists are interested in.

It is important, then, to examine the extent to which the results already derived in the EU analysis of the choice under uncertainty can be extended to generalized models. The purpose of this chapter is to show that most EU comparative static results can be carried over to the RDEU model. The fact that the major comparative static results can be extended to the RDEU model, but not to the case of general smooth preferences, arises because RDEU maintains the separation between probabilities and utilities that is abandoned in the general case. The RDEU model is general enough to accommodate most of the anomalies observed in EU theory, while retaining enough structure to preserve the standard comparative static results.

As a by-product of the analysis, some generalizations of existing results in the EU literature concerning increasing risk are obtained. These arise because certain generalizations of EU concepts are natural in the RDEU context. The most important are the replacement of multiplicative increases in risk with the monotone spreads defined in Section 6.5, and the extension of a number of results to cover the case of preferences that are not necessarily risk averse.

7.2 Extension Methods

There are three main methods of extending results from EU to RDEU. First, a number of results can be extended simply by repeating the EU proof and imposing conditions on q where appropriate. In Quiggin (1986), this approach was used to generalize the main results of the EU theory of the firm under price uncertainty.

The second extension method relies on the fact that an analog to Machina's (1982) local utility function can be defined for this model. Machina (1989a) has shown that for an important family of economically significant control problems, EU analysis can be satisfactorily generalized in terms of properties of the local utility function. This class of control problems is characterized by an objective function in which the control variable is separable from the random variable of economic interest. However, this is a fairly restrictive condition, which excludes most of the problems discussed in Chapter 3. For example, in the theory of portfolio choice, the risky rate of return and the control variable (the amount allocated to the risky asset) interact to determine the distribution of total returns. The separation property does, however, apply to situations of temporal choice such as those examined in Machina (1984). The use of the local utility function associated with an RDEU functional provides an elegant method of extending a range of EU results. It does not, however, exploit the specific features of the RDEU model, most notably the separation between probabilities and utilities inherent in (5.1) and (5.2).

The third, and most powerful, method of generalization exploits a correspondence principle for comparative statics. A typical comparative static result states that if the movement from the initial to the final distribution of some relevant random variable θ satisfies the relation R, all Expected Utility maximizers with $U \in \boldsymbol{U}$ will alter their optimal action in a particular way e.g. by increasing the value of some control variable.

For any given θ, the decision-maker in the standard comparative static problem chooses over random variables of the form $y_\alpha = \phi(\alpha, \theta)$. Suppose, as is standard, that ϕ is increasing in θ, and consider the case when θ, and hence also y_α, takes on only finitely many values. If $y_\alpha = \{\boldsymbol{x}; \boldsymbol{p}\}$, the transformed variable $\tilde{y}$ takes the form $\tilde{y}_\alpha = \{\boldsymbol{x}; h(\boldsymbol{p})\}$, where, in each case $x_i = \phi(\alpha, \theta_i)$. Hence, if we denote by $\tilde{\theta}$ the result of applying the transformation q to the random variable θ, we have $\tilde{y}_c = \phi(\alpha, \tilde{\theta})$. Suppose that whenever $y_0\, R\, y_1$, $\tilde{y}_0 \mathrm{R}\, \tilde{y}_1$. Then, also whenever $\theta_0\, R\, \theta_1$, $\tilde{\theta}_0 \mathrm{R}\, \tilde{\theta}_1$. Hence, any EU comparative static result concerning R will carry over to the RDEU case.

This argument implies a correspondence principle for comparative statics that may be stated as follows:

Correspondence principle for comparative statics : Provided the outcomes from every action are better, the higher is the realization of the relevant random variable, the conclusion of the comparative static result will be true for RDEU maximizers whenever $U \in \boldsymbol{U}$ and $q \in Q^*(R)$.

A formal proof may be given for the general class of comparative static problems analyzed in Chapter 3, for which the general form is given by equation (3.6).

PROPOSITION 7.1: *Let R be a relation on $\mathcal{D}$, let $\mathcal{U}$ be a family of utility functions, and let $q \in Q^*(R)$. Suppose that whenever $(F_1, F_2) \in R$, $U \in \mathcal{U}$ a shift from F_1 to F_2 in the distribution of θ leads to an increase (decrease) in the optimal value for α in a problem of the form* (3.6). *Then, provided ϕ is strictly monotone increasing in θ, a shift from F_1 to F_2 in the distribution of θ leads to an increase (decrease) in the optimal value for α in the corresponding problem with RDEU preferences.*

Proof: Let $G_i = q^\circ F_i$ $i = 1, 2$. Since $q \in Q^*(R)$ and ϕ is strictly monotone increasing in θ, $(G_1, G_2) \in \mathrm{R}$ by the argument given above. Hence, a shift from G_1 to G_2 leads to an increase (decrease) in the optimal value for α in a problem of the form (3.6). But these are precisely the RDEU problems corresponding to a shift from F_1 to F_2.■

This simple result is sufficient to yield extensions of most of the main results of EU theory to the RDEU model. The major remaining problem is the characterization of appropriate relations R and the corresponding classes of transformations $Q^*(R)$.

Given the correspondence principle derived above, the majority of EU results for the economic control problem described in Chapter 3 may be carried over in a fairly straightforward

The general form of the problem is

$$\text{Max}_\alpha \, \text{E}[U(\phi(\theta, \alpha, W_0))].$$

As in Chapter 3, it will be assumed that the utility function displays decreasing absolute risk aversion. This implies that $U''' \geq 0$. Then:

PROPOSITION 7.2:

(a) *Let F_1 be the initial distribution and F_2 the final distribution, and let θ_1 and θ_2 be the corresponding random variables. Given the assumptions above, the following are sufficient conditions for an* EU *maximizer to choose an increase in α^*.*

(i) $\theta_2 = \theta_1 + \delta$ *for some* $\delta > 0$;

(ii) $F_2 = \delta_c$, $E[F_1] \leq c$; *and*

(iii) F_1 *is derived from* F_2 *by a monotone spread,* $E[F_2] \geq E[F_1]$

(b) *An increase in W_0 leads to an increase in α^*.*

Proof: For all except a(iii) this is the same as Proposition 3.5. For a(iii) see the Appendix to this chapter. ■

This result extends Proposition 3.5 by replacing the multiplicative spread in part (ii) with a monotone spread. The reasoning behind this extension follows from the Correspondence Principle. There is no natural class of transformation functions that preserves the multiplicative spread relation. However, any of the well behaved classes of risk averse transformation functions will transform multiplicative spreads into monotone spreads. Furthermore, any monotone spread may be obtained by applying an appropriate transformation to a multiplicative spread.

The result in part (iii) appears to be the most general that can be obtained for increases in risk. The notion of mean–preserving spreads has generally proved intractable in comparative static problems of this kind. The use of the monotone spread definition of an increase in risk in part (iii) generalizes a number of results in the literature, including those of Rothschild and Stiglitz (1971b), Coes (1977) and Meyer and Ormiston (1983).[17] It is noteworthy that (iii) does not hold if the monotone spread condition is replaced by the requirement that F_2 second stochastically dominate F_1.

7.3 The Extension to RDEU

For RDEU maximizers, the general control problem may be rewritten as:

$$\text{Max}_a \int U(\phi(\theta, \alpha, W_0)) \, dq \circ F(\theta)$$

In most cases, by virtue of the Correspondence Principle, it is fairly straightforward to

[17] This result has been developed independently, in the EU case, by Meyer and Ormiston (1989).

obtain a formal extension of EU results derived to the RDEU case. However, the economic interpretation of these extended results is not the same as in the EU case. In particular, the results suggest a re–interpretation of notions of risk aversion and risk seeking.

First, it is desirable to derive conditions for the existence of a finite optimum. To carry the EU existence results over to the RDEU case, it is necessary to impose a continuity condition, namely that $q'(p)$ be bounded. If this condition is not satisfied, it is possible to design a sequence of lottery tickets with constant expected value and an unbounded certainty equivalent. One example of a weighting function that does not satisfy this condition is that proposed by Karmarkar (1978), namely

$$q(p) = p^{\alpha}/[p^{\alpha} + (1-p)^{\alpha}],\ 0 < \alpha \leq 1. \tag{7.1}$$

In this case, as p approaches zero or unity, $q'(p)$ increases without bound. If functions of this kind are excluded, it is possible to prove

PROPOSITION 7.3: *Let $q'(p)$ be bounded and define*

$$K = \lim_{\alpha \to \infty} \partial V/\partial\alpha = U_1 \int_{\phi_{\alpha}^{\infty}>0} \phi_a^{\infty}\, q'(F(\theta)) - U_2 \int_{\phi_{\alpha}^{\infty}\leq 0} \phi_a^{\infty}\, q'(F(\theta)) \tag{7.2}$$

Then a finite optimum will exist if $K < 0$ and not if $K > 0$

Proof: See the Appendix to this chapter. ■

The main result of this section is:

PROPOSITION 7.4:

(a) *Let F_1 be the initial distribution and F_2 be the final distribution, and let θ_1 and θ_2 be the corresponding random variables. Let the assumptions on U be the same as for Proposition* 7.1. *Then the following are sufficient conditions for an* RDEU *maximizer to choose an increase in α^*.*

(i) $\theta_2 = \theta_1 + \delta$ *for some* $\delta > 0$, $q \in Q$;

(ii) $F_2 = \delta_c$, $E[F_1] \leq c$, $q(p) \geq p\ \forall\ p$; and

(iii) F_1 *is derived from* F_2 *by a monotone spread.*

(b) *An increase in x_0 leads to an increase in α^*, $q \in Q$.*

Proof: The result follows from Proposition 7.2 and the Correspondence Principle .■

The decreasing absolute risk aversion condition may be relaxed in the case of a *monotone spread about the origin,* that is, a change in which all the bad outcomes get worse and all the good outcomes get better. A number of the standard ways in which risk might increase fall into the category of monotone spreads about the origin. For example, in a share or futures contract a shift to trading on margin would make good outcomes better and bad outcomes worse. A second example is that of price–band stabilization, which involves a change in distribution by which all prices lying outside some upper and lower bounds are set equal to those bounds. Several authors including Eeckhoudt and Hansen (1980), Quiggin and Anderson (1981) and Meyer and Ormiston (1983) have independently proved the result that price–band stabilization will always lead to an increase in the output of a risk averse producer and the same logic carries over to the two asset portfolio problem.

Nevertheless, the condition that the monotone spread should be centered on the origin is quite restrictive. In particular, since risk averse investors will only hold the risky asset if the expectation of θ is positive, it excludes the case of a multiplicative spread about the mean.

PROPOSITION 7.5: *For any RDEU risk averse individual, if θ_2 is derived from θ_1 by a monotone spread about the origin, the optimal level of investment will fall.*

Proof: See the Appendix to this chapter. ■

This result is consistent with the conditions derived by Rothschild and Stiglitz (1971) for an increase in risk, in the sense of second stochastic dominance, to yield a reduction in holdings of the risky asset. Their condition is expressed in terms of the difference between the original cumulative distribution function F_0 and the final distribution F_1. Meyer and Ormiston (1983) also investigated the issue of conditions on the difference between two cumulative distribution functions that may yield a reduction in allocation to the risky asset for all risk averse individuals. Their results were primarily negative. However, these negative conclusions apply only to conditions on the difference between two cumulative distribution functions. Because the monotone spread condition is expressed in relation to the mapping of the state space into the outcome space rather than in terms of the difference between cumulative distribution functions, these negative results do not apply here.

7.4 Risk Aversion, Risk Seeking and Comparative Statics

None of the results derived in the previous section requires SSD risk aversion, the concept proposed by Machina (1982) for the smooth model and Chew, Karni and Safra (1987) for the RDEU model. The results in Proposition 7.4, parts a(i) and (b), do not even require RDEU risk aversion in the weaker sense that a certain outcome is preferred to a risky variable having the same expectation. Although risk aversion is the predominant form of behavior for both firms and individuals, one of the main reasons for the development of RDEU theory was the desire to resolve the paradox (in terms of EU theory) of simultaneous gambling and insurance.

The main case of interest where risk aversion does not apply arises with an 'S–shaped' function q, and a distribution for the variable θ that is skewed to the right. An example is that of a speculative asset that will probably yield a zero return, but which will yield a high return if the associated venture is successful. An RDEU–maximising investor may purchase such an asset even if expected profits are negative. Similar examples apply in the theory of the firm and in the theory of labor supply for high risk professions such as acting and politics.

The presence of this type of risk taking behavior raises a number of questions of interest. For example, for a given expected rate of return, what price distribution is the most attractive to investors with preferences of this kind. This problem is closely related to that of the optimal prize structure for lotteries (see Chapter 8). The optimal prize structure is characterized by a fairly small probability of winning a few large prizes. However, there are also a large number of small prizes that do not contribute much to the expected return but act to reduce the probability of loss to a level where the probability weight is lowest.

There are a number of ways in which the study of lotteries is relevant. First, if significant numbers of individuals have preferences of this kind, entrepreneurs will have incentives to create and market shares in enterprises with return structures similar to the prize structure in a lottery. This certainly appears to take place with examples including 'blue sky' mineral exploration ventures and some types of highly geared futures contracts.

Second, these considerations are relevant to the construction of a portfolio of investments. The standard theory, developed in a mean–variance context by Lintner (1965) and Sharpe (1970) and in an EU context by Hildreth (1974), suggests that additional investments will be evaluated at a discount if their returns are positively correlated with those of the existing portfolio and at a premium if the correlation is negative. One way of interpreting this is to regard the discount as a charge for moving the distribution of returns away from its preferred shape – namely a probability mass concentrated at a single point.

In the present model, a discount for correlation with the existing portfolio will apply for 'downside' risks, but not necessarily for correlations between highly favorable outcomes. The most preferred shape of the distribution for preferences of the kind examined here consists of a concentrated mass at the lower end combined with a long tail to the right.

7.5 Monotone Spreads and Comparative Risk Aversion

The problem of increasing risk was examined in Chapter 6. A dual problem arises with consideration of increasing risk aversion. Pratt (1964) showed the equivalence, under EU, of a number of definitions of increasing risk aversion. One individual is more risk averse than another if the first has a coefficient of risk aversion that is everywhere higher, or the first utility function is a concave transform of the second. These conditions are both equivalent to the requirement that the first individual should require a larger risk premium (have a lower certainty equivalent) for any risky prospect. By comparing the same utility function combined with a translation (a change in base wealth) these results may also be applied to yield results for the case of decreasing absolute risk aversion.

However, as was shown by Ross (1981), increasing risk aversion does not imply a higher premium for a partial reduction in risk, that is, a shift from an initial distribution to one that is less risky in the sense of Rothschild and Stiglitz. Ross showed that the results of Pratt may be generalized to this case using an alternative, stronger definition of increasing risk aversion. A further development of this line of reasoning is given by Machina and Neilson (1987).

The second stochastic dominance interpretation of increasing risk also yields restrictive results in relation to the problem of increasing risk aversion. It is natural to suppose that the risk premium associated with a given increase in risk would be larger for a more risk averse individual than for a less risk averse one. In fact, as Ross (1981) has shown by counterexample, this is not necessarily true if increasing risk aversion is interpreted in the natural sense proposed by Pratt (1964). Ross's counterexample involves adding noise to the upper tail of a distribution while the lower tail remains unchanged. Clearly this is not a monotone spread.

In fact, the monotone spread concept offers an alternative to Ross' suggestion that a more restrictive concept of increasing risk aversion be adopted. Because a monotone spread may be regarded as a concave mapping on the outcome space, it is straightforward to show, in the EU model, that the risk premium for such a spread will increase with concave transformations of the utility function.

Let U^A and U^B be utility functions with $U^A = G \circ U^B$ for some concave function G. Thus, U^A is more risk averse than U^B in the sense of Arrow and Pratt. Now let y_0 and $y_1 = y_0 + \psi$ be random variables related by a mean-preserving monotone spread. Then, for the EU case the following generalization of the Pratt result may be obtained:

PROPOSITION 7.6: *Let π^A and π^B be risk premia defined such that*

$E[U^A(y_0 - \pi^A)] = E[U^A(y_1)]$, $E[U^B(y_0 - \pi^B)] = E[U^B(y_1)]$. *Then* $\pi^A \geq \pi^B$

Proof: We may define a y_λ, $\lambda \in [0, 1]$, such that

(i) $y_\lambda = y_0 + \lambda\psi + \pi(\lambda)$, with $\pi(0) = -\pi^B$, $\pi(1) = 0$; and

(ii) $\partial/\partial\lambda\, E[U^B(y_\lambda)] = 0 \;\forall\; \lambda \in [0, 1]$.

Now

$$\begin{aligned}\partial/\partial\lambda\, E[U^A(y_\lambda)] &= \partial/\partial\lambda\, E[G(U^B(y_\lambda))] \\ &= E[G'(U^B)\, U^{B\prime}(y_\lambda)(\psi + \pi'(\lambda))].\end{aligned}$$

By the monotone spread assumption there exists, for each λ, some value ω^* such that $\psi(\omega) \geq -\pi'(\lambda)$ if and only if $\omega \geq \omega^*$. Let G^* be the value of $G'(U^B)$ for $\omega = \omega^*$. By the concavity of G, $G \geq G^*$ if and only if $\omega \leq \omega^*$. Partition the expectation as

$$E[G'(U^B)U^{B\prime}(y_\lambda)(\psi + \pi'(\lambda))] = E[(G'(U^B) - G^*)\, U^{B\prime}(y_\lambda)(\psi + \pi'(\lambda))] + G^* E[U^{B\prime}(y_\lambda)(\psi + \pi'(\lambda))]$$

The first term on the RHS is everywhere negative, since $(G'(U^B) - G^*)$ has the opposite sign to $(\psi + \pi'(\lambda))$. The second term is equal to $\partial/\partial\lambda\, E[B\,(y_\lambda)]$ and is zero by condition (ii). Hence $\partial/\partial\lambda\, E[A\,(y_\lambda)]$ is everywhere negative and hence

$$E[U^A(y_0 - \pi^B)] \geq E[U^A(y_1)].$$

Hence, by the monotonicity of U^A, $\pi^A \geq \pi^B$. ■

A similar argument suffices to establish Ross main result for portfolio theory. Ross shows that, if one individual is more risk averse than the other in the strong sense he proposes, that individual will hold less of the riskier asset. This is not true for the usual definition of increasing risk aversion if general mean preserving spreads are considered. The alternative is to confine attention to monotone spreads. Suppose the return θ_2 is derived from θ_1 by a monotone spread (not mean-preserving). Let α be the proportion invested in the riskier asset, and let $\pi = W[\alpha\theta_2 + (1-\alpha)\theta_1]$ be the total return. A slight modification of the proof of Proposition 3 yields

Corollary: Let $U^A = G \circ U^B$ for some concave function G. Then an individual with utility function U^A will hold less of the riskier asset than an individual with utility function U^B.

Proof: The first order condition for U^B is given by

$$E[U^{B\prime}(\pi)\,(\theta_2 - \theta_1)] = 0.$$

Applying the argument of Proposition 7.6 to $U^A = G(U^B)$ shows that

$$E[U^{A\prime}(\pi)\,(\theta_2 - \theta_1)] \geq 0,$$

and the second order condition for the optimization problem yields the required result. ■

7.6 Comparative Risk Aversion in RDEU

The extension of results on comparative risk aversion to the RDEU case is complicated by the fact that two definitions of risk aversion must be considered. The case of SSD risk aversion is simplest. In Section 6.2, it was shown that SSD risk aversion is equivalent to the requirement that U and q be concave. It is natural to consider a notion of comparative risk aversion based on the idea of concave transforms of U and q. Chew, Karni and Safra (1987) show that Machina's analysis may be extended to yield:

PROPOSITION 7.7: *The following conditions on a pair of RDEU preference functionals V^A and V^B are equivalent:*

(i) *$U^A(x)$ is at least as concave a function of x as is $U^B(x)$, so that if these functions are twice differentiable in x, $-U^{A\prime\prime}(x)/U^{A\prime}(x) \geq U^{B\prime\prime}(x)/U^{B\prime}(x)$ and $q^A(p)$ is at least as concave a function of p as is $q^B(p)$, so that if these functions are twice differentiable in p, $-q^{A\prime\prime}(p)/q^{A\prime}(p) \geq q^{B\prime\prime}(p)/q^{B\prime}(p)$;*

(ii) *If F^* differs from F by a simple compensated increase in risk from the point of view of V^B, $V^A(F) \leq V^A(F^*)$; and*

(iii) *If V^A is indifferent between a p: $1-p$ chance of F or F^* and a p: $1-p$ chance of the sure amount c or the distribution F^*, and V^B is indifferent between a p: $1-p$ chance of F or F^* and a p: $1-p$ chance of the sure amount c^* or the distribution F^*, $c \leq c^*$.*

There does not appear to be a comparably simple analysis for RDEU risk aversion. The risk premium and probability weighting coefficient may be used in comparisons of risk aversion between individuals. Given two RDEU preference functionals V^A and V^B, respectively, V^A may be said to more RDEU risk averse than V^B if

(i) U^A is a concave transform of U^B and $q^A(p) \geq q^B(p)\ \forall\ p \in [0, 1]$;

or, equivalently, if

(ii) $\Delta_q^A(y) \geq \Delta_q^B(y)$ and $\Delta_U^A(y) \geq \Delta_U^B(y)\ \forall\ y \in \mathcal{Y}$.

Moreover, V^A is more RDEU risk averse than V^B if and only if

(iii) $\rho^A(p) \geq \rho^B(p)\ \forall\ p$ and $-U^{A\prime\prime}(x)/U^{A\prime}(x) \geq -U^{B\prime\prime}(x)/U^{B\prime}(x)\ \forall\ x \in W$.

If V^A is more RDEU risk averse than V^B, the risk premium $\Delta^A(y) \geq \Delta^B(y)$, $\forall\ y \in \mathcal{Y}$. However, the results of Cohen and Chateauneuf (1991), cited in Section 6.2, show that the reverse implication does not hold. If $q^A(p)$ is sufficiently greater than $q^B(p)$, it may be that $\Delta^A(y) \geq \Delta^B(y)$, $\forall\ y \in \mathcal{Y}$, even though U^A is not a concave transform of U^B.

By the Correspondence Principle, Proposition 7.6 may be extended to the case of RDEU risk averse preferences, since any pessimistic transformation function preserves the monotone spread relationship. Whenever two RDEU preference functionals differ only by a concave transformation of the utility function, risk premia will be well behaved for monotone spreads. It is not clear whether this result holds generally when V^A is more RDEU risk averse than V^B.

Concluding Comments

The results given in this chapter indicate that the generalization obtained by the RDEU model is achieved without a significant loss of power. RDEU theory can generate results in areas such as portfolio theory and the theory of the firm under uncertainty that are just as sharp as those derived from EU theory. The fact that results of this kind can be carried over to RDEU theory should increase confidence in the validity of much of the analysis using EU theory that has been performed in the past two decades, since it is likely that most of these results do not rely crucially on the independence axiom.

It is however, important to note that although the behavior of risk averse individuals will be similar in both EU theory and RDEU theory, RDEU theory does not give the same support to the presumption that most rational people will be globally risk averse. Whereas the behavior of an EU risk seeker seems strange, the behavior of an individual whose preferences are described by an RDEU functional with a concave outcome utility function and an S–shaped probability weighting function seems quite plausible. Of course, such an individual will display risk aversion except when confronted with probability distributions that are skewed to the right.

Appendix:

The first order condition for the general model is

(A.1) $$\partial V/\partial\alpha = \mathrm{E}[\,\partial U/\partial\alpha] = 0$$

or

(A.2) $$\mathrm{E}[U'(\phi(\theta,\ \alpha,\ x_0))\ \partial\phi/\partial\alpha] = 0$$

and the second order condition is

(A.3) $$D = \mathrm{E}[\,\partial^2 V/\partial\alpha^2] < 0$$

Proof of Proposition 7.2 (a(iii)) :

Let λ be the monotone spread parameter. Implicitly differentiating (A.2) with respect to λ yields

(A.4) $$\partial\alpha/\,\partial\lambda = \partial\alpha/\partial\delta = (-1/D)\,\partial^2 \mathrm{V}/\partial\alpha\partial\lambda$$

$$= -1/D\int_X \{U''(\phi(\theta,\ \alpha,\ x_0))\partial\phi/\partial\theta\ \partial\theta/\partial\lambda\ \partial\phi/\partial\alpha + U'(\phi(\theta,\ \alpha,\ x_0))\partial^2\phi/\partial\theta\partial\alpha\ \partial\theta/\partial\lambda\}\ dF(\theta).$$

Lemma 3.1 may be used to show that the second term in the integral is negative. By (Φ.3) and (Φ.5), $\partial^2\phi/\partial\theta\partial\alpha$ is a positive constant. Applying Lemma 3.1 with $g = U'$ and $f = \partial\theta/\partial\lambda$ yields the required result.

It remains to consider the first. Denote by ϕ_0 the value of ϕ evaluated at $\lambda = 0$. Let θ^* be the value of θ in the state of the world such that $\partial\phi_0/\partial\alpha = 0$, and let δ be the value of $\partial\theta/\partial\lambda$ evaluated at θ^*. Then there are two cases to be considered depending on whether δ is positive. If not, we may partition the integral

(A.5) $$\int_X U''(\phi)\partial\phi/\partial\theta\ \partial\theta/\partial\lambda\ \partial\phi/\partial\alpha\ dF(\theta) \quad \text{as}$$

(A.6) $$\int U''(\phi)\partial\phi/\partial\theta(\delta+\partial\theta/\partial\lambda - \delta)\partial\phi/\partial\alpha\ dF(\theta)$$

or

$$\int U''(\phi)\partial\phi/\partial\theta(\partial\theta/\partial\lambda - \delta)\partial\phi/\partial\alpha\, dF(\theta) + \delta \int U''(\phi)\partial\phi/\partial\theta\partial\phi/\partial\alpha\ dF(\theta).$$

By (Φ.3), the first integrand is negative everywhere. The second integral has already been shown to be positive, and the non–positivity of δ now yields the required result.

If δ is positive it is more convenient to partition the domain of integration rather than the integrand. For $\theta \geq \theta^*$, the integrand in (A.5) is negative, so it is sufficient to consider the integral of $U''(\phi)\partial\phi/\partial\theta\ \partial\theta/\partial\lambda\ \partial\phi/\partial\alpha$ over the range $[-\infty,\ \theta^*]$. Since $-U'(\phi)\partial\phi/\partial\alpha$ is monotone decreasing over this range and $\partial\theta/\partial\lambda$ is monotone increasing, Lemma 3.1 implies that

(A.7) $$\int -\partial\theta/\partial\lambda\ U'(\phi)\partial\phi/\partial\alpha\ dF(\theta) \leq \int \partial\theta/\partial\lambda\ dF(\theta) \int -U'(\phi)\partial\phi/\partial\alpha\ dF(\theta) = 0.$$

The integrand $U''(\phi)\partial\phi/\partial\theta\ \partial\theta/\partial\lambda\ \partial\phi/\partial\alpha$ may be written as

(A.8) $$-\int_{-\infty}^{\theta^*} A\ U'(\phi)\partial\phi/\partial\alpha\partial\theta/\partial\lambda\ dF(\theta)$$

By the Mean Value Theorem, there exists a value θ^{**}, such that $-\partial\theta/\partial\lambda\ U'(\phi)\partial\phi/\partial\alpha$, evaluated at θ^{**} takes the value

(A.9) $$M = \int_{-\infty}^{\theta^*} -\partial\theta/\partial\lambda\ U'(\phi)\partial\phi/\partial\alpha\ dF(\theta) \leq 0$$

Now $-\partial\theta/\partial\lambda\ U'(\phi)\partial\phi/\partial\alpha$ is monotone increasing over the range where it takes negative values. Thus, $-\partial\theta/\partial\lambda\ U'(\phi)\partial\phi/\partial\alpha > M$ if and only if $\theta > \theta^{**}$. Hence, it is possible to apply Lemma 3.1 with $f = -\partial\theta/\partial\lambda U'(\phi)\partial\phi/\partial\alpha$ and $g = A$ to show that the integral in (A.8) is less than

(A.10) $$\int_{-\infty}^{\theta^*} A\ dF(\theta) \int_{-\infty}^{\theta^*} -U'(\phi)\partial\phi/\partial\alpha\partial\theta/\partial\lambda\ dF(\theta),$$

which has already been shown to be negative. ■

Proof of Proposition 7.3

Because of the concavity of U, U_1 must be finite, and the results follow trivially for the cases when U_2 or ϕ_a^∞ is infinite. Let δ^* be the maximum value attained by $|\partial\phi/\partial\alpha|$. Then, for given θ

(A.11) $$\begin{aligned} |\partial/\partial\alpha(U(\phi)q'(F))| &= |U'(\phi)\partial\phi/\partial\alpha q'(F)| \\ &\leq U_2 q'(F)\ \delta^* \end{aligned}$$

The right hand side is integrable with respect to r since q' is bounded, so the Dominated Convergence theorem may be applied to the left hand side. Thus,

(A.12) $$\begin{aligned} \lim_{\alpha\to\infty} \partial V/\partial\alpha &= \lim_{\alpha\to\infty} \partial/\partial\alpha \left(\int U(\phi)q'(F)dF(r)\right) \\ &= \int \lim_{\alpha\to\infty} (\partial/\partial\alpha(U(\phi)q'(F)))dF(r) \\ &= \int \lim_{\alpha\to\infty} (U'(\phi)\partial\phi/\partial\alpha\ q'(F))dF(r) \\ &= K. \end{aligned}$$ ■

Proof of 7.5:

By the correspondence principle, it is necessary only to prove this result for the case of risk averse EU preferences.

Let λ be the spread parameter. Implicitly differentiating (A.2) with respect to λ yields

(A.13) $$\partial\alpha/\partial\lambda = -1/D \{ \int_\Omega U'(\pi) (\partial\theta/\partial\lambda) dF(\omega) + \alpha \int_\Omega U''(\pi)(\partial\theta/\partial\lambda)\theta \, dF(\omega) \}$$

In the first integral, $U'(\pi)$ is monotone decreasing, and $\partial\theta/\partial\lambda$ is increasing. Hence,

(A.14) $$\int_\Omega U'(\pi) (\partial\theta/\partial\lambda) dF(\omega) \leq \int_\Omega U'(\pi) dF(\omega) \int_\Omega \partial\theta/\partial\lambda \, dF(\omega)$$
$$\leq \int_\Omega U'(\pi) dF(\omega) \int_\Omega \partial\theta/\partial\lambda \, dF(\omega) \leq 0,$$
since $U'(\pi)$ is strictly positive and $E[\partial\theta/\partial\lambda] \leq 0$.

As regards the second integral, $U''(\pi)$ is everywhere negative, and θ $(\partial\theta/\partial\lambda)$ is everywhere positive, so the result must be negative. ■

CHAPTER 8

Risk Seeking and Lottery Design

In the previous two chapters, it has been shown that the majority of the EU analysis of choice under uncertainty may be carried over to the RDEU framework. It has also been shown that some results, notably those concerning second order risk aversion and those relying on the equivalence between risk aversion and second stochastic dominance, may not hold in the more general setting.

The third, and perhaps the most important, role of generalized utility theories is their potential contribution to the development of new theoretical analysis. This arises from the treatment of problems that are not amenable to analysis using EU theory and from the application of new theoretical tools, such as alternative concepts of stochastic dominance.

To show that the increased generality of RDEU and related theories is more than mere formalism, it is necessary to demonstrate that RDEU theory not only resolves anomalies that have arisen in EU analysis, but also that it permits the extension of economic analysis into new areas of behavior. Perhaps the most important aspect of behavior where EU theory is inadequate is that of risk taking. Although risk taking is a pervasive feature of economic activity, the conflict between EU theory and observed behavior is most clearly evident in the analysis of gambling. In this chapter, based on Quiggin (1991c), the RDEU model is applied to the problem of lottery design.

Despite a number of attempts, most notably that of Friedman and Savage (1948), it has not been possible to produce an adequate explanation of observed gambling behavior within the EU framework. The fundamental difficulty is that observed in Section 3.5, the lack of an adequate account of risk seeking behavior in the EU context. As noted in Section 4.5, attempts to explain gambling behavior using devices such as utility functions with convex segments imply extreme sensitivity of gambling behavior to initial wealth. Similar comments apply to models such as those of Ali (1977) and Ng (1975), in which gambling is a response to indivisibilities in consumption or constraints on the consumption set.

All of the approaches cited above have focused on the value of the outcomes. This is a natural consequence of the use of the EU framework, but it seems far more reasonable to suppose that participation in lotteries has to do with attitudes to probabilities and, in particular, with the placing of a high weight on extremely favorable, low probability events. Adam Smith (1776, pp. 164–165) stated:

> That the chance of gain is naturally over–valued, we may learn from the universal success of lotteries. The world neither ever saw, nor ever will see, a perfectly fair lottery; or one in which the whole gain compensated the whole loss; because the undertaker could make nothing by it. In the

> state lotteries, the tickets are not worth the price which is paid by the original subscribers, and yet commonly sell in the market for twenty, thirty and sometimes forty per cent advance. The vain hope of getting some of the great prizes is the sole cause of this demand. The soberest people scarce look upon it as folly to pay a small sum for the chance of gaining ten or twenty thousand pounds; though they know that even that small sum is perhaps twenty or thirty per cent more than the chance is worth. In a lottery in which no prize exceeded twenty pounds, though in other respects it approached nearer to a perfectly fair one than the common state lotteries, there would not be the same demand for tickets. In order to have a better chance for some of the great prizes, some people purchase several tickets, and others, small shares in a still greater number. There is not, however, a more certain proposition in mathematicks, than that the more tickets you adventure upon, the more likely you are to be a loser. Adventure upon all the tickets in the lottery, and you lose for certain; and the greater the number of your tickets the nearer you approach to this certainty.

This passage encapsulates a number of objections that have been made to the EU explanations of gambling and a number of requirements for a successful explanation. In particular, it is necessary that the theory should explain preference for lotteries with a few large prizes, that it should not suggest that people are unaware that the game in which they are participating is (actuarially) unfair, and that it should explain the purchase of one or a few tickets.

8.1 Lotteries with a Single Prize

The discussion above has indicated that the RDEU model is capable of explaining both risk seeking and risk averse behavior. Given a concave utility function and a transformation function that displays optimism for at least some distributions, RDEU is consistent with simultaneous gambling and insurance. However, such an explanation is only valuable if the model can generate sharp and (at least in principle) testable predictions of behavior. Although some individual testing has been carried out (see Quizon, Binswanger and Machina 1984 and Quiggin 1981), the most useful tests are those that relate to behavior in actual gambling and insurance markets. Gambling markets are of particular interest because they have previously been outside the scope of effective economic analysis. It is important to see whether the observed structures of gambling markets and, in particular, the gambles offered and accepted, are consistent with the predictions of the theory.

In this section, the RDEU model is applied to the problem of determining the optimal prize structure for a lottery, given that all consumers have identical RDEU preferences. It will be assumed that the operator's return is predetermined, either by government regulation or by market competition, and that the problem is to maximize the perceived net value of the ticket to the potential purchaser. This appears to correspond to the actual situation for lottery–type gambles. If the RDEU model is correct, we would expect that the prize structure actually prevailing will be fairly similar to the optimal solution derived here.

Before proceeding to the general solution of the problem, it is useful to consider two sub-problems. Consumption of any commodity is determined by individual demand schedules and the market price. In this context, it is useful to think of the demand curve being determined by the anticipated utility[18] of the (net) prize payouts on the winning tickets, and the price being the anticipated utility loss associated with the losing tickets. To optimize lottery design, the operator should maximize the anticipated gains and minimize the anticipated losses.

The simpler of these two sub-problems is that of minimizing anticipated losses. Since ticket prices are normally small in relation to total wealth, the utility function U can be approximated by a function linear in the ticket charge c. Units can be chosen so that the required average revenue is 1, and the decision problem becomes

$$\text{Min } c\, q(p) + \lambda(1-cp), \tag{8.1}$$

where p is the probability of a losing ticket. This problem is equivalent to minimizing $q(p)/p$ and the first and second order conditions on p are

$$pq'(p) - q(p) = 0,$$

and

$$pq''(p) > 0$$

respectively. These conditions will be satisfied at point A in Figure 8.1, where a ray drawn from the origin is tangent (from below) to the weighting curve.

Although data are scanty and not very reliable, the evidence that is available, such as Edwards (1962), suggests that this point will lie somewhere between 0.75 and 0.95. The solution derived here has direct application to one class of gambles, namely promotions for a product in which purchasers have some chance of having the purchase price refunded, that is, of getting the product for nothing. Obviously, this involves an effective increase in price, since the promotional funds could equally be applied to an across the board price reduction. The evidence given by Edwards suggests that promotions of this kind will be most effective in increasing demand if the proportion of refunds lies between 1 in 4 and 1 in 20.

The problem of maximizing the anticipated value of the payout is somewhat more complex because of the need to take both probability and risk attitudes into account. If only probability attitudes were considered, the problem would be one of maximizing $q^*(p^*)/p^*$, where p^* is the probability of a winning ticket. However, the assumptions behind the function illustrated in Figure 8.1 mean that this value increases as p^* decreases, converging to $(q^*)'(0)$ as p^* converges to zero. The optimal solution would be an infinitely large prize with an infinitesimally small chance of winning. The diminishing marginal utility of income offsets this and implies that a finite optimal prize will exist for a lottery with a single prize and a fixed average return.

[18] The term 'anticipated utility' is used, as in the original presentation of RDEU, to reflect the idea that the weighting function is integrated to yield an anticipated value of $U(x)$, which may be different from the mathematical expectation.

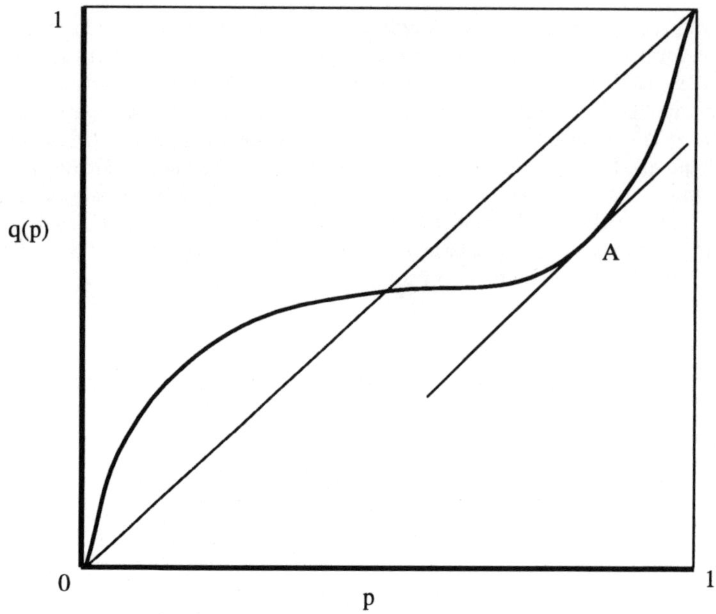

Figure 8.1: Optimum winning probability for lotteries

Expressing the utility function in terms of deviations from initial wealth, the problem may be expressed as

$$\text{Max } U(x)q^*(p^*) + \lambda(1 - xp^*).$$

Deriving the initial conditions and solving for λ yields

$$\frac{x\,U'(x)}{U(x)} = \frac{p^* q^{*\prime}(p^*)}{q^*(p^*)}\,. \tag{8.2}$$

The LHS of (8.2) may be interpreted as a measure of relative risk aversion. It is different from $r_r(x)$, the standard Arrow–Pratt coefficient of relative risk aversion, which refers to risks in a neighborhood of x. The measure given here compares the marginal utility of additional wealth at x with the average utility over the whole range $[0, x]$. Nonetheless, the two are closely related. In particular, for the class of constant relative risk aversion utility functions $U(x) = x^\alpha$, we have

$$r_r(x) = 1 - \alpha\,,\ \frac{x\,U'(x)}{U(x)} = \alpha,\ \ \forall x.$$

A similar interpretation may be given to the RHS of 8.2. It is a measure of the weight given to a small change in p compared to the weight on the total probability of winning $q^*(p^*)$.

Before considering the properties of this solution, it is necessary to establish that a solution does, in fact, exist. This may be shown as follows, subject to fairly weak conditions. First, in order for an increase in the prize to be profitable, it is necessary that the LHS of (8.2) be greater than the RHS. Given the shape of the weighting function in Figure 8.1, some gambles are favorable, so this condition must be satisfied somewhere. The concavity of U implies that the LHS is always less than one, and, provided $r_r(x)$ is bounded away from zero, the LHS will be bounded away from 1. The boundedness condition on q' implies that the RHS approaches 1 as p^* approaches zero, and hence that (8.2) must be satisfied for some finite x and p^*.

This discussion also gives an indication of the comparative static properties of the solution. In general, the optimal prize will be larger, the larger is the overweighting of small probabilities and the lower is the level of relative risk aversion.

8.2 The General Case

The most important point to note from the analysis of the previous section is that there is no necessary relationship between the probability of winning that maximizes the anticipated value of the prize and the probability of losing that minimizes the anticipated loss. For plausible values of the coefficients, the former will be very close to zero, and the latter is likely to be significantly less than 1. This provides an intuitive justification for the existence of multiple prizes in lotteries, and, in particular, for the frequently adopted practice of giving a large number of fairly small prizes that do not contribute much to the expected value of the ticket. By reducing the probability of losing from near certainty to a value of p for which significant underweighting applies, this practice reduces the anticipated loss associated with the ticket.

The rationale for multiple prizes given here must be distinguished from the discussion of this issue by Friedman and Savage (1948). Friedman and Savage justified the final concave segment in their utility function by the observation that lotteries have multiple prizes and hence that people are presumably not risk preferrers for unbounded wealth levels. However, what they were really concerned about here was the fact that there is a finite optimal bet, and this can be inferred more satisfactorily from the observation that otherwise there would be only one big lottery in any given time period. The Friedman–Savage theory does not predict multiple prizes unless it is assumed that there is a fixed minimum size for the lottery pool. Even then, it would predict a number of identical prizes rather than the observed pattern of a maximum prize and a series of smaller prizes.

With these considerations in mind, it is possible to analyze the general problem of optimal lottery design. It will be assumed that there is a fixed number of tickets n. Provided n is large, this is not a very severe restriction on the generality of the results. For any lottery with say, 1000 tickets at \$10 each, a fairly close substitute can be designed having 10 000 tickets at \$1 each. There are, therefore, n outcomes each occurring with probability $1/n$. These will be denoted $x_1, \dots x_n$, and ordered from worst to best, so that x_n is the first prize, and x_1 is the maximum loss (in a normal lottery, this will be the price of a ticket). The optimization problem must take account of both the constraint on the operator's rake–off and the ordering of the x_i. To simplify the former constraint, it will be assumed that the lottery is constrained to break even. (The introduction of positive profits does not lead to major changes in the solution.) The problem may be formulated as

$$\text{Max} \sum_{i=1}^{n} h_i\, U(x_i) + \lambda\left(\sum_{i=2}^{n} x_i\right) + \sum_{i=1}^{n} \mu_i\,(x_i - x_{i-1}), \tag{8.3}$$

where the μ_i are Kuhn–Tucker multipliers.

The first order conditions are

$$h_i\, U'(x_i) + \lambda + \mu_i - \mu_{i+1} = 0 \qquad \forall\, i \qquad (\text{setting } \mu_0 = 0), \tag{8.4}$$

and

$$\mu_i(x_i - x_{i-1}) = 0,\ \mu_i \geq 0,\ (x_i - x_{i-1}) \geq 0 \qquad \forall\, i.$$

The interpretation of these conditions is straightforward for the upper tail of the distribution, where (8.4) can be satisfied with the μ_i equal to zero. There will be a declining sequence of prizes starting at x_n and satisfying the relationship

$$U'(x_i)\, /\, U'(x_k) = h_k/h_i. \tag{8.5}$$

This relationship is particularly tractable for the constant relative risk aversion functions of the form $U(x) = x^{\alpha}/(1 - \alpha)$, discussed above. The relationship reduces to

$$x_i/x_k = (h_k/h_i)^{\beta} \qquad \text{where } \beta = -(1/1-\alpha) = -1/r_r. \tag{8.6}$$

Although the ordering of the x_i is essential for a tractable solution to the problem, there are some difficulties in determining the precise nature of the solution over the range where the μ_i are not necessarily zero. The most obvious solution is one where $x_1, \ldots x_k$ are all equal (and, of course, negative, being equal to the ticket price) and $x_{k+1}, \ldots x_n$ are an increasing sequence of prizes satisfying (8.5). In this case, it would appear that the analysis of the first sub-problem can be carried over to show that k/n, the probability of a losing ticket, will be chosen to minimize $q(p)/p$. The next proposition shows that this is, in fact, the optimal solution under natural conditions.

PROPOSITION 8.1: *Let the utility function be U be concave and let q be such that $q'(p)$ is convex in p. Then the optimal prize structure is as described above.*

Proof: See Appendix to this chapter. ■

8.3 Evidence from observed lottery designs

The prize structure described above seems to correspond fairly well to that prevailing in actual lotteries. There are, however, a number of qualifications that should be taken into account. First, in most lotteries, the small prizes do not form a strictly increasing sequence but are bunched together, with, say one set of $10 prizes, another of $50 prizes and so on. This prize structure is presumably adopted for simplicity. The precise structure of the set of small positive prizes does not make much difference to either the statistical expectation or the anticipated value of the lottery. These will be determined primarily by the probability of losing and by the value of the main prizes at the extreme upper tail of the distribution.

Second, the solution above is derived on the assumption that all lottery purchasers have identical preferences. The obvious market response to heterogeneous consumers is product differentiation. Consumers with limited risk aversion and heavy overweighting of extreme low probability events will prefer lotteries dominated by one large prize. Those with higher risk aversion and more weight on events not quite so close to the tail will prefer a more even distribution of prizes. Obviously, a large group will simply abstain. This group includes both global risk averters and those risk seekers whose anticipated utility gain from actuarially fair lotteries is insufficient to offset the operator's margin in an unfair lottery. If product differentiation is not possible, the solution would involve a compromise between different groups, with the weight depending both on numbers in different groups and the elasticity of demand with respect to deviations from the preferred prize structure.

Third, the analysis presented here assumes that the individual's income is known with certainty apart from a single lottery purchase. In practice there are numerous other sources of uncertainty and most people typically make a sequence of lottery purchases. As regards the first point, the upper tail of the wealth probability distribution will, for many people, be contributed primarily by the possibility of winning the lottery, since there is no prospect of their attaining substantial wealth. As regards the second, it is useful to consider the position of someone who is presented with a sequence of lotteries being resolved at regular intervals, for example, weekly, but whose time horizon is longer, say a year. A somewhat more complex version of the analysis presented above is applicable, in which the individual's anticipated utility is determined by the probability distribution yielded by the sum of the different lotteries in which they participate. The sum of the lotteries will yield a distribution similar to that of the optimal single lottery derived above. This implies that the optimal winning probability for any one lottery is smaller, as is the optimal ticket price. The rational strategy in this case will be one in which a small number of tickets is purchased each week. The most obvious alternative would be one in which a large number of tickets were purchased in the first available lottery and no more subsequently. However, this strategy would be dynamically inconsistent since, unless a major prize was won, the position after the lottery was resolved would again be one in which it was rational to buy tickets.

Fourth, lotteries are only one of a number of gambling forms and others do not obviously fit the pattern predicted here. This reflects the fact that lotteries are a very pure form of gambling with no element of skill and little of the entertainment available from time–consuming forms of gambling such as bingo and slot machines. The analysis of lotteries presented here forms a useful basis for the treatment of more complex cases such as that of racetrack betting. An analysis of this problem is presented as an indication of the way in which the insights derived from the simple model presented here may be applied to more complex cases.

8.4 Racetrack Betting

Whereas the main interest in lotteries is in bets at very long odds, racetrack betting involves a wide range of odds from very short (odds–on) to very long (such as doubles and trebles). A pure gambling explanation of the kind advanced for lotteries will not work in this case and it is necessary to introduce other explanatory factors. The central distinguishing feature of racetrack betting is that there are no objectively given odds, and there is considerable room for disagreement about the prospects of particular horses. The existence of such disagreements would provide a reason for bets between risk neutral or risk averse individuals. On the other hand, the incentives for information collection and the well established markets for information provision mean that it is unlikely that the market odds for bets between risk neutral individuals could differ greatly from the objective probabilities. It appears that an explanation based on disagreements over odds must be integrated with an analysis of risk preferences of the type presented for lotteries.

A number of writers including Griffiths (1949) and Ali (1977) (see Bird and McCrae 1984 for a summary of the literature) have examined the structure of returns to racetrack bets. These writers examine the average return per dollar invested on bets at particular odds or on horses in order of favoritism. Essentially the same features are found by all writers. First, all bets of this kind are actuarially unfair. This is not surprising, since otherwise there would exist a profitable betting strategy requiring no information about the individual characteristics of the horse involved. Second, the return to punters is near unity for short–priced horses, but falls as low as 60 cents in the dollar for long–priced horses. This is consistent with the previous discussion. Bets on long–priced horses are a substitute for lottery tickets, for people who know nothing about the prospects of the horses concerned. Thus, their rate of return should approach that of a lottery ticket as the odds increase. As a result of taxes and operating expenses, this latter return is typically of the order of 60 cents in the dollar. The general pattern of returns on 'exotic' bets such as doubles is similar (Asch and Quandt 1987).

This suggests that the returns structure may be regarded as being determined in the following fashion. As a first approximation, the return on a bet on a particular horse may be regarded as being determined by the objective odds and the amount people are willing to pay for a bet at those odds in the general gambling market. This would yield exactly fair returns for bets at evens with a gradually decreasing rate of return as odds lengthen. Because of disagreements regarding the appropriate odds for a particular horse, bookmakers are able to offer odds slightly less favorable than those suggested by this rule and, in particular, to lay bets on short–priced horses, which are, on average slightly unfavorable to punters.

RDEU theory permits a fairly straightforward explanation of the demand side of the market for racetrack bets. There are, however, a number of interesting problems on the supply side. The fact that the margins differ substantially between the different bets suggests that bookmakers are able to exercise a degree of price discrimination, which in turn implies the exercise of market power. In the case of pari–mutuel (totalisator) betting, this pattern of payments is generated automatically in response to bettor demand, but it is not clear precisely how the same result is achieved by on–course bookmakers, since the market appears to be fairly competitive. As with other discriminating monopoly solutions, the existing pattern is profitable for bookmakers as a group, but appears to offer incentives for any individual to defect. At first sight, it would appear profitable for an individual bookmaker to specialize in taking bets on long–priced horses, and offer slightly better odds than those who took bets on the field. A number of possible explanations for the stability of racetrack betting markets may be advanced, including the existence of informational difficulties or the operation of informal sanctions that act to preserve a cartel, but none appears completely convincing at this stage.

Concluding Comments

Risk seeking is an important aspect of economic behavior that has not been amenable to analysis under EU. At least in the case of lotteries, RDEU theory appears to give a very satisfactory account of risk seeking behavior and gambling markets.

The potential scope of the theory is much wider. A wide range of investments, such as shares and futures contracts include low probability high return events at the upper tail of the distribution of possible outcomes. It seems likely that use of an EU model with coefficients derived from standard questionnaire methods will lead to underestimates of the attractiveness of such investment. Conversely, EU methods may give an excessively favorable evaluation of private investments or public policy choices involving low probability events with extreme losses attached. Decisions associated with the siting of nuclear power plants provide an example.

Observed behavior in the face of risk is dominated by risk aversion, but contains elements that seem to imply risk preference. Under EU theory, this seems contradictory or irrational. The RDEU approach permits the development of a portfolio analysis that will include elements of risk seeking along with risk aversion.

Appendix

Proof of Proposition 8.1:

Two lemmas are required before the main result is proved.

LEMMA **8.1:** Let p^* be the probability that solves the problem (8.1) for minimization of the weighted probability of loss, and let $[i/n, (i+1)/n]$ be the interval of measure $1/n$ containing p^*. Let Z be any prize structure such that the probability, $\bar{p}$, of the lowest prize does not lie within this interval. Then there exists a preferred prize structure that does satisfy this condition.

Proof: Assume without loss of generality that the lowest prize is -1, and denote the next prize by z_1. Suppose $\bar{p} = k/n$, $k< i$. Then $h_{k+1}(p) < q(k/n)/(k/n)$.
Hence,

$$q(k/n)\, U(-1) + h_{k+1}(p)\, U(z_1) < (q(k/n) + h_{k+1}(p))\, ((k\, U(-1) + U(z_1)/(k+1))$$
$$< q((k+1)/n)\, U\, ((-k+z_1)\, /\, (k+1)),$$

by the concavity of U.

Hence Z will be dominated by a lottery with lowest prize $(-k+z_1)/(k+1)$ arising with probability $(k+1)/n$. The converse case, where $\bar{p} = k/n$, $k > i+1$, follows similarly with the observation that in a sufficiently small neighborhood of any point U is 'close enough' to linearity. ■

LEMMA **8.2:** Let Z be a lottery in which the probability of the minimum prize satisfies the optimality condition derived in Lemma 8.1, and let i be such that

(i) $x_i > x_{i-1}$; and

(ii) $x_{i+1} = x_i$.

Then there exists a preferred lottery with $x_{i+1} > x_i$.

Proof: By the conditions on the minimum prize $q'(p)$ is increasing over the relevant range and $h_{i+1} > h_i > h_{i-1}$.

Hence there exists some δ such that

(i) $x_i - \delta > x_{i-1}$; and

(ii) $h_i\, U(x_i) + h_{i+1}\, U(x_{i+1}) < h_i\, U\, (x_i - \delta) + h_{i+1}\, U(x_{i+1} + \delta)$.

If $x_{i+1} + \delta < x_{i+2}$, the preferred lottery may be constructed by reducing prize i by δ, and increasing prize i+1 correspondingly. If this condition is not satisfied, it is necessary to spread the increased prize money over a range of higher valued prizes to preserve the non-decreasing sequence of prizes, but a condition analogous to (ii) will still hold. ■

The main result may now be proved inductively. After the sequence of minimum prizes satisfying Lemma 8.1, consider the two subsequent prizes in an optimal design. By Lemma 8.2, they will form part of an increasing sequence. Lemma 8.2 may now be applied to each of the subsequent prizes in turn.

PART 3

FURTHER PROPERTIES OF THE MODEL

The previous four chapters dealt with properties specific to the RDEU model. In the next three chapters, the model is considered in relation to issues raised by the broader literature on generalized expected utility theory.

Chapter 9 contains a discussion of issues including betweenness concepts, dynamic consistency and the value of information. In general, these issues reflect rationality concepts more stringent than those of transitivity and preservation of first stochastic dominance. The EU model obeys these rationality concepts, whereas generalized models usually do not. This reflects the fact that most of these rationality concepts are restatements or modifications of the independence axiom.

In Chapter 10, it is shown that RDEU can account for most of the well known violations of EU predictions, such as the Allais problem , the common ratio effect and preference reversal. Recent empirical evidence and attempts to estimate RDEU functional forms are also discussed.

Chapter 11 presents various axiomatic approaches to the model. In most cases these involve the replacement of the EU independence axiom with one or more weaker axioms. An alternative approach, useful in the analysis of ambiguity is to maintain the independence axiom but to drop the reduction of compound lotteries axiom.

CHAPTER 9

Some Normative Properties of RDEU

The motivation for the development of RDEU theory and other generalizations of EU theory was twofold. First, there was the desire, in view of the well known violations of the predictions of EU theory, to produce a more adequate descriptive model of choice under uncertainty. Second, there was a widespread view that the independence axiom lacked the normative appeal of the dominance and transitivity axioms (the continuity and completeness axioms are primarily technical). Historically the second concern came first. The Allais 'paradox' was developed to illustrate problems with the von Neumann–Morgenstern independence axiom. Savage's sure thing principle was a reformulation of the independence axiom designed to enhance its normative appeal.

The appeal of the sure thing principle rested to a significant extent on the apparent link between the independence axiom and the more generally accepted first stochastic dominance rule. It was undermined by the development of RDEU and other models that preserved first stochastic dominance, but not the independence axiom.

Advocates of EU have responded by proposing examples of multi-stage dynamic[19] choice problems in which decision-makers who violate the independence axiom may be shown to be dynamically inconsistent, to display negative value for information or, worse, to be vulnerable to *Dutch books*, that is, acceptance of (multi-stage) gambles involving a certain loss.

The object of this chapter is to discuss these issues, and the responses that have been put forward by proponents of generalized models, with particular reference to the RDEU model. To present an adequate discussion of the issues, it is necessary to introduce the related concepts of quasiconcavity and quasiconvexity. These concepts are dual to the notion of diversification, which will be discussed first.

9.1 Diversification

Some of the most important results in portfolio theory concern the benefits of diversification. In EU theory, risk averse decision-makers will always prefer a diversified portfolio to "putting all their eggs in one basket." In this section, it will be shown that similar results hold for RDEU decision-makers who are risk averse in the SSD sense.

Consider a set $y^1, y^2 \ldots y^n$ of random variables, not necessarily comonotonic, which are interpreted as assets such that y^i yields $y^i(\omega)$ in state ω. For any vector α, $\sum_{i=1}^{n} \alpha_i = 1$, a mixture

[19] Note that these problems are not dynamic in the sense that the passage of time is an inherent element of the analysis. Progress on a truly dynamic representation of problems of choice under uncertainty has been limited. See Machina (1984) for a summary of some of the difficulties.

y^α of these variables yielding $\alpha \bullet y = \sum_{i=1}^{n} \alpha_i y^i(\omega)$ in state ω may be formed by diversification. In EU theory, with quasilinear preferences, preference for diversification is equivalent to risk aversion.

An individual is referred to as a *diversifier* if

$$y^1 \sim y^2 \sim \dots \sim y^n \Rightarrow y^\alpha \succcurlyeq y^i \,\forall\, i. \tag{9.1}$$

This definition applies for any RDEU preferences (and for any preferences that yield a weak order on $\mathcal{Y}$). However, for the remainder of this section, the utility function will be assumed linear, so that attention may be confined to probability attitudes. Consider first the case of comonotonic random variables over a finite state space. The condition that all the random variables be equally attractive may be written

$$\sum_{j=1}^{n} y^i_j h_j = V \;\forall\, i, \tag{9.2}$$

where h_j is the weight on state j. Given comonotonicity, $h_j = q(\sum_{k=1}^{j} p_k) - q(\sum_{k=1}^{j-1} p_k)$ and is independent of i. Hence the LHS of (9.2) is linear in the y^i_j and the individual will be indifferent regarding diversification across comonotonic prospects. This result was proved by Roell (1987).

Yaari (1987) introduced the notion of *hedging* to analyze the case where the variables y^j are not comonotonic. Pessimism implies a preference for hedging. The simplest form of hedging arises with a state space consisting of two states i, j (each occurring with probability 0.5) and two variables y^1, y^2 such that $y^1_i > y^1_j$, but $y^2_j > y^2_i$. Pessimism implies $h_1 > 0.5 > h_2$.

$$y^1 \sim y^2 \Rightarrow V^1 = h_1 y^1_j + h_2 y^1_i = h_1 y^2_i + h_2 y^2_j = V^2 ,$$

where V^i is the evaluation of y. Suppose without loss of generality that state i yields the worse outcome in the mixed prospect, $\alpha y^1 + (1-\alpha)\, y^2$, so that

$$\alpha y^1_i + (1-\alpha)\, y^2_i < \alpha y^1_j + (1-\alpha)\, y^2_j.$$

Now, let V^α be the evaluation of the mixed prospect. Collecting terms yields the desired result.

$$V^\alpha = h_1(\alpha y^1_i + (1-\alpha)\, y^2_i) + h_2(\alpha y^1_j + (1-\alpha)\, y^2_j) > \alpha V^1 + (1\text{-}\alpha) V^2 ,$$

since $h_1 > h_2$ and $(1-\alpha)\, y^2_i > (1-\alpha)\, y^2_j$.

The converse result holds in the case of optimism, when $h_2 > 0.5 > h_1$.

The argument presented above goes through with minor modifications if the probabilities of the states i and j are p_i and $p_j = 1\text{-}p_i$ for arbitrary p_i. We now have

$$y^1 \sim y^2 \Rightarrow V^1 = h_1(p_j, p_i) y^1_j + h_2(p_j, p_i) y^1_i = h_1(p_i, p_j) y^2_i + h_2(p_i, p_j) y^2_j = V^2 = V.$$

If state i yields the worse outcome in the mixed prospect, collecting terms yields:

$$V^{\alpha} = h_1(p_i, p_j)(\alpha y^1_i + (1-\alpha)\, y^2_i) + h_2(p_i, p_j)(\alpha y^1_j + (1-\alpha)\, y^2_j)$$
$$= h_1(p_i, p_j)\alpha y^1_i + h_2(p_i, p_j)\alpha y^1_j + (1-\alpha)V^2$$
$$\alpha V^1 + (1-\alpha)V^2 = V.$$

When there are only two states of the world, the basic and SSD definitions of pessimism are equivalent. Also, any two prospects are either comonotonic or anti-comonotonic (that is, the best state under one prospect the worst under the other and so on). These equivalences do not hold when there are more than two states.

The SSD definition of pessimism yields a general extension of the result that risk averters prefer diversification. Assume for simplicity that there are n equiprobable states. Concavity of the weighting function is now equivalent to the requirement that $i > j \;\Rightarrow\; h_i \leq h_j$. Consider now two prospects with rankings which differ only with respect to states i and j. The argument presented above requires only notational changes. Since any rank ordering can be obtained by successive interchanges of pairs of states and since any prospect can be approximated by a prospect with n equiprobable states, the general result may be established.

The basic definition of pessimism yields a more limited extension. Decision-makers who are risk averse in this sense will always prefer mixtures between prospects that are anti-comonotonic. Although this requirement is restrictive, it covers many cases of interest. In particular, many of the classic examples of hedging in commodity and insurance markets involve mixtures between anti-comonotonic prospects.

Wakker (1990b) extends the analysis presented above to give a direct characterization of optimism and pessimism in terms of comonotonicity. He shows that the transformation function is concave if and only if for any y^1, y^2, y^3 with y^2, y^3 comonotonic, and any $\alpha \in [0, 1]$

$$V(y^1) \geq V(y^2) \Rightarrow V(\alpha y^1 + (1-\alpha)y^3) \geq V(\alpha y^2 + (1-\alpha)y^3)$$

Also, the transformation function is concave if and only if the implication above holds whenever y^1 and y^3 are comonotonic. The only-if part of Wakker's result follows from the argument presented above. The converse implication arises by considering the case when y^2 is a degenerate random variable (hence trivially comonotonic with y^3 and y^1) such that $V(y^1) = V(y^2)$.

All of these results, except the converse implication in Wakker's result, hold *a fortiori* when the utility function is concave rather than linear. In this case, diversification across comonotonic prospects will yield an increase in welfare. For each i, the concavity of U means

$$U\Big(\sum_{j=1}^{n} \alpha_j y^j_i\Big) \geq \sum_{j=1}^{n} \alpha_j U(\alpha_j y^j_i).$$

Summing across the states yields $V^{\alpha} \geq V$.

9.2 Quasiconcavity, Quasiconvexity and Betweenness

Diversification may be regarded as a linear mixture of random variables in the outcome space $\mathcal{Y}$, arising from, say, an allocation of wealth across a portfolio. A good deal of attention in the literature on generalized utility theories has been paid to various properties of the underlying preferences with respect to probability mixtures in $\mathcal{D}$. Such mixtures arise naturally in multi-stage lotteries and decision problems.

The notions of quasilinearity, betweenness, and quasiconcavity have all been examined. *Quasi–linearity* is the EU property of linearity with respect to probability mixtures. In the terminology of Chew (1989), EU represents the quasilinear mean on $\mathcal{D}$.

Quasilinearity may be weakened to *betweenness*, the property that

$$\forall\, F, G \in \mathcal{D},\ \alpha \in [0, 1],\ F \sim G \Rightarrow \alpha F + (1-\alpha)\, G \sim F.$$

A number of functional forms displaying betweenness have been examined in the literature, most notably the weighted utility model of Chew (1983).

The notions of quasiconcavity and quasiconvexity arise naturally in this context. Preferences are *quasiconcave* if

$$\forall\, F, G \in \mathcal{D},\ \alpha \in [0, 1],\ F \sim G \Rightarrow \alpha F + (1-\alpha)\, G \succcurlyeq F,$$

and *quasiconvex* if

$$\forall\, F, G \in \mathcal{D},\ \alpha \in [0, 1],\ F \sim G \Rightarrow \alpha F + (1-\alpha)\, G \preccurlyeq F.$$

Preferences display betweenness if and only if they are both quasiconcave and quasiconvex.

A number of EU results have been generalized using the concept of quasiconcavity. Karni and Safra (1989a) have examined optimal stopping rules and behavior in auctions. Dekel (1989) examined the equivalence between risk aversion (in the SSD sense) and preference for diversification. He showed that this equivalence is preserved for general quasiconcave preferences, and, by example, that there are general preferences displaying risk aversion but not diversification.

It may appear surprising then, that, in RDEU theory, risk aversion (in the strong sense of aversion to second stochastically dominated random variables) implies quasiconvexity. Chew (1989) shows that concavity of q implies quasiconvexity of preferences. A simple proof of this result may be provided in the case of a probability mixture between a two-outcome bet $y = \{(x_1,\ x_2);\ (p,\ 1\text{-}p)\}$ and its certainty equivalent c.

$$\alpha y \oplus (1\text{-}\alpha)c = \{(x_1,\ c,\ x_2);(\alpha p,\ 1\text{-}\ \alpha,\ \alpha(1\text{-}p))\}.$$

For concave q,

$$\begin{aligned} V(\alpha y \oplus (1\text{-}\alpha)c) &= q(\alpha p)U(x_1) + q^*(\alpha(1\text{-}p))\, U(x_2) + (q(1\text{-}\alpha + \alpha p) \ - \ q(\alpha p))U(c) \\ &\le \alpha\, (q(p)U(x_1) + q^*(p)U(x_2)) + (1\text{-}\alpha)U(c) \\ &\le \alpha\, V(y) + (1\text{-}\alpha)\, V(c). \end{aligned}$$

The converse result, that quasiconvexity implies concavity of q, is proved by Wakker (1991a). Since Dekel's results require both quasiconcavity and risk aversion, they cannot be applied to the RDEU model. Nevertheless, as has already been shown, the equivalence between risk aversion and diversification carries over to this model.

Another factor which has led some writers to see quasiconcavity as a desirable property has been its use in the derivation of equilibrium concepts. Debreu (1952) showed that quasiconcavity in preferences is sufficient for the existence of a mixed-strategy Nash equilibrium in non-cooperative games. This result does not carry over to quasiconvex preferences because decision-makers with such preferences are averse to the randomization usually assumed to be inherent in a mixed strategy. However, Crawford (1990) points out that randomization, in the sense that the decision-maker is subject to uncertainty about her own choice, is unnecessary. All that is required is that the other player(s) should be unable to predict the decision-maker's choices. Crawford formalizes this idea to yield a more general equilibrium concept and shows that an equilibrium will exist for both quasiconvex and quasiconcave preferences.

It is difficult to obtain a clear intuition about the plausibility of quasiconvexity or quasiconcavity in preferences. Analogy with diversification over outcome mixtures, and the results of Dekel seem to suggest that quasiconcavity is the appropriate assumption. However, the example of RDEU theory, where preference for diversification over outcome mixtures arises without quasiconcavity, suggests that this analogy is misleading.

An alternative view arises from considering probability mixtures as two–stage lotteries. For people with an aversion to probability risk, these will generally be less attractive than single–stage lotteries. This provides an argument for quasiconvexity in preferences as a concomitant of risk aversion.

9.3 Dynamic Consistency

One of the most important unresolved issues for generalized utility theories arises with sequential choice problems. The problem may be illustrated by an example. Suppose an individual has RDEU preferences with a linear utility function and a weighting function such that $q^*(0.01) > 0.01$ but $q^*(0.1) < 0.1$. Such an individual will accept fair gambles where the chance of winning is 1/100, but will reject fair gambles where the chance of winning is 1/10. Now consider a situation where the individual has the chance to participate in two successive gambles, each with a winning probability of 1/10. *Ex ante*, the dominant strategy is to accept the first gamble, then place any winnings on the second gamble, yielding a winning probability of 1/100. Suppose, however, that the individual can choose at the end of the first gamble whether or not to participate in the second. If he optimizes on the basis of the preferences outlined above, he will choose not to accept the second gamble. Thus the individual's preferences are *dynamically inconsistent.*

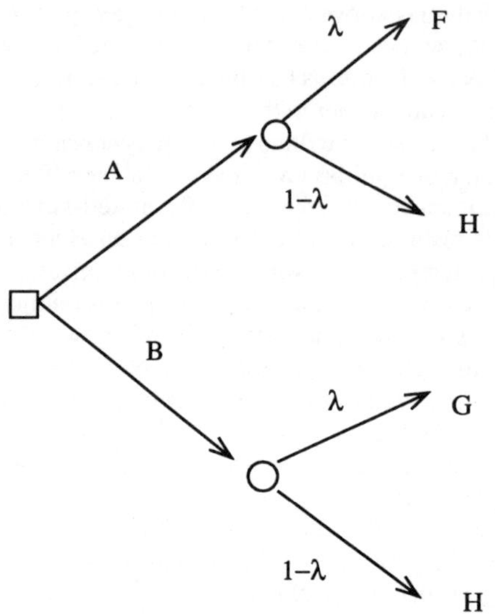

Figure 9.1: Two-stage choice problem

The notion of dynamic consistency is derived from the theory of intertemporal choice, where preferences may be dynamically inconsistent if the discounting structure is myopic. For example, suppose an individual places a high value on present consumption, but treats consumption in all future periods as equally valuable. Then, if the rate of interest is positive, and income is equal in all periods, the optimal time path for consumption will involve high consumption in period 1, followed by savings in period 2 for consumption in later periods. However, when the individual arrives in period 2, she will have a strong preference for consumption in that period, and hence will not carry out the plan which appeared optimal in period 1.

This issue cannot arise with EU preferences, which are linear in the probabilities. However, anyone who violates the independence axiom must exhibit dynamic inconsistency in some cases. If the independence axiom (EU.5) is violated, there exist F, G, $H \in \mathfrak{D}$ and $\lambda \in (0, 1)$ such that

(a) $F \succ G$ and

(b) $\lambda G + (1-\lambda)H \succ \lambda F + (1-\lambda)H$.

Suppose an individual with preferences of this kind is faced with a choice between two-stage prospects. In prospect A, the first stage gamble yields distribution H with probability $(1-\lambda)$ and distribution F with probability λ. In the second stage the individual receives a random realization of the selected distribution. Prospect B is the same except that F is replaced by G (see Figure 9.1). Given the preference in (b), prospect B will be preferred. Suppose however, that the first stage is played out and the individual is then offered a chance to switch from B to A. If the first-stage gamble yielded H, she will be indifferent. If the first-stage gamble yielded G, she will be willing to pay a positive amount. Hence, regardless of the outcome of the first-stage gamble, the individual will pay a non-negative amount to reverse her choice.

The example can be made a little sharper. By continuity, (b) can be replaced by

$$\text{(b}'\text{)}\ \lambda G + (1\text{-}\lambda)H \succ \lambda F + (1\text{-}\lambda)(H - \delta)$$

where $(H - \delta)$ denotes the distribution H combined with a fixed negative payment δ. The individual is now willing to pay a strictly positive amount to reverse her initial choice.

Dynamic inconsistency can be used to generate examples where a person with non-linear preferences may be the subject of a Dutch book, that is, a gamble which yields losses with probability 1. When initial wealth is known with certainty, risk averse RDEU maximizers, and, more generally, people with quasiconvex preferences, are not vulnerable to Dutch books (Green 1987). The central point may be seen by supposing that $F = H$ in Figure 9.1 and that this distribution yields a given outcome with probability 1. That is, the individual has available a given certain wealth and has the 'do nothing' option of retaining that wealth. Then we may rewrite condition (b) as $\lambda G + (1\text{-}\lambda)F \succ F$. Given quasiconvexity, this can only hold if $G \succ F$. Thus, the Dutch Book presented in Figure 9.1 can never arise.

The negative value of information observed in risk seeking RDEU maximizers may be regarded as the necessary counterpart of a desire for gambling.[20] If one enjoys gambling for its own sake, then at least in some cases, one would prefer not to have all possible information. These considerations reduce the problem posed for RDEU theory by the phenomenon of dynamic inconsistency, but the assumption of known initial wealth is very restrictive. For other models, in which quasiconcavity is the preferred behavioral postulate, dynamic inconsistency is a more critical issue.

There have been three main reactions to the problems posed by dynamic inconsistency. Advocates of EU theory have concluded that, at least at a normative level, the attempt to abandon the independence axiom has been unsuccessful. A succinct statement of this viewpoint is given by LaValle and Wapman (1986).

A second approach, employed by Karni and Safra (1989b), is based on the notion of *behavioral consistency*, also derived from the theory of intertemporal choice. Here the idea is that the individual treats the sequential decision process as a non-cooperative game with the 'players' being the same individual at different points. Thus, at the first stage, the individual makes an optimal choice, given that each subsequent stage her future self will also be choosing in the same fashion. In the example above, the behaviorally consistent individual faced with the initial gamble will choose knowing that the second-stage individual will always reject a gamble at the given odds. Hence, the first-stage choice is between a certain sum of money and a gamble with a 1/10 chance of winning. Since the gamble is unfavorable, the individual will reject it at the first stage. Karni and Safra have used the notion of behavioral consistency to model behavior in a sequential decision contexts such as auctions. In their results, quasiconcavity is necessary for the existence of an equilibrium, which will normally be a mixed strategy equilibrium. However, it seems probable that the approach of Crawford (1990), presented in the previous section, could be used to derive a more general equilibrium concept.

[20] More precisely, since a desire for gambling is equivalent to quasi-concavity of preferences, we may refer to a desire for randomization.

Machina (1989b) adopts a quite different approach. He rejects the assumption that individuals will choose, at each point on the decision tree, in a manner which takes no account of the past decisions which led to that point, and of the outcomes which were possible at the beginning of the decision processes but have not been realized. This assumption, which Machina refers to as *consequentialism*, is closely tied to the independence axiom. Machina argues that, if people reject the independence axiom in making choices over simple prospects, they will also reject consequentialism in making sequential decisions.

Machina illustrates this claim with the parable of 'Mom' who must give a (non-divisible) treat to one of her two children, Abigail and Benjamin. Mom prefers choice by a random coin flip denoted $\{A, B);(1/2, 1/2)\}$ to a choice (A or B), which gives the treat to one of the children with certainty. She flips the coin and the treat is allocated to Abigail. However, Benjie now argues that, since Mom has shown a revealed preference for $\{A, B);(1/2, 1/2)\}$ over A, she should flip the coin again. Mom naturally rejects this claim. Machina argues that Mom, along with decision-makers who reject the independence axiom has rejected consequentialism, and is not obliged to 'snip off the decision tree' by ignoring the existence of the unrealized outcome that would have allocated the treat to Benjamin.

Machina's argument is a convincing rebuttal of the normative critique of generalized utility theories. However, it does not yield a fully specified theory of sequential decision-making. The obvious dynamically consistent choice pattern is to select the plan which is optimal *ex ante* and to stick to that plan subsequently. There are two main objections to this solution. The first, due to LaValle (1991), is that its informational requirements are extreme. If applied in full rigor, it would require us to estimate, and keep track of the consequences, in every possible state of the world, of each option one might have chosen for any decision in the past. This is clearly impractical. However, if it is desired to keep track of some unrealized consequences and ignore others, then it is necessary to specify a rule by which this may be done.

A second objection is that this solution requires individuals to make very unattractive choices at late points in the decision tree, solely to keep faith with earlier decisions which may have yielded only marginal benefits over available alternatives. Suppose in the example given above that $q^*(0.01)$ is only slightly greater than 0.01, but $q^*(0.1)$ is much less than 0.1. Then the optimal *ex ante* strategy of accepting both gambles yields only marginal benefits, and the required gamble at stage 2 is highly unattractive. Further, if the individual at the initial decision point is not sure that he will have the strength of will to carry out the planned course of action at stage 2, then considerations of behavioral consistency suggest that he should refuse the first gamble.

However, the notion of dynamic consistency does not require that the selected plan should be the one which is most attractive to the individual at the initial decision point. A more general dynamically consistent solution arises if the non-cooperative game solution proposed by Karni and Safra is replaced by some form of cooperative game solution. In such a solution, the individual would choose and stick to a plan which maximized a welfare function which took account of preferences at all points in the decision tree. Such an approach could also be applied to problems of dynamic inconsistency in intertemporal choice.

9.4 RDEU and Information

A defence of the independence axiom, closely related to the Dutch book and dynamic consistency arguments, has been proposed by Wakker (1988). He observes that anyone who violates the independence axiom will have a negative value for information in certain circumstances. The value of information problem is closely related to the dynamic inconsistency problems considered in the previous section.

As before, if the independence axiom (EU.5) is violated, there exist F, G, $H \in \mathfrak{D}$ and $\lambda \in (0, 1)$ such that

(a)$F \succcurlyeq G$ and

(b) $\lambda G + (1\text{-}\lambda)H > \lambda F + (1\text{-}\lambda)H$.

Wakker's example involves the choice problem depicted in Figure 9.1 with $F_1 = F$, $G_1 = G$ and $F_2 = G_2 = H$. The agent chooses an action α yielding a lottery that depends on the state of the world θ. If $\alpha = 1$ is chosen the agent receives F when $\theta = 1$, and H when $\theta = 2$. If $\alpha = 2$ is chosen the agent receives G when $\theta = 1$, and H when $\theta = 2$. In the absence of information, (b) indicates that the agent will choose $\alpha = 2$, and receive $\lambda G + (1\text{-}\lambda)H$. If the agent is informed that $\theta = 1$, she will choose $\alpha = 1$ and receive F. If the agent is informed that $\theta = 2$, her choice makes no difference; she receives H. Thus, an agent who chooses to become informed of the value of θ, faces, *ex ante*, the distribution $\lambda F + (1\text{-}\lambda)H$. *Ex ante*, the agent prefers $\lambda G + (1\text{-}\lambda)H$, which is obtained by remaining uninformed. Hence, the agent prefers not receiving information and assigns negative value to information.

One difficulty with Wakker's example has been observed by Kelsey (1990). The value of information for an EU maximizer in this case is zero, since the optimal action is always that which maximizes expected utility given that $\theta = 1$. The event $\theta = 2$ is, as the name of the axiom suggests, an irrelevant alternative, since the choice of action has no effect in this event. However, an appeal to continuity suggests that there must exist cases in which a non-EU maximizer would have negative value, but EU maximizers would have positive value.

Ex ante, the agent would like to commit herself to choose $\alpha = 2$ regardless of the information that is revealed. Given the ability to make such commitments, the value of information would always be non-negative. (In the present example, however, the value would be zero, just as it is for an EU maximizer.) Thus, if Machina's criticism of the dynamic inconsistency arguments is accepted, it also yields the conclusion that the value of information can never be negative.

Schlee (1990) considers Wakker's argument as it applies to the RDEU model. He shows that under RDEU, willingness to pay for perfect information is always positive, though willingness to pay for imperfect information may not be. He also considers Segal's derivation of RDEU from violations of the axiom of reduction of compound lotteries, rather than from violations of the independence axiom (see Section 11.5). He shows that, although Wakker's argument is not applicable in this case, examples of negative willingness to pay for imperfect information will still arise.

Schlee considers the general control problem, discussed in Chapter 7. His argument is given for the discrete case, but applies equally for the continuous case. Denote by α^{**} the optimal action under uncertainty and by $\alpha^*(\omega)$ the optimal action when the state of the world is known to be ω. For any ω, the definition of optimality requires that $\phi(\alpha^*(\omega), \theta(\omega)) \geq \phi(\alpha^{**}, \theta(\omega))$.

Hence,

$$\int_{\Omega} U(\phi(\alpha^*(\omega), \theta(\omega)))\, dq(F(\theta)) \geq \int_{\Omega} U(\phi(\alpha^{**}, \theta(\omega)))\, dq(F(\theta))$$

Schlee's argument applies, not only to RDEU, but to any preference functional that preserves first stochastic dominance. The fact that the argument is based on first stochastic dominance suggests that other stochastic dominance concepts may be used to derive conditions under which imperfect information will have positive value. The approach would involve showing that, conditional on any possible value of the information received, the distribution obtained from the optimal choice of α with information first (or second) stochastically dominated that obtained using any other value of α. The result would then follow from the fact that the standard stochastic dominance relationships are preserved by probability mixtures.

Consider, for example, the case when $\theta = \eta + \varepsilon$ is the sum of two independent random variables and the return from a given choice α is linear in $(\alpha - \theta)$. Suppose that ε is symmetric, and that information on the value of η, the choice $\alpha^*(\eta) = \eta + E[\varepsilon]$, second stochastically dominates any alternative choice of α. This implies that, for individuals whose preferences preserve second stochastic dominance, whether or not they obey EU, the value of information is strictly positive.

Concluding Comments

The recent generalizations of EU theory have been developed primarily to explain observed preferences in atemporal single-stage lotteries. The debate over dynamic consistency indicates some of the complexities that arise when attention is broadened to cover sequential choices and sequential acquisition of information. The EU theory of sequential choice, and the associated Bayesian decision theory represent the only fully developed body of thought on this topic.

Although the term 'dynamic' is used here, the choices in the EU model are atemporal. Choices take place in sequence, but there is no passage of time between them, and hence no subjective experience of being exposed to uncertainty about the future. The fundamental problem for a descriptive and normative theory of choice under uncertainty must be to capture the fact that sequential choices are embedded in time.

CHAPTER 10

RDEU and Experimental Evidence

The primary motivation for the development of generalized theories of choice under uncertainty was the empirical observation of behavior inconsistent with the EU model. The most notable examples include the Allais problem, the common ratio effect, the coincidence of gambling and insurance, the Ellsberg problem and the phenomenon of preference reversal. It is therefore of interest to consider how well the RDEU model explains these various observations. Except for the Friedman–Savage problem, discussed in Chapter 8, all of these observations are based primarily on experimental studies.

This chapter commences with a discussion of the general problems associated with experimental studies of choice under uncertainty. This is followed by a discussion of the way in which the RDEU model has been used to explain the main classes of behavior inconsistent with EU. The final two sections contain a summary of recent empirical tests of RDEU and other generalized models, and a discussion of some issues involved in estimating RDEU functionals.

10.1 The Experimental Approach

In the literature on EU and its generalizations, empirical evidence, is almost exclusively, experimental evidence. A typical experiment would involve 100 or so college students being asked their reactions to a series of variants on the classic Allais and common ratio problems.

The obvious (at least to economists) objection to experimental studies of this kind is that subjects have no incentive to answer correctly. Since the choices are purely hypothetical, it may be doubted whether the choices reported are those that would actually be made in a real-life decision. The simplest response is to use real money problems instead of hypothetical problems. Although hypothetical experiments dominated the early literature, a number of researchers, beginning with Mosteller and Nogee (1951) undertook trials in which real gambles for small sums were offered.

A number of problems arise here. First, ethical constraints are usually taken to mean that it is impossible to pose problems that could leave subjects financially worse off than if they had not participated in the experiment. This difficulty is most salient in tests of prospect theory, with its hypothesis of risk seeking in the domain of losses.

Second, and most important, limits on experimental budgets mean that the payoffs in experiments of this kind must be quite small. Moreover, the differences in expected value or expected utility between any two gambles will be an order of magnitude smaller than the prizes themselves. As a result, the incentive to make accurate choices is quite limited. For most problems, the difference in expected value between the options is less than a dollar, and often only a few cents. Since there is usually a trade-off between risk and return, the difference in certainty equivalent terms is usually even less.

Perhaps the most important difficulty arising from the use of small payoffs is that choices in problems of this kind are dominated by first order risk preferences. Models that display only second order risk preferences, including EU, smooth preference models and regret theory, predict risk neutrality in choices of this kind. That is, in a choice between small gambles, the one with the higher expected value should always be chosen. It is possible to test this prediction, and in general it does not appear to be upheld. However, no other prediction of EU (or any other theory implying risk neutrality in a neighborhood of certainty) can be tested using small-money gambles unless the local risk neutrality property is ignored and it is assumed that the subjects are choosing 'as if' the gambles were large in relation to their actual wealth.

Finally, the gaming atmosphere inherent in many studies of this kind, combined with the small amounts at stake, encourages the adoption of heuristics such as 'maximize the probability of winning,' where winning is defined, say, as finishing with more money than the sum initially allocated by the experimenter. Conversely, risk averse strategies such as taking the initial stake and refusing all gambles are likely to be rejected on the basis that they are 'not playing the game.' The result is that experiments of this kind are likely to overstate the degree of risk seeking, particularly in the domain of losses, where a risky strategy may offer the only chance of finishing ahead.

One way of stretching experimental budgets, and permitting the use of somewhat larger payoffs, it to pose a larger number of questions, and announce that one of them, selected at random, will be played out 'for real.' The problem with this procedure is that, if participants consider only the real money payoffs, they are faced with a two-stage compound lottery. Suppose that a subject is asked to choose between $\{(0, 1000); (0.2, 0.8)\}$ and $\{500; 1\}$, but is told in advance that there is only a 1 per cent chance of the gamble actually being played out. The true choice is therefore between $\{(0, 1000); (0.992, 0.008)\}$ and $\{(0, 500); (0.99, 0.01)\}$. EU theory suggests that the one choice logically implies the other (indeed, this type of problem is the basis of Savage's sure thing argument), but the well confirmed common ratio effect shows that this is not true of observed choices. If the EU independence axiom (or the reduction of compound lotteries axiom) is not satisfied, choices may differ from those which would be made if it were known for certain that a given gamble involved real money. Similar problems arise with the Becker–de Groot–Marschak procedure, discussed in Section 10.4. Many subjects appear to ignore the two-stage nature of the gamble although they do not necessarily conform to the EU axioms. Kahneman and Tversky (1979) refer to this as the *isolation effect*. Experimenters frequently use the isolation effect as a justification for the use of two-stage procedures. However, as will be discussed below, reliance on the isolation effect raises as many problems as it solves in experimental work.

There does not appear to be any way of avoiding these problems, except for the possibility of undertaking research in very poor countries. Binswanger (1981) presented subjects with a series of real money prospects, some of which involved payments equivalent to a month's income. Quizon, Binswanger and Machina (1984) observed that some difficulties with the interpretation of Binswanger's data could be resolved by moving from an EU framework to a more general framework.

It is open to question, however, whether these extensive attempts to provide real incentives are necessary. In studies where both hypothetical and real-money questions have been asked, there have rarely been significant differences between the two sets of responses. The issue has been most hotly debated in relation to the preference reversal phenomenon. A series of experimental tests involved substantial increases in the sums at stake (Lichtenstein and Slovic, Grether and Plott 1979, Pommerehne Schneider and Zweifel 1982). This process yielded a slight reduction in the proportion of preference reversals, but the phenomenon was still observed consistently.

A better test of the seriousness of choice was employed by MacCrimmon and Larsson (1979), but unfortunately has not been adopted by subsequent experimenters. After obtaining responses to Allais-type problems, they presented subjects with arguments from 'Professor S' and 'Professor A', arguing the merits of EU and Allais-type choices respectively. Subjects were then offered the chance to change their choices. Some subjects with Allais-type responses switched their choices to conform with the independence axiom. However, a similar proportion of subjects who initially conformed to EU were persuaded by the arguments of Professor A to make Allais-type choices.

This may be contrasted with the experience of Tversky (1969), who elicited violations of transitivity from a number of subjects. When the intransitivity was pointed out, all wished to change their choices and several denied that they could ever have made such obviously irrational decisions. For completeness, Tversky should have presented arguments in favor of intransitivity. (The obvious problem would be finding arguments that carried any weight.) Lichtenstein and Slovic (1971) also found that most subjects revised choices involving preference reversals when presented with arguments against their initial position. Like Tversky, Lichtenstein and Slovic did not attempt to persuade initially consistent subjects to choose preference reversals.

The violations of EU theory elicited by the classic experiments of Kahneman and Tversky, MacCrimmon and Larsson and others had two effects on the development of the theory of choice under uncertainty. First, they undermined the position of EU theory as a positive theory, and, to a lesser extent, as a normative theory. Second, they created a set of criteria for alternative, more general models. Theorists developing such models aimed to show that they could account for the Allais paradox and the common ratio effect, along with their generalized versions, while preserving the desirable properties of EU theory. Attempts have also been made to encompass ambiguity and the preference reversal effect, though these have proved somewhat more resistant to analysis within the general framework of preferences represented by a single functional on $\mathcal{Y}$.

The volume of experimental work has expanded since the publication, around 1980, of a number of alternatives to, and generalizations of, EU theory. Most of this work has involved small real payments in one form or another. There has been a general confirmation of the previously observed violations of the independence axiom, most notably the Allais paradox and the common ratio effect. However, the main pattern has been that there has been no pattern. Almost all the proposed models have yielded predictions that have been violated. However, it should be noted that the original form of RDEU theory, with an S-shaped transformation function, has rarely been subject to test. Some experimenters have reported a rejection of RDEU although their data is quite consistent with the original form of the model (see Section 10.5).

An important difference must be noted between the experiments performed prior to the development of alternatives to EU and those undertaken subsequently. The early experiments tested for behavior patterns that seemed intuitively plausible but were inconsistent with EU theory. The later experiments tested for properties that distinguished the various generalized theories. These typically related to abstract concepts such as betweenness, fanning out and ordinal independence, for which intuition provided little guidance.

The fact that theories constructed, at least in part, in response to experimental violations of EU theory have themselves been subject to experimental violations must be of some comfort to advocates of an unreconstructed EU approach. However, the 'classical' violations of EU theory are more substantive than this. The introspection that suggested these tests is matched by violations of EU theory in observed economic behavior. Most notably, the overweighting of small probabilities, which is an inherent feature of many of these examples, implies behavior in gambling and insurance markets inconsistent with EU theory.

10.2 The Allais Problem

The Allais problem is the *pons asinorum* of theories of choice under uncertainty. Almost all of the many authors who have introduced new models of choice under uncertainty in the last ten years have included a demonstration that the model is consistent with the behavior revealed in this problem. In the case of RDEU, the first explicit solution was given by Quiggin (1985), and subsequent presentations of the model have included similar solutions. Interest must rest, not with the existence of a solution *per se* but with the intuitive appeal of the solution — the extent to which it captures the essence of the reasons why people choose not to obey the independence axiom in their responses to the Allais problem.

The spirit of RDEU theory is illustrated by the solution it yields for the Allais 'paradox.' The problem will be restated here for convenience.

The subject is first asked to choose between

A_1 {\$1m; 1};

and

B_1 {(0, \$1m, \$5m); (0.01, 0.89, 0.1)},

and then between

A_2 {(0, \$1m); (0.89, 0.11)};

and

B_2 {(0, \$5m); (0.9, 0.1)}.

These may be evaluated using a utility function with

$$U(0) = 0,\ U(\$1m) = 1,\ U(\$5m) = 1.4.$$

This captures the idea that, although \$5m is preferred to \$1m, both outcomes are so high that the marginal utility of wealth is very low, and the risk of getting a zero outcome is regarded very seriously. Nevertheless, an EU–maximizer will choose to take the risk in both cases, selecting B_1 and B_2.

Now consider a weighting function such that

$$q(0.01) = 0.04,$$

$$q(0.89) = 0.93,$$

$$q(0.9) = 0.94.$$

This is consistent with a concave transformation such as that illustrated in Figure 5.2 or with an S-shaped transformation function as in Figure 5.1. Evaluation according to (5.1) and (5.2) yields

$$V(A_1) = 1.$$

$$V(B_1) = U(0)*q(0.01) + U(\$1m)*(q(0.89)-q(0.01)) + U(\$5m)*(1-q(0.89))$$

$$= 0.89 + 1.4* 0.07$$

$$= 0.988.$$

$$V(A_2) = U(\$1m)*(1 - q(0.89)) = 0.07.$$

$$V(B_2) = U(\$5m)*(1 - q(0.9)) = 0.084.$$

Hence, choices in the Allais problem are consistent with the observed majority choice. The crucial feature of this example is the overweighting of the extreme low probability outcome in prospect B_1, yielding zero and occurring with probability 0.01.

To see the intuition behind these result, consider the kind of objections that can be made to this resolution of the Allais problem using a 'sure thing' formulation of the EU independence axiom. Organize the two choices as lotteries with 100 prizes .

Table 1.A Problem 1

	Ticket No		
	1–89	90–99	100
Prospect *A*	$1m	$1m	$1m
Prospect *B*	$1m	$5m	0

Table 1.B Problem 2

	Ticket No		
	1–89	90–99	100
Prospect *A*	0	$1m	$1m
Prospect *B*	0	$5m	0

These choice problems may be restated as two-stage lotteries, with the first stage allocating either a lottery L_1 over tickets 1–89 or a lottery L_2 over tickets 90–100. It is a natural extension of the sure thing principle, on which stochastic dominance rules are based, to suggest that if L_1^B is indifferent to L_1^A and L_2^B is preferred to L_2^A, choice B must be preferred to choice A. In both choices, L_1^2 is identical to L_1^A, and the general decision on the second problem indicates that L_2^B is preferred to L_2^A. Anyone who chooses prospect *A* in the first problem is giving up a sure thing. This type of criticism underlies Savage's rejection of the Allais problem.

Since no information on the relationship between states of the world and outcomes was given in the verbal presentation of the problem, the 'sure thing' presentation makes implicit use of the assumption that any rearrangement of equiprobable states is permissible. This view is inconsistent with the intuition underlying RDEU. On the basis of rank ordering, it would be natural to interpret the problem as follows:

Table 2.A Problem 1 (with tickets ordered by value)

	Ticket No		
	1	2–90	91–100
Prospect *A*	\$1m	\$1m	\$1m
Prospect *B*	0	\$1m	\$5m

Table 2.B Problem 2 (with tickets ordered by value)

	Ticket No		
	1–89	90	91–100
Prospect *A*	0	\$1m	\$1m
Prospect *B*	0	0	\$5m

Since there is no necessary equivalence between state 90 and state 1, there is no reason why preference for prospect *B* in Choice 1 should have any direct implications for Choice 2. In terms of the two–stage lottery interpretation, suppose that a lottery may be formed by combining any subset of the set of tickets {1 ... 100}, but that the same subset must be used in each problem. With the arrangement presented above, there is no partition of the set {1 ... 100} that yields a sure thing argument for choosing in conformity with EU theory. The relationship between independence rules and re-arrangements of states is discussed further in Chapter 13.

The Allais problem has played an important rôle in the debate over the appropriate form of the RDEU transformation function q. The resolution presented above is consistent with either an S-shaped function or a globally concave function. However, some extensions are consistent only with a globally concave function.

Segal (1987a) defined the Generalized Allais Paradox (GAP) as follows: Let A, B, C, D be lotteries such that C and D stochastically dominate A and B respectively, and $F_D - F_C \equiv F_B - F_A$. Assume moreover, that B differs from A by a simple compensated spread, and let x^* be such that, for $x \le x^*$, $F_B(x) \ge F_A(x)$ and for $x \ge x^*$, $F_B(x) \le F_A(x)$. If, for $x \ge x^*$, $F_C(x) = F_A(x)$ (and $F_D(x) = F_B(x)$), C is preferred to D. The standard Allais paradox arises with $A = A_2$, $B = B_2$, $C = A_1$, $D = B_1$. The GAP is broadly consistent with Machina's interpretation of the MacCrimmon–Larsson data, based on the notion of 'fanning out,' although the GAP does not imply fanning out. Segal proves that RDEU preferences display the GAP if and only if q is concave. There does not appear to be any direct empirical evidence on the prevalence or otherwise of GAP behavior, although evidence on fanning out may be suggestive.

10.3 The Common Ratio Effect

The RDEU model also provides a natural explanation of the common ratio effect, at least in the examples presented by Kahneman and Tversky (1979). Consider Problem 2 in Chapter 3, repeated here for ease of reference.

Problem 2:
Part 1: Choose between
A_1 {(0,\$4000);(0.2, 0.8)}
and
B_1 {\$3000, 1}
Part 2: Choose between
A_2 {(0,\$4000);(0.8, 0.2)}
and
B_2 {(0,\$3000);(0.75, 0.25)}

The crucial requirement is that $q^*(0.2)/q^*(0.25) > q^*(0.8)/q^*(1) = q^*(0.8)$. This will always be the case when q is S–shaped as in Figure 5.1. The fact that q lies above the diagonal for small p means $q^*(p) < p$ for large p, so $q^*(0.8) < 0.8$. The fact that $q^*(p)$ is concave for small p means $q^*(p)/p$ is initially declining, so $q^*(0.2)/q^*(0.25) > 0.2/0.25 = 0.8$.

Segal (1987a) considers the more general question of when the transformation function will have $q^*(\alpha p)/q^*(p)$ increasing in p for every $\alpha > 1$. This occurs if and only if the elasticity $pq^{*\prime}(p)/q^*(p)$ is increasing in p. Segal's elasticity condition may be satisfied either by S-shaped or by concave transformation functions. For example, the condition holds for

$$q(p) = q^*(p) = p^\alpha/(p^\alpha + (1\text{-}p)^\alpha),\ 0 < \alpha < 1$$

and for

$$q(p) = p^\alpha,\ 0 < \alpha < 1$$

It is immediate that, for symmetric functions, the elasticity of q^* is increasing if and only if the elasticity of q is increasing. For concave functions, no general relationship holds. The condition proposed by Segal is consistent with the MacCrimmon–Larsson observation that preference for the safe bet increases with p, as in Figure 4.1.

Machina (1982, *p*. 305) extended the MacCrimmon–Larsson approach further by suggesting the Generalized Common Ratio Effect, which may be stated as follows: Let F_1, F_2, F_3, $F_4 \in \mathfrak{D}$ be such that F_1 FSD F_3, F_2 FSD F_4, and $F_1 - F_2 = k(F_3 - F_4)$ for some $k > 0$. Then if $F_3 \sim F_4$ and F_3 may be obtained from F_4 by a simple spread, $F_1 \succ F_2$.

Machina shows that under the GCRE, indifference curves display 'fanning out' as in Figure 4.2b. Segal (1987a) shows that RDEU is inconsistent with the GCRE. This would be a serious problem if there were strong empirical support for 'fanning out.' However, the studies discussed in Section 10.6 have not, in general, found 'fanning out' to be a universal pattern, and several have found that RDEU models outperform 'fanning out' models.

10.4 Ambiguity and Reduction of Compound Lotteries

Most presentations of the RDEU model, and other generalized EU models, are based on a relaxation of the independence axiom. However, Segal (1987b, 1990) shows that the RDEU model may be regarded as consistent with the independence axiom if the reduction of compound lotteries axiom is dropped. This axiom, implicit in the notation adopted here, means that the value of a multi-stage lottery depends only on the probability with which any final outcome is received and not on any intermediate lottery. This axiom seems plausible, at least as a normative rule, in a setting where probabilities are known. Segal challenges its applicability in situations characterized by ambiguity, where probabilities are unknown.

Segal (1987b) suggests that such situations may be regarded as two-stage lotteries. The first stage is a lottery over the probabilities which are to be used in the second stage. In the Ellsberg problem, for example, it might be assumed that any possible number of red balls, from 1 to 100, was equally likely. The probability would be randomly determined and, in the second stage, a ball would be chosen at random. For simplicity, attention will be confined to problems where the second stage of the lottery is of the form

$$x_p = \{(0, x);(1\text{-}p, p)\}.$$

For any probability p in the second stage lottery, denote the corresponding first-stage probability by $P^*(p)$. Using the reduction of compound lotteries axiom, the final probability of receiving the prize x is given by

$$p^{**} = \sum P^*(p)p$$

and

$$V = q^*(p^{**})\, U(x).$$

Segal, however, suggests an alternative method of evaluating such two-stage prospects. Denote the certainty equivalent of x_p by c_p. Under RDEU,

$$c_p = U^{-1}(q^*(p)\, U(x)).$$

Note that c_p is increasing in p. Segal suggests evaluating ambiguous prospects, and, more generally, all two-stage lotteries, as if they were single stage prospects yielding outcome c_p with probability $P^*(p)$. Segal's main result is the derivation of conditions under which the single-stage lottery $\{\boldsymbol{x};\, \boldsymbol{p}^{**}\}$, derived using the reduction axiom, is preferred to the lottery $\{\boldsymbol{c}_p;\, \boldsymbol{P}^*\}$.

He shows the following to be a set of sufficient conditions in the case where the distribution of possible values of p is symmetric around some mean value $p^{**} = \Sigma\ P^*(p)p$:

- q is concave
- the elasticity of q with respect to p is non-increasing
- the elasticity of q^* with respect to p is non-decreasing

These conditions are fairly restrictive and Segal gives some examples where it might not be expected that the unambiguous lottery is to be preferred to the ambiguous one. For example, if the probability of receiving a desirable outcome is very small, one might prefer a measure of ambiguity to a situation where the unpalatable truth is clearly presented.

Schmeidler (1989) takes an alternative, normatively motivated, approach to the problem of ambiguity and two-stage lotteries. He proposes that individuals should act as EU-maximizers when probabilities are given, but may employ non-additive measures (that is, RDEU) in cases of ambiguity.

10.5 Preference Reversal

The Allais and common ratio problems were designed as challenges to the EU independence axiom, and provided a natural motivation for the development of generalized models. By contrast, the preference reversal phenomenon was long seen as a challenge to any theory based on the notion of a preference ordering. Even the abandonment of transitivity would not be sufficient to account for the data. However, the standard interpretation rested on the implicit assumption that rational respondents would reveal true valuations when faced with the Becker–de Groot–Marschak (BDM) mechanism. As was observed in Section 4.4, the standard reasoning behind the mechanism rests on the independence axiom.

Consider a subject who has the right to a prospect $\{(x_1, x_2); (1\text{-}p, p)\}$, and is asked to state a price in some range $[0, \bar{x}]$. If the price stated is π, and the BDM mechanism is applied, the individual is effectively faced with a two stage lottery With probability $\pi/\bar{x}$, the bid is above the randomly drawn price, and the original prospect is received. With probability $1\text{-}\pi\bar{x}$, the bid is below the randomly drawn price and the subject receives a uniform distribution over the range $[\pi, \bar{x}]$. Independence ensures that if the subject would rather receive a given δ_π than the prospect $\{(x_1, x_2); (1\text{-}p, p)\}$, he should announce a price no less than π.

Karni and Safra (1987, 1990) used the RDEU model to illustrate the argument. Karni and Safra (1987) showed that the independence argument did not apply to the RDEU model, and that preference reversals were possible. Karni and Safra (1990) showed that the observed pattern, in which preference reversals are common when the P-bet is chosen over the corresponding \$-bet, is consistent with a concave utility function and an S-shaped transformation function, as in Figure 5.1.

The idea is an extension of the explanation offered for the common ratio effect. If the initial probability is sufficiently high for both the P-bet and the \$-bet, both the transformation function and the utility function will be concave. Since the P-bet second stochastically dominates the \$-bet, it will be chosen. The effect of the BDM procedure is to reduce the probability of receiving the main prize $\bar{x}$. As in the common ratio problem, this implies less risk averse choices, because the ratio $q^*(\alpha p)/q^*(p)$ is increasing in p . The analysis is complicated by the existence of the uniform distribution of prizes in the second lottery. As is shown by Karni and Safra, this permits some possibility of preference reversal for subjects who initially chose the

$-bet. Safra, Segal and Spivak (1990a) show that this pattern of choice is also consistent with Machina's GCRE hypothesis.

Safra, Segal and Spivak (1990b) examined the comparative statics of the choice problem for RDEU maximizers. They showed that the BDM mechanism could be used, at least in principle, to elicit an RDEU preference functional. As the interval $[0, \overline{x}]$ becomes large, the optimal offer price approaches the pseudo certainty equivalent π^* satisfying

$$U(\pi^*) = pU(x_1) + (1\text{-}p)\, U(x_2)$$

computed using EU rather than the transformed probability distribution. Hence the BDM mechanism can elicit the utility function. The standard reference contract or other methods may then be used to elicit the probability transformation function.

Segal (1988) observed that the BDM mechanism would also break down if the independence axiom held but the reduction of compound lotteries axiom did not. In Segal's analysis, attention is focused on the two-stage nature of the lottery associated with the BDM mechanism.

As was noted in the introduction, a broadly similar criticism may be levelled at the common experimental procedure of asking questions about a large number of gambles, then selecting one at random to be played out. Experimenters using this method have relied on the isolation effect observed by Kahneman and Tversky, who found that subjects in this situation reported the same choices as when the gamble was certain to be played out.

However, an appeal to the isolation effect does not guarantee the effectiveness of the Becker–de Groot–Marschak mechanism. If subjects ignore the two-stage aspect of the gamble, it seems reasonable to assume that they will respond to the mechanism in the same way as to the simple question "How much are you willing to accept in return for giving up your right to play this gamble?" The large literature on WTA and WTP measures indicates that subjects will respond with an over-estimate of their true valuation.

10.6 The Recent Empirical Evidence on RDEU

The general tenor of the conclusions of recent empirical studies has been subdued, to say the least. Violations of EU predictions have been confirmed, but no single model has emerged as a satisfactory alternative.

The conclusion of Battaglio, Kagel and Jiranyakul (1990, p. 46) is typical

> Our overall conclusion is that none of the alternatives to expected utility considered here consistently organize the data, so we have a long way to go before having a complete descriptive model of choice under uncertainty.

The models analyzed were RDEU, regret theory, prospect theory and Machina's generalized smooth preferences model. In relation to RDEU, their pessimism is unwarranted. Battaglio et al. test RDEU theory in conjunction with the hypothesis of a concave weighting function, as in Figure 5.2. An S-shaped weighting function, as in Figure 5.1, fits the data quite well.

Battaglio et al. offered their undergraduate subjects a number of pairwise choices between gambles. For example, their Question 4 is a choice between ($14, 1) and ($0, 0.3; $20, 0.7). A noteworthy feature of their questioning procedure is a test of the 'reflection hypothesis' and the 'reference point' hypothesis of Kahneman and Tversky (1979). Subjects were presented with two sets of questions, a loss series and a gain series. Subjects selected to play loss questions received a starting balance of \$30, while those selected to play gain questions received a balance of \$5. Tests of the reflection hypothesis involved paired gain and loss questions with equal and opposite payoffs. For example question 4 was paired with 4′ in which all payoffs were negative. Tests of the reference point hypothesis involved paired questions in which all payoffs differed by \$25 between the gain and loss series. Offset against the differences in starting balances, this meant that the two gambles implied the same distribution of outcomes.

Given the fairly simple questions used by Battaglio et al., it is straightforward to derive and test the predictions of the original form of RDEU theory. Since all of the money amounts used are small, even in relation to the wealth of the average undergraduate, it seems reasonable to impose a linear utility function. In combination with the assumption that the weighting function is S-shaped, as Figure 5.1, this is sufficient to give unambiguous predictions for the majority of the questions reported by Battaglio et al.

Consider, for example, the choices offered in Question 4. The RDEU evaluations of these prospects, with the utility function set to the identity, are 14 and $20(1 - q(0.3))$ respectively. Since, by hypothesis, $q(0.3) > 0.3$, the (\$14, 1) bet is to be preferred. Similar reasoning shows that when the payoffs are negative, as in Question 4′, (-\$20, 0.7; \$0, 0.3) should be preferred to (-\$14, 1).

The main cases where the conditions imposed thus far do not yield a clear preference are

(i) A group of fair, even money bets where the RDEU model predicts indifference

(ii) A group of choices of the form (±\$18, p), (±\$27, $0.8p$)

In case (i), it seems reasonable to model the predictions by the hypothesis that the responses were purely random. In case (ii), the expected value of the bets is positive, but the effects of RDEU probability weighting tend to counteract this. However, given the empirical estimates reported in Quiggin (1981), where it was suggested $q(0.75) \approx 0.73$, it seems reasonable to propose that the expected value effect will predominate except, perhaps, for very small p.

Given these assumptions, it is possible to test the predictions of the standard RDEU model against the results of the 23 questions reported in Battaglio et al., Tables 1-4. In the 19 cases where a definite prediction was made, the RDEU model is correct in 17 (Quiggin 1993). In all 4 even-money bets, the results are consistent, at the 0.05 level, with random choice, as predicted by RDEU.

In summary, the pessimism expressed by Battaglio et al. is unwarranted, at least for this data set. The RDEU model, in its original form, provides a quite satisfactory description of observed behavior in this case.

These conclusions are supported by the work of Harless (1990). Harless examined the impact of presenting subjects with choices from the interior of the unit probability triangle. He examines a number of theories including RDEU. For the RDEU case, Harless considers both concave and convex transformation functions. Although he does not consider the S-shaped transformation function analyzed above, the majority of the prospects involve a low probability for the best outcome, so that preferences may be approximated by a convex transformation.

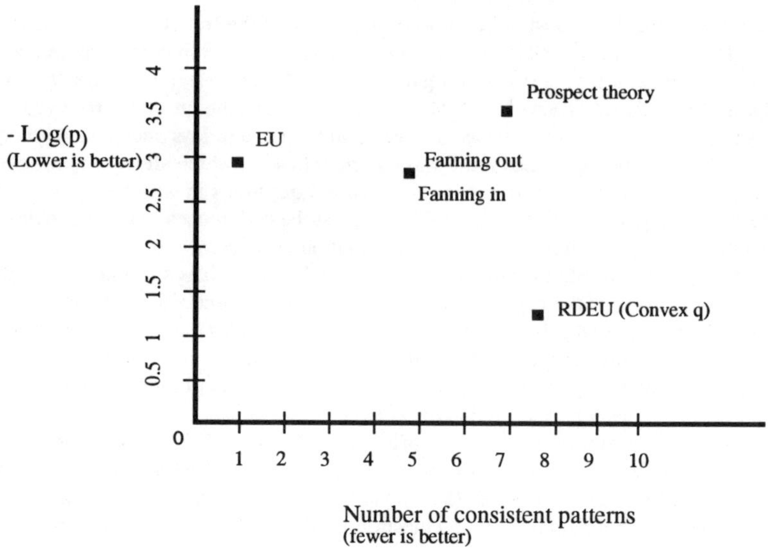

Figure 10.1: Performance of utility theories (Harless)

As with Battaglio et al., Harless rejected the concave version of the RDEU model, along with competing hypotheses including fanning out, prospect theory and EU. He concludes that

> Choices over real money lotteries ... show that inside the triangle subjects reveal indifference curves with properties corresponding to RDEU with convex indifference curves.

He also finds that the convex form of RDEU is the only model for which it appears that inconsistent choice patterns are only randomly selected by subjects. The good performance of the RDEU model is derived primarily from problems involving gains. No consistent pattern seemed to emerge from the problems involving losses.

The test proposed by Harless involves a comparison of the observed number of response patterns consistent with a given model and the number of patterns permitted by that model. EU tends to perform reasonably well in comparisons of this kind. A large proportion of subjects exhibit responses inconsistent with EU, but this is offset by the fact that EU only permits a small number of patterns. Harless' results are shown in Figure 10.1. The results of a re-analysis of the results of Chew and Waller (1986) are presented in Figure 10.2. Chew and Waller confirmed the superiority of convex RDEU over concave RDEU and found that the best of the RDEU models was a convex model satisfying Segal's declining elasticity hypothesis. Unlike Harless, however, Chew and Waller found that fanning out and weighted utility theory outperformed RDEU.

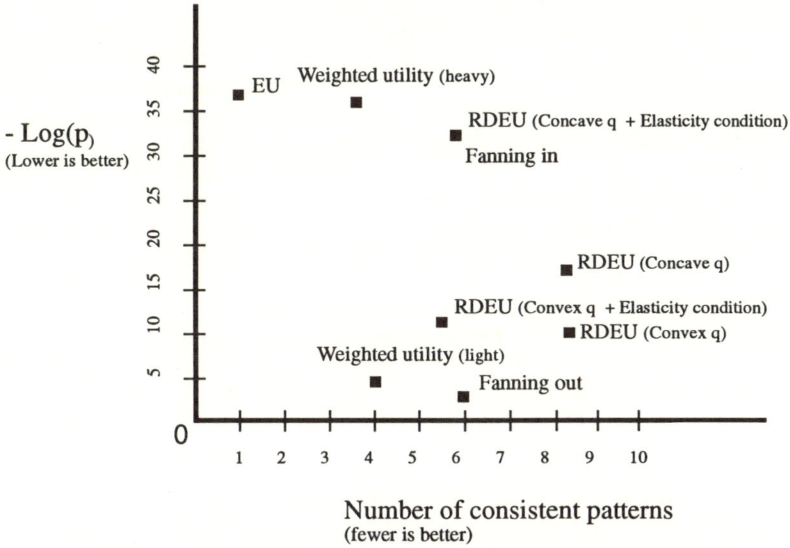

Figure 10.2: Performance of utility theories
(Harless, from Chew and Waller data)

Camerer (1989) also tests a number of decision theories using a unit triangle approach. Like Harless, he considers concave and convex q, but not the original proposal for S-shaped q. He does not present any formal tests of RDEU theory. He presents separately results for prospects involving large (hypothetical) gains, small gains and small losses. Camerer's results appear to be broadly consistent with those of Harless. RDEU theory performs well for the large gains prospects, moderately well for the small gains prospects and poorly for the prospects involving losses.

Prelec (1990) examines a modified version of the Allais problem. His results are inconsistent with Machina's Hypothesis 2 (fanning out). His data support the conclusion that

$$q^*(0.02) - q^*(0.01) > q^*(0.34)\text{-}q^*(0.33).$$

This is consistent with either a globally convex transformation or with an S-shaped transformation.

Starmer and Sugden (1987) present evidence from a series of experiments conducted at the University of East Anglia. The experiments in question were designed primarily as a test of the 'fanning out' hypothesis in common ratio problems (the hypothesis was rejected). However, Starmer and Sugden observed that a limited test of RDEU was possible, since a number of problem sets involved the same probabilities with different payoffs. RDEU predicts that violations of EU predictions should depend only on the probabilities and the rankings of the payoffs.

Consistency was observed for most of the positive payoff problems, but results for problems with negative payoffs showed no consistent pattern.

In summary, the available data from empirical evidence is inconsistent with the hypothesis of global risk aversion implied by the use of a concave transformation function. At least for gains, however, the data is consistent with an S-shaped transformation function involving overweighting of small probabilities. The main problem would appear to be that the probability weighting function depends to some extent on the magnitude of the payoffs and not merely on their ranking. This could be handled by moving to generalizations such as that proposed by Green and Jullien (1988) and Puppe (1990). However, the standard RDEU model is tractable, relatively parsimonious and seems to fit the data adequately.

On the other hand, the model does not perform well in dealing with prospects involving losses. Two responses are possible here. First, it is possible to modify RDEU so that it incorporates the key features of prospect theory, namely that changes in wealth are the carriers of value and that preferences over losses are systematically different from preferences over gains. This approach has been proposed by a number of writers (Starmer and Sugden 1987, Tversky and Kahneman 1990) and most rigorously axiomatized by Wakker and Tversky (1991) (see Section 11.7). The resulting model avoids the violations of dominance associated with the probability weighting scheme used in the original presentation of prospect theory.

Second, it may be argued that the experimental data on problems involving losses is simply unsatisfactory. Such problems appear to increase the likelihood of random errors by subjects as well as sensitivity to framing effects. On this view, the challenge is to develop experimental techniques which permit the extraction of useful information from the noise associated with problems involving losses.

Both approaches are worth pursuing. However, at least as far as economic analysis is concerned, there are good reasons for pursuing the second. As was shown in Chapters 7 and 8, the RDEU model permits a straightforward generalization of the comparative static results of EU theory while adding the flexibility needed to incorporate risk seeking behavior. By contrast, a model involving reference points seems unlikely to prove tractable in economic analysis. Of course, if systematic reference points can be reliably shown to exist there will be no choice but to employ models that incorporate them.

10.7 Estimating a Functional Form

None of the studies discussed above involved the estimation of functional forms. Also, for reasons that are not altogether clear, none of them offered a test of the hypothesis of overweighting of low probability extreme events, which motivated the original development of the RDEU model. Questionnaire evidence provided the basis for a specific test of the overweighting hypothesis in an RDEU context, presented in Quiggin (1981). In this paper, a survey of risk attitudes amongst Australian farmers (Bond and Wonder 1980) was re-analyzed to fit an RDEU preference function, and overweighting of low probability events was found to be predominant. This study was based on a model incorporating the requirement $q(1/2)= 1/2$, and thus the possibility of a concave weighting function was excluded from consideration. If, however the true function q had been concave, it is unlikely that satisfactory results would have been obtained.

Before examining this evidence, it is useful to consider how the problem of estimating RDEU preference functionals using a questionnaire approach might be tackled. Given that $q(1/2) = 1/2$, the utility function, U, can be evaluated using an ELCE or ELRO approach. Once U is known, the decision weighting function q can be determined by eliciting certainty equivalents for prospects with a range of probabilities $(p, 1 - p)$. If $x_3 = \mathrm{CE}(x_1, x_2, p, 1 - p)$,

$$q(p)U(x_1) + (1 - q(p))U(x_2) = U(x_3),$$

so that:

$$q(p) = (U(x_2) - U(x_3))/(U(x_2) - U(x_1)).$$

Estimation of RDEU functionals via specifically designed questionnaires is practicable. However, a great deal of research has already been undertaken in the context of EU theory and other models such as prospect theory. It is, therefore, of interest to examine possibilities of re-analyzing the Bond and Wonder data in an RDEU framework.

The data was derived from a study of risk attitudes in Australian agriculture undertaken as part of the 1975-76 Australian Grazing Industry Survey. Although there are some problems with the use of this data, it provides some useful illustrations of the implications of the RDEU theory for the analysis of risk attitudes. Bond and Wonder attempted to analyze risk attitudes of Australian farmers using a modified von Neumann–Morgenstern approach. Due to the small number of questions asked and other difficulties associated with limited interview time, only tentative conclusions could be drawn from their analysis. In addition, some of the analytical methods used by Bond and Wonder have been criticized (Drynan 1981). Nevertheless, this study provides a useful illustration of the methods by which data of this kind may be re-interpreted in an RDEU framework.

Bond and Wonder presented two series of four gambles and respondents were asked to choose that which most closely corresponded to their own experience. The first series (response code 1), representing 'income steady in most years, occasionally high', contained gambles of the form $y = (x_1, x_2; 0.75, 0.25)$ where x_2 was fixed at \$40 000 and x_1 took the values \$5000, \$10 000, \$15 000 and \$20 000. In each case, the questioner attempted to elicit certainty equivalents. The second series, representing 'income steady in most years, occasionally low', contained gambles of the form $y = (x_1, x_2; 0.25, 0.75)$ where x_1 was fixed at \$2000 and x_2 took the values \$5000, \$10 000, \$15 000 and \$20 000. Of the 201 respondents, 82 chose response code 1, 103 chose response code 2, and 16 answered both sets of questions. Bond and Wonder did not construct utility functions for their respondents. Rather, for each individual response to a given prospect, they computed risk coefficients, the most useful of which was

$$\mathrm{A} = (\mathrm{E}(y) - \mathrm{CE}(y))/\mathrm{Var}(y). \tag{10.1}$$

If the utility function displays constant absolute risk aversion, then A is approximately equal to one half of the coefficient of absolute risk aversion. RDEU preferences may be incorporated into equation (10.1) for a two-outcome prospect $y = (x_1, x_2; p_1, 1 - p_1)$, yielding:

$$\text{CE}(y) = \text{E}(y) + (q(p_1) - p_1)(x_1 - x_2) + \text{A Var}(y).$$

It is impossible to estimate the coefficients A and $q(p_1)$ on the basis of the response to a single question. Even for the four answers to either set of questions, the high correlation between $(x_1 - x_2)$ and Var(y) makes accurate estimation of the coefficients very difficult. This problem may be overcome to some extent by imposing the symmetry assumption $q(p) = q^*(p)$. The information from all of the questionnaires may then be used to estimate mean values of the two coefficients. These may be taken as characterizing the preferences of a representative respondent.

The mean estimates are (with standard errors in parentheses):

$$r_a = 7.51 \, x \, 10^{-6}, \text{ and}$$
$$(1.18 \, x \, 10^{-6})$$

$$q\,(0.25) - 0.25 = 1.79 \, x \, 10^{-2},$$
$$(6.24 \, x \, 10^{-3})$$

so that the estimated value of $q(0.25)$ is 0.268, and is significantly different from 0.25. The risk aversion coefficient, r_a, is roughly similar to those calculated by Bond and Wonder. These results give some support to the claim that people are, on the whole, risk averse and tend to over-weight small probabilities.

Most questionnaire procedures do not involve the elicitation of certainty equivalents, but are based on simple pairwise choices over prospects. The least-squares approach outlined above is inapplicable. Fortunately, the steady increase in available computing power means that maximum likelihood approaches may be used. This approach has been employed by Camerer and Ho (1991). Like Quiggin (1981), Camerer and Ho estimated the set of parameters that would best characterize the 'representative' preferences of a large group of respondents. They estimated the functional form $q(p) = p^\gamma/(p^\gamma + (1\text{-}p)^\gamma)^{1/\gamma}$ in combination with the constant relative risk aversion utility function $U(x) = x^\alpha$. Since the same parameters were estimated for all respondents, it is necessary to account for variations in preferences through an error term. Camerer and Ho assumed a stochastic choice process based on the usual logit form. Their estimation approach involved maximizing the associated likelihood function by grid search. Camerer and Ho estimated γ using data from eight separate studies. Subdivisions within these studies yielded a total of eleven data sets. In all except one, the estimated value satisfied $0 < \gamma < 1$ and in all except two of the remaining cases a likelihood ratio test rejected the EU model in favor of an RDEU model of the type illustrated in Figure 5.1. The estimate of γ obtained by pooling the data from all of the studies was $\gamma = 0.56$. The resulting transformation function is illustrated in Figure 10.3.

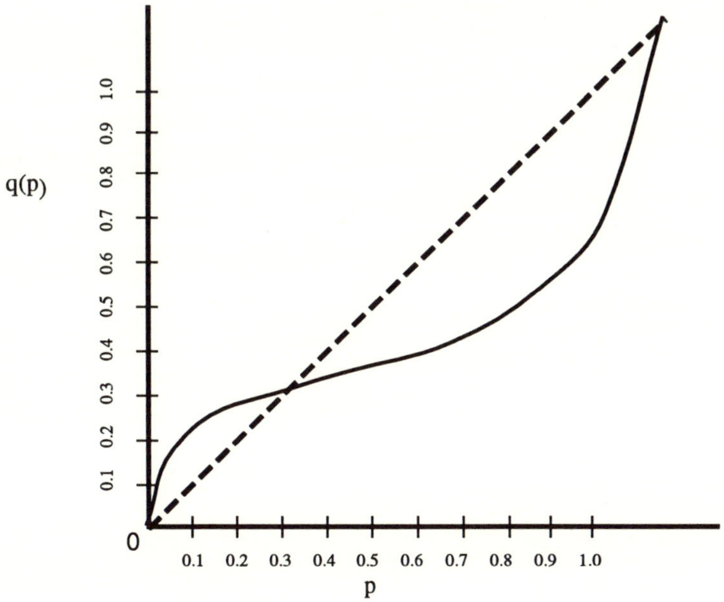

Figure 10.3: Estimated transformation function
(Camerer and Ho)

Camerer and Ho also estimated parameters for the disappointment aversion model of Gul (1991) and the original version of prospect theory. They found theory performance to be similar to that of the RDEU model. This is perhaps unsurprising, since both models coincide with a special case of RDEU for the two-outcome case, and the questions were not, in general, designed with the objective of distinguishing the models. In particular, the dominance violations predicted by prospect theory were not tested.

CHAPTER 11

Axiomatic Approaches to RDEU

There has been some debate over the appropriate role of axiomatic systems in generalized expected utility. This debate has run parallel, to some extent, with the split between normative and descriptive approaches to the theory of choice under uncertainty. At one extreme are those for whom the ideal approach is to write down an appealing set of axioms, then derive the functional form implied by those axioms. A large part of the research agenda then consists of weakening and modifying the axioms and of exploring the logical relationships between sets of axioms. The outstanding exemplar of this approach is Fishburn (1982, 1988).

At the alternative extreme are those for whom only the functional form, and its ability to fit the data, are important. Here the main research task is the analysis of the behavioral implications of different specifications of utility and transformation functions. The derivation of an axiomatic basis for the model is of secondary importance, and primarily of pedagogic interest. For example, Machina (1982) dispensed with the EU independence axiom, but did not provide an axiomatic basis for his generalized model. Nor did he express any concern at the lack of such a basis.

The RDEU model has been approached from both viewpoints. At one extreme, Allais (1987) did not present any axiomatic basis for his model and stated (p. 274)

> *I have a deep aversion for useless mathematical refinement, and experience seems to me the only criterion.* As for me, piling axiom on axiom does not make a theory true, and any mathematical construction is useless if it is toppled down by the facts. (emphasis in original)

By contrast, Yaari (1987) approached the topic primarily from an axiomatic viewpoint. He showed how dual forms of the EU axioms yielded a special case of RDEU.

In Quiggin (1982a), I took a middle course. The RDEU model was initially derived, as in Section 5.8, as an extension of the simple probability weighting models that preserved first stochastic dominance. I hedged my bets, however, by producing a set of axioms from which the model could be derived. Perhaps unfortunately, this introduced the requirement that $q(1/2) = 1/2$. Chew (1989) generalized the axioms in Quiggin (1982a), dropping the requirement that $q(1/2) = 1/2$. Segal (1989) and Wakker (1991a) similarly generalized Yaari's approach to incorporate non-linear utility.

The axiomatic approach has also led to the development of a number of generalizations of the RDEU model.

11.1 The Probability Weighting Approach

We begin by recalling the axioms for EU theory

(EU.1) If y_1 and y_2 have the same cumulative distribution function, $y_1 \sim y_2$.

(EU.2) $\succcurlyeq$ is a weak order.

(EU.3) If y_1 FSD y_2, $y_1 \succcurlyeq y_2$.

(EU.4) The preference relation $\succcurlyeq$ is continuous in the topology of weak convergence.

(EU.5) If $F, G, H \in \mathfrak{D}$ and $F \succcurlyeq G$, for any $\alpha \in [0, 1]$, $\alpha F + (1-\alpha)H \succcurlyeq \alpha G + (1-\alpha)H$.

It has already been shown that preferences represented by an RDEU functional (with continuous q and U) are consistent with axioms (EU.1)–(EU.4). In most of what follows these axioms are taken as a starting point. To derive the RDEU model, it is necessary to impose an additional, modified independence axiom.

The first set of axioms for RDEU theory was presented in Quiggin (1982a). The main novelty was the weakened independence axiom, which may be stated as follows:

(AU.5) Let $y = \{\boldsymbol{x};\boldsymbol{p}\}$ and $y' = \{\boldsymbol{x}';\boldsymbol{p}\} \in \mathcal{Y}$ and let $y_c = \{\boldsymbol{c};\boldsymbol{p}\}$ be defined such that

$$c_i = \mathrm{CE}\{(x_i, x'_i); (1/2, 1/2)\}.$$

Then

$$y_c \sim \{(\mathrm{CE}(y), \mathrm{CE}(y')); (1/2, 1/2)\}.$$

This axiom, in combination with (EU.1) to (EU.4), guarantees a representation of the form given by (5.1) and (5.2), with the additional requirement that $q(1/2) = 1/2$.[21] This requirement is motivated by the intuition, backed up by some empirical evidence, that both parts of a 50–50 bet will be given equal weight. It is closely tied to the interpretation of RDEU theory in terms of probability weights. The certainty equivalent c_i may be seen as yielding the unweighted average utility of the outcomes x_i, x'_i. The existence of these unweighted averages permits the construction of the utility function. It is then a simple matter to construct the probability transformation function using prospects of the form $\{(x_0, x_1); (1\text{-}p, p)\}$. If we set $U(x_0) = 0$, $U(x_1) = 1$, then

$$q(p) = U(CE\{(x_0, x_1); (1\text{-}p, p)\}). \tag{11.1}$$

This is simply the von Neumann–Morgenstern standard reference contract approach. This argument requires the existence of a rich set of prospects, and, in particular, a complete set of certainty equivalents. This was explicit in Quiggin (1982a) and implicit in some other formulations.

[21] Some other issues relating to the original axioms, and in particular the dominance axiom, are discussed in the Appendix to this chapter.

Chew (1989) weakened axiom (AU.5) and provided an axiomatization for the general case of RDEU theory without the restriction $q(1/2) = 1/2$. His approach is based on the idea of a mean value developed in the work of Hardy, Littlewood and Polya (1952) and de Finetti (1963). In this work, a wide range of measures of central tendency, including arithmetic, geometric and harmonic means are treated in an integrated framework. In de Finetti's terminology, the expected utility functional is a quasilinear mean, because of the property of linearity in probability mixtures. In earlier work, Chew (1983) proposed a generalization of the quasilinear mean resulting in the weighted utility model. Chew (1989) showed that the RDEU model may be regarded as an alternative generalization of the quasilinear mean. He gives a statistical interpretation showing that the RDEU estimate of utility includes as special cases the median and 'trimmed' or winsorized means.

The expression of the problem primarily in terms of 'mean values', which in the present context are certainty equivalents, is a characteristic feature of Chew's exposition. Although the present work has adopted the more traditional approach based on a preference functional, the use of a mean value approach is, in many ways, more suggestive.

Chew's generalized 'Weak Commutativity' axiom is derived by considering pairs of prospects $y = \{\boldsymbol{x};\boldsymbol{p}\}$, $y' = \{\boldsymbol{x}';\boldsymbol{p}\}$ over the same vector of probabilities, and such that $x_i \leq x'_i \ \forall i$. For any α, define $\boldsymbol{x}^{\alpha}$ such that

$$\boldsymbol{x}^{\alpha}_i = \text{CE}\{(x_i, x'_i); (\alpha, 1-\alpha)\},$$

and

$$y^{\alpha} = \{\boldsymbol{x}^{\alpha};\boldsymbol{p}\}.$$

Chew's modified axiom is:

(AU.5a) Let y, y', y^{α} be as defined. Then for any $\alpha \in [0, 1]$,
$\{(\text{CE}(y), \text{CE}(y'); (\alpha, 1-\alpha))\} \sim y^{\alpha}$.

It may be checked that any functional of the form (5.1, 5.2) satisfies this axiom.

The crucial change from (AU.5) is the imposition of the restriction $x_i \leq x'_i \ \forall i$. This ensures that, for an RDEU representation

$$U(\boldsymbol{x}^{\alpha}_i) = q(\alpha)\, U(x_i) + q^*(\alpha) U(x'_i) \ \forall\ i.$$

An argument from the theory of functional equations may be used to show that, if axiom (AU.5a) holds, preferences may in fact be represented by an RDEU functional (see Krantz et al. Chapter 6). If the transformation q is symmetrical, so that $q(p) = q^*(p) \ \forall\ p$, the restriction $x_i \leq x'_i \forall i$ is unnecessary. In the original axiomatization of RDEU theory, the symmetry condition is satisfied for $p = 1/2$. A generalization of Chew's approach is given by Nakamura (1982).

11.2 The Dual Approach

Yaari (1987) offered a different approach. He observed that just as $\mathcal{D}$ is a mixture space with respect to probability mixtures, $\mathcal{Y}$ is a mixture space with respect to linear mixtures of the outcomes. Furthermore, by (EU.1), $\mathcal{Y}$ and $\mathcal{D}$ are isomorphic, and any two elements of $\mathcal{Y}$ may be regarded, without loss of generality, as comonotonic. The EU independence axiom may therefore be replaced by a dual axiom

(EU.5*) If $y_1, y_2, y_3 \in \mathcal{Y}$ are comonotonic and $y_1 \succ y_2$, for any $\lambda \in [0, 1]$, the random variable with outcome mixture $\lambda y_1 + (1-\lambda)y_3$ is preferred to $\lambda y_2 + (1-\lambda)y_3$.

Because of the exact duality between Yaari's axioms and those of standard EU theory, the proof of the usual EU representation theorem may be used to yield a model that is linear in the outcomes but not in the probabilities.

Axiom (EU.5*) may also be expressed in terms of cumulative (or decumulative) distribution functions. Yaari shows that, given (EU.1), a convex outcome mixture of random variables is equivalent to a *convex harmonic mixture* of cumulative distribution functions. Using the inverse notions defined in Section 2.4, we may write such a mixture as

$$\lambda F_1 \oplus (1\text{-}\lambda)\, F_2 = (\lambda F_1^{-1} + (1\text{-}\lambda)\, F_2^{-1})^{-1}. \tag{11.2}$$

Yaari (1986) extends the dual axioms to the case of multivariate outcomes. Given n-tuples of independent random variables, he proposes an additional independence axiom. This requires that for multivariate distributions that differ only with respect to the i-th component, preferences should be independent of the distributions y^j, $j \neq i$. (This assumption is meaningless if the random variables are not independent). With appropriate extensions of the continuity and order axioms to the multivariate case, Yaari shows that preferences may be represented by a functional of the form

$$V(y^1, y^2, \ldots y^n) = U(V^1, V^2 \ldots V^n) \tag{11.3}$$

where

$V^i = \int_X x\, dq^{i}\circ F^i(x)$ is a dual functional;

$q[0, 1] \rightarrow [0, 1]$ is a transformation function; and

U: $\mathfrak{R}^n \rightarrow \mathfrak{R}$ is a riskless utility function.

If a cardinal utility function over X is already given without considerations of uncertainty, the axioms for the dual model, applied to probability distributions of utilities, yield the general RDEU model. This is, in essence, the approach espoused by Allais. Hence the Allais version of RDEU could be axiomatized using (EU.5*) and a set of axioms yielding an interval measure of utility on X.

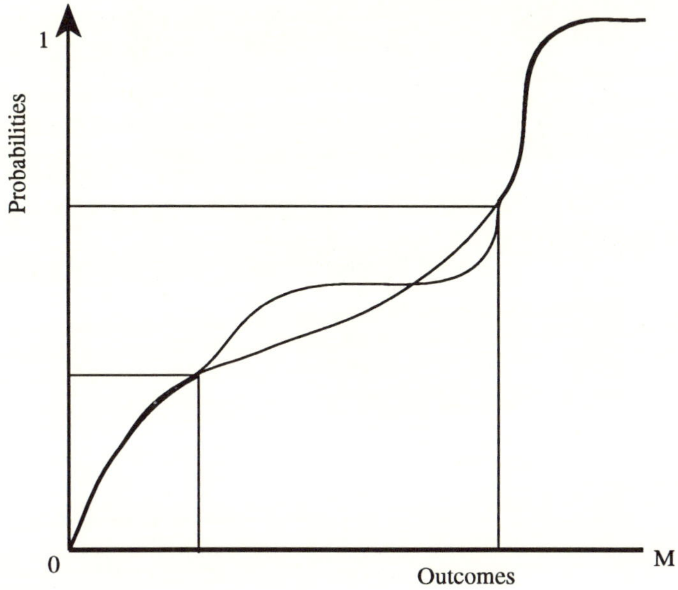

Figure 11.1: Ordinal independence

11.3 Ordinal Independence and Measure Representation

An alternative approach, followed by Green and Jullien (1988), Segal (1989) and Quiggin (1989b) begins with the notion of ordinal independence. The crucial axiom may be presented as

(RLU.5) If F, $G \in D$, $F \succcurlyeq G$, S is a measurable subset of $\mathcal{X}$, and
(i) $F^*(x) = G^*(x)$, $F(x) = G(x)$ $x \in S$,
(ii) $F^*(x) = F(x)$, $G^*(x) = G(x)$ $x \notin S$
Then $F^* \succcurlyeq G^*$.

The implication of this independence rule is that if two random variables agree on a given segment of the cumulative distribution function, the values they take on that segment should not affect their ranking (see Figure 11.1). This is a considerably weaker assumption than the EU independence axiom.

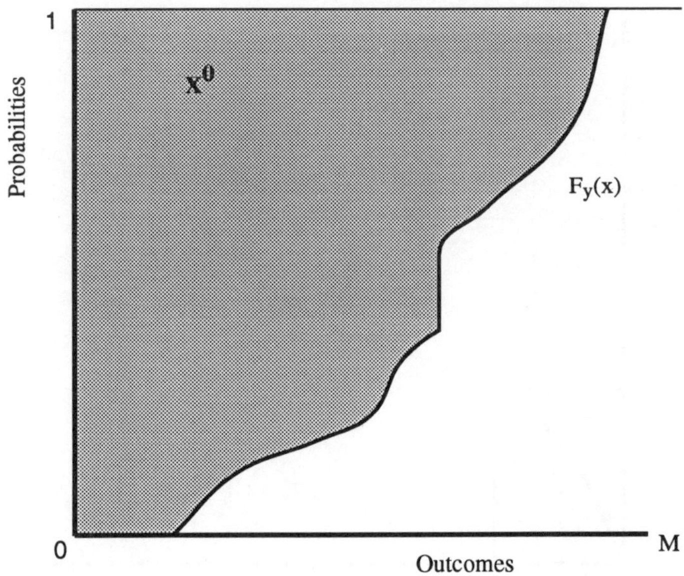

Figure 11.2: The epigraph of a cumulative distribution function

Segal (1989) proposes an axiomatization of RDEU theory using a measure representation approach that takes (RLU.5) as its starting point. He first observes[22] that, if (RLU.5) holds, preferences may be represented by a measure on [0, 1] × [0, *M*]. A given random variable is evaluated by the measure of the epigraph (the area to the left of the graph) of its cumulative distribution function (see Figure 11.2). The ordinal independence assumption (RLU.5) ensures that the preference functional does behave like a measure in that the difference in the evaluation of two cumulative distribution functions cannot depend on areas that their graphs have in common.

In this representation, EU preferences correspond to the product of the Lebesgue measure on [0, 1] with a measure, induced by the utility function, on [0, *M*]. Yaari's dual model corresponds to the product of Lebesgue measure on [0, *M*] with a measure, induced by the transformation function, on [0, 1]. RDEU preferences correspond to the general class of product measures. (Compare the informal discussion of Figures 5.5 and 5.6).

[22] Wakker (1991b) has observed a number of technical difficulties, primarily associated with continuity, in Segal's formal statement and proof of this result. Similar difficulties apply to the related work of Green and Jullien (1988) and Quiggin (1989). Segal and Wakker (pers. comm.) have made progress in resolving these difficulties.

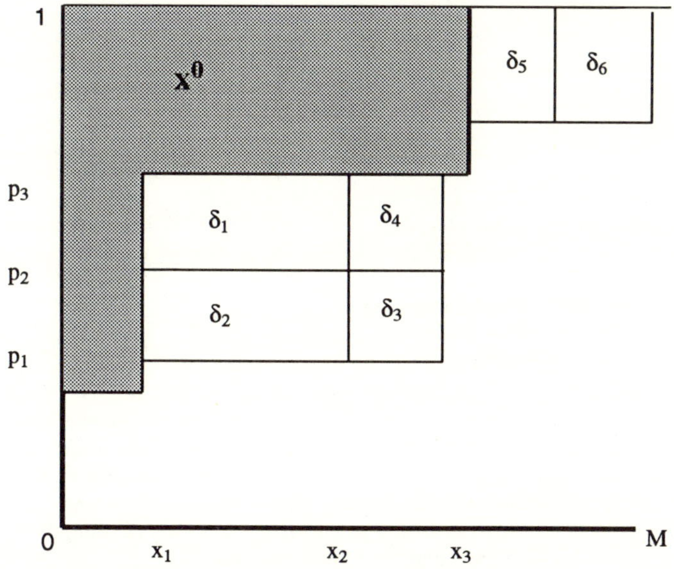

Figure 11.3: Projection independence

One additional axiom is needed to characterize RDEU preferences. Since preferences are represented by a measure, it is possible to compare arbitrary subsets of $[0, 1] \times [0, M]$, and, in particular, rectangular subsets such as those illustrated in Figure 11.3. For a product measure ν, $\nu(\delta_1) > \nu(\delta_2)$ if and only if $\nu(\delta_3) > \nu(\delta_4)$. Similarly, we may observe, for RDEU preferences, that we may define a partial ordering $\succcurlyeq^*$ on subsets of $[0, 1] \times [0, M]$ based on the idea that $\delta_1 \succcurlyeq^* \delta_2$ if and only if for some F, $F+\delta_1 \succcurlyeq F+\delta_2$.

RDEU preferences satisfy the condition

$$(q(p_3)\text{-}q(p_2))(U(x_2) - U(x_1)) \geq (q(p_2)\text{-}q(p_1))(U(x_2) - U(x_1))$$

if and only if

$$(q(p_3)\text{-}q(p_2))(U(x_3) - U(x_2)) \geq (q(p_2)\text{-}q(p_1))(U(x_3) - U(x_2)) \qquad (11.4)$$

Segal refers to this property as *projection independence*. It is obvious that RDEU preferences satisfy projection independence. Conversely, given projection independence, any measure representing preferences must be a product measure and hence must have an RDEU representation. For a measure ν, define

$$U(x) = \nu([0, 1] \times [0, x])$$

and

$$q(p) = \nu([0, M] \times [0, p]).$$

Projection independence now implies that for $0 \le x_1 < x_2$, and $p_1 < p_2$

$$\nu([p_1, p_2] \times [x_1, x_2]) = (q(p_2)-q(p_1))(U(x_2) - U(x_1)). \qquad (11.5)$$

In the same paper, Segal considers the extension of RDEU to the case of vectorial outcomes. Using a functional analysis approach, he shows that there exists a unique extension.

11.4 Trade-Off Consistency

The axiomatic systems discussed so far imply a separation between outcomes and probabilities. As shown in Chapter 6, this permits us to distinguish between risk attitudes associated with the probability transformation function and risk attitudes associated with the utility function. However, this distinction depends on the functional representation of preferences, and is only indirectly related to the axiomatic framework. Wakker (1991a) offers an axiomatic basis for the distinction between probability attitudes and the utility function. He begins with the notion of derived trade-offs, which may be regarded as a revealed ordering of strengths of preferences. He defines $[\alpha; \beta] \succcurlyeq^* [\gamma; \delta]$ if there exist $\boldsymbol{x}$, $\boldsymbol{y}$, $\boldsymbol{p}$, i such that

$$\{(x_1, \dots x_{i-1}, \alpha, x_{i+1}, \dots x_n); \boldsymbol{p}\} \succcurlyeq \{(y_1, \dots y_{i-1}, \beta, y_{i+1}, \dots y_n); \boldsymbol{p}\}, \qquad (11.6)$$

and

$$\{(x_1, \dots x_{i-1}, \gamma, x_{i+1}, \dots x_n); \boldsymbol{p}\} \preccurlyeq \{(y_1, \dots y_{i-1}, \delta, y_{i+1}, \dots y_n); \boldsymbol{p}\}. \qquad (11.7)$$

Assuming that RDEU holds, this condition may be interpreted as saying that the utility difference between α and β is greater than the utility difference between γ and δ. Evaluating the RDEU preference functionals and cancelling common terms yields

$$h_i(\boldsymbol{p})\,(U(\alpha) - U(\beta)) \ge h_i(\boldsymbol{p})\,(U(\gamma) - U(\delta)). \qquad (11.8)$$

Because both the probabilities and the rank ordering of the outcomes are constant, the change in evaluation from (11.6) to (11.7) must be explained by the change in outcomes. It follows that, for any choice of $\boldsymbol{x}$, $\boldsymbol{y}$, $\boldsymbol{p}$, i, with $x_i = \alpha$ and $y_i = \beta$, replacing x_i by γ and y_i by δ must make $\{\boldsymbol{x}; \boldsymbol{p}\}$ less attractive relative to $\{\boldsymbol{y}; \boldsymbol{p}\}$[23]. This motivates

[23] A comparison between (11.5) and (11.8) shows that this is essentially the dual of the Projection Independence requirement imposed by Segal (1989).

(RDEU.6) Preferences satisfy trade-off consistency if there do not exist α, β, γ, δ such that

$$[\alpha; \beta] \succcurlyeq^* [\gamma; \delta] \text{ and } [\gamma; \delta] \succcurlyeq^* [\alpha; \beta]$$

with at least one inequality strict.

This condition exactly characterizes the relationship between EU and RDEU. In EU theory, the cancellation argument presented above would apply regardless of the rank order of the outcomes. The choices in the Allais problem, which involves a change in the rank order of outcomes, violate the EU axioms but not trade-off consistency.

Wakker's proof that the axioms (EU.1)–(EU.4) and (RDEU.6) imply that preferences can be represented by an RDEU functional may be summarized as follows. He first shows, using methods similar to the standard proofs of EU theory, that, for any given $\boldsymbol{p}$, the axioms imply the existence of a utility function U and a set of weights $\boldsymbol{h}(\boldsymbol{p})$ representing preferences. Next he observes that for any $\boldsymbol{p}$, $\boldsymbol{p}'$, it is possible to consider a third, 'more refined' $\boldsymbol{p}''$ such that all prospects obtained from $\boldsymbol{p}$ or $\boldsymbol{p}'$ may also be obtained from $\boldsymbol{p}''$. For example, if $\boldsymbol{p} = (1/2, 1/2)$ and $\boldsymbol{p}' = (1/3, 1/3, 1/3)$ we may set $\boldsymbol{p}'' = (1/6, \ldots, 1/6)$. The cardinal utility function U and weighting vector $\boldsymbol{h}$ derived from $\boldsymbol{p}''$ are shared by $\boldsymbol{p}$ and $\boldsymbol{p}'$. A simple limiting argument extends this representation to the case of general cumulative distribution functions. Wakker also considers a range of continuity conditions. Although primarily of technical interest, his analysis shows that the weighting function may, if desired, be discontinuous at 0 or 1, thereby allowing for a pure preference for certainty.

The most appealing feature of Wakker's axiomatization is that it permits the characterization of declining marginal utility and probabilistic risk aversion directly in terms of preferences, without reference to the properties of the RDEU functional itself. Let $\succcurlyeq^A$ and $\succcurlyeq^B$ be two preference orderings. Wakker defines $\succcurlyeq^B$ to exhibit a *stronger decrease of marginal utility* than $\succcurlyeq^A$ if there do not exist α, β, γ, δ with $\alpha > \beta > \gamma > \delta$ such that $[\alpha; \beta] \succcurlyeq^{A*} [\gamma; \delta]$ and $[\alpha; \beta] >^{B*} [\gamma; \delta]$. That is, if the utility difference between α and β is less than that between γ and δ for $\succcurlyeq^A$, it cannot be greater for $\succcurlyeq^B$.

Wakker proves that, for any preferences $\succcurlyeq^A$ and $\succcurlyeq^B$ satisfying (EU.1)–(EU.4) and (RDEU.6), $\succcurlyeq^B$ exhibits *stronger decrease of marginal utility* than $\succcurlyeq^A$ if and only if the utility function representing $\succcurlyeq^B$ is a concave transform of that representing $\succcurlyeq^A$. In particular, this result applies if $\succcurlyeq^A$ describes the preferences of a risk neutral individual. More generally, it applies if $\succcurlyeq^A$ satisfies the axioms of the dual theory, so that it can be represented by a linear utility function. Thus, the derived trade-off approach permits a straightforward characterization of diminishing marginal utility in terms of preferences.

The characterization of probabilistic risk is more complicated. The problem is to provide a behavioral characterization of the probabilistic attitudes of individuals who may have different utility functions. Using the derived trade-offs approach, Wakker first defines the notion of a mid-point outcome μ between outcomes $\alpha > \beta$ by the requirement that $[\alpha, \mu] \sim^* [\mu, \beta]$. Given RDEU preferences, this implies $U(\mu) = 1/2(U(\alpha) + U(\beta))$. More generally, for prospects y_1, y_2 the midpoint outcome is defined as the midpoint outcome of $CE(y_1)$, $CE(y_2)$.

One individual shows greater probabilistic risk aversion than another (in the SSD sense) if q^A is a concave transformation of q^B. That is, for any p_1, p_2, λ,

$$q^A(\lambda(p_1) + (1-\lambda)(p_2))/(q^A(p_1) + q^A(p_2)) \geq q^B(\lambda(p_1) + (1-\lambda)(p_2))/(q^B(p_1) + q^B(p_2)). \quad (11.9)$$

Conversely q^{A*} must be a convex transformation of q^{B*}, and (11.9) must hold with the inequality reversed for the q^{i*}. This condition may be expressed in terms of derived trade-offs. The condition is simplest if we set $U(0) = 0$ and $U(M) = 1$. Consider prospects of the form $y_i = \{(0, M); (1-p_i, p_i)\}$, $i = 1, 2$. These are evaluated as $V(y_i) = q^*(p_i)$. Hence a mid-point outcome μ_i for individual i satisfies

$$U^i(\mu_i) = 1/2\,(q^{i*}(p_1) + q^{i*}(p_2)). \quad (11.10)$$

Now suppose that for some $\lambda \in [0, 1]$, the degenerate prospect δ_{μ_1} is preferred to $\lambda y_1 \oplus (1-\lambda)y_2$. From (11.10), this implies

$$q^{A*}(\lambda(p_1) + (1-\lambda)(p_2))/(q^{A*}(p_1) + q^{A*}(p_2)) \geq 1/2.$$

Now, by (11.9) the same inequality must hold for q^B. Wakker shows that this is a complete characterization of probabilistic risk aversion. That is, individual A has greater probabilistic risk aversion than individual B if and only if whenever $\delta_{\mu_1} \succcurlyeq^A \lambda y_1 \oplus (1-\lambda)y_2$, it is also true that $\delta_{\mu_2} \succcurlyeq^B \lambda y_1 \oplus (1-\lambda)y_2$.

11.5 The Reduction of Compound Lotteries Axiom

Another approach to the RDEU model has involved the abandonment of the 'Reduction of Compound Lotteries Axiom' (RCLA) implicit in the notation used here, in which preferences are expressed over final probability distributions of outcomes, without regard to the way in which these may have been derived from sequences of gambles. If this postulate is dropped, the sure thing principle may be retained and a model similar to RDEU will result. This approach is followed by Luce and Narens (1985) and Luce (1989) and Segal (1990). The analysis of Segal will be followed here.

Segal's central point is that the equivalence between the EU independence axiom and the Savage sure thing principle depends on RCLA. Given RCLA, (EU.5) implies *Compound Independence*, which may be written as:

(EU.5a) Let $y^i = \{\mathbf{x}^i; \mathbf{p}^i\}$, $i = 1, 2, 3$ be single-stage lotteries and let $\lambda \in [0, 1]$. Then $y^1 \succcurlyeq y^2$ if and only if the single-stage lottery yielding each x^1_j with probability λp^1_j and each x^3_j with probability $(1-\lambda)p^3_j$ is preferred to the single-stage lottery yielding each x^2_j with probability λp^2_j and each x^3_j with probability $(1-\lambda)p^3_j$.

Given RCLA, the second part of the Compound Independence axiom may simply be written as $\lambda y^1 + (1-\lambda)y^3 \succcurlyeq \lambda y^2 + (1-\lambda)y^3$. This property will be referred to as *Mixture Independence*.

Segal shows that RDEU preferences over two-stage lotteries may be derived from a set of axioms in which the independence axiom (EU.5) is retained, but RCLA is dropped. Segal shows that this version of RDEU may account for the Ellsberg paradox and preference reversal as well as yielding the usual RDEU resolution of the Allais and common ratio problems. Some empirical support for the notion that violations of compound independence arise from failures of RCLA rather than of mixture independence is given by Conlisk (1989). On the other hand, the results of Conlisk (1987) seem to indicate quasiconvex preferences (that is, aversion to randomization) over explicit 50-50 mixtures of prospects.

In an atemporal framework, the normative status of RCLA seems unquestionable. The observation that people violate RCLA might be ascribed to the fact that most people are not very good at multiplying probabilities (whether in fractional or decimal form). In this context, it is unfortunate that studies of RCLA violations have not included the check of providing all subjects with arguments for and against RCLA and the opportunity to revise choices. The provision of an appealing argument against RCLA would appear to require an explicit temporal framework. The task of developing such a framework is outlined in Segal (1990).

11.6 Ordinally Independent Generalizations

The RDEU functional form given by (5.1) and (5.2) is appealing and tractable. However, because it depends only on rank order to determine decision weights, it does not fully capture the intuition that weighting should be greatest for extreme events. This suggests that weighting should be more important for outcomes that are in some general sense 'extreme' than for those that merely happen to fall at the bottom tail of a probability distribution with a narrow range. Moreover it is difficult to find an appealing axiomatic basis for the model. Most of the axiom schemes that have been proposed contain at least one axiom that is hard to motivate.

A more general class of rank order models of the form

$$V(y) = \int \eta(x, F(x))\, dF(x), \tag{11.11}$$

has been referred to as Rank–Linear Utility (RLU) or ordinally independent utility. This function was presented independently by Green and Jullien (1988), Quiggin (1989b) and Segal (1989).

A dual representation is

$$V(y) = \int_0^1 \phi(p, z(p))\, dp, \tag{11.12}$$

where

$$z(p) = \inf\{x \in X \mid F(x) \geq p\},$$

and

$$\phi(p, z(p)) = \int_0^{z(p)} \zeta(x,p)\, dx.$$

This may be related to the RDEU model by considering the special case when $\zeta(x,p)$ takes the multiplicatively separable form

$$\zeta(x, p) = \zeta_1(x)\zeta_2(p). \tag{11.13}$$

Here $\zeta_1(x)$ corresponds to the utility function $U(x)$ and $\zeta_2(p)$ corresponds to $q'(p)$. In this case, we have

$$V(F) = \int U(x)\, d(q^\circ F(x)) = \int U(x) q'(F(x))\, dF(x).$$

The crucial change between RDEU and RLU is the abandonment of separability between probabilities and outcomes. This involves a loss of simplicity and a corresponding gain in flexibility.

The most important increase in flexibility arises because the RLU model is consistent with a behavioral pattern in which (for some range of initial wealth levels) all small actuarially fair bets are rejected although certain long–odds bets, such as lottery tickets, with large positive prizes, are accepted.

In the special case where Ω is a set of n states of the world (11.11) may be written as

$$V(y) = \sum_{i=1}^{n} U_r(w_i),$$

where $r = r(i, y)$ is the rank of state i under the prospect y. This formulation has an obvious kinship with the state–dependent model of Karni (1983). Note, however, that when two prospects are being compared, the rank of state i will not in general be the same.

The results for risk aversion derived by Green and Jullien are a straightforward extension of those of Chew, Karni and Safra (1987). They show that an RLU functional is risk averse (in the SSD sense) if and only if ζ_{11}, $\zeta_{22} \leq 0$, just as would be expected from (11.13).

Green and Jullien claim that the RDEU model is inconsistent with the Friedman–Savage observation of simultaneous gambling and insurance, and that the extension to RLU is necessary to capture this important empirical violation of EU predictions. The incorrectness of this claim may be seen from the analysis presented in Chapter 8. It appears to arise from the assumption that the boundedness properties of the local utility function used in Machina's (1982) example of Friedman–Savage behavior are a necessary feature of any solution to the problem.

Puppe (1990) extends the results of Green and Jullien in several directions. He first shows that an arbitrary preference functional defined over all prospects of the form $\{(0, x); (1-p, p)\}$ may be extended to a functional over Y satisfying ordinal independence. In fact, his proof shows more than this. There is a 1-1 correspondence between the two classes of functionals.

Second, Puppe considers the specific functional form

$$v(x, p) = u(x)p^{g(x)}. \tag{11.14}$$

It may be observed that this is an RDEU functional whenever g is a constant function, and an EU functional whenever g is identically equal to 1. A constant value greater than (less than) 1 implies convexity (concavity) of q. Puppe proposes the condition $g'(x) < 0$. The resulting weighting function will vary according to the distribution, but will always be S-shaped.

11.7 Cumulative Prospect Theory

One of the original motivations for the development of RDEU was the observation of violations of dominance in the prospect theory of Kahneman and Tversky (1979). The replacement of weights on individual probabilities by a transformation of the cumulative distribution function eliminated these violations. It is natural to ask whether a version of prospect theory can be developed which incorporates cumulative decision weights while maintaining the other key features of prospect theory — risk preference in the domain of losses and the expression of preferences in terms of a deviations from a reference point rather than in terms of final wealth.[24]

A number of authors (Starmer and Sugden 1989, Tversky and Kahneman 1990, Luce and Fishburn 1991), have proposed cumulative versions of prospect theory, with a reference point of 0 (that is, the initial wealth level). However, these representations do not permit changes in the reference point. The examples given by Kahneman and Tversky suggest that reference point effects must either arise from framing effects (involving violations of EU.1) or must imply violations of first stochastic dominance.

Wakker and Tversky (1991) provide an axiomatization of a rank-dependent sign-dependent model which they refer to as *cumulative prospect theory*. The approach is based on the axiomatization of RDEU presented in Section 11.4. The only modification needed to the trade-off consistency axiom (RDEU.6) is that it is required to apply only when α, β, γ, δ have the same sign. The result is a model with two transformation functions, one, denoted q^-, for negative values of x and one, denoted q^+, for positive values. Since the utility function has x as an argument, it automatically captures sign-dependence. However, the hypothesis of risk preference in the domain of losses implies that the utility function will have a point of inflexion at the origin. Further and without loss of generality, $U(0) = 0$.

Suppose that, for a given prospect expressed $\{(\boldsymbol{x};\boldsymbol{p})\}$ in the usual rank-ordered form, there exists k such that $x_k \leq 0 \leq x_{k+1}$. Then

$$V\{(\boldsymbol{x};\boldsymbol{p})\} = \sum_{i=1}^{k} h^-_i(\boldsymbol{p})\, U(x_i) + \sum_{i=k+1}^{n} h^+_i(\boldsymbol{p})\, U(x_i).$$

where

$$h^-_i(\boldsymbol{p}) = q^-(\sum_{j=1}^{i} p_i) - q^-(\sum_{j=1}^{i-1} p_i) \quad i \leq k, \text{ and}$$

$$h^+_i(\boldsymbol{p}) = q^+(\sum_{j=k}^{i} p_i) - q^+(\sum_{j=k}^{i-1} p_i) \quad i > k..$$

Note that, since $U(0) = 0$, it does not matter if there is more than one k satisfying the requirement that $x_k \leq 0 \leq x_{k+1}$.

A closely related model, based on the concept of disappointment aversion, is presented by Gul (1991). The distinguishing feature of Gul's model is that the prospect's certainty equivalent, rather than the zero outcome, plays the rôle of the reference point. Since the certainty equivalent

[24] The original presentation of prospect theory included reference to a number of other phenomena. Some of these, most notably framing effects were never explicitly modelled (see Section 14.5). Others, such as editing of dominated prospects, are irrelevant if the model does not exhibit violations of dominance.

is itself dependent on preferences, the result is an implicitly defined preference functional. Gul provides an algorithm by which the values of the preference functional may be calculated. The most noteworthy feature of Gul's model is the fact that it displays betweenness while involving probability weighting broadly similar to that in RDEU.

All of the models presented in this section coincide with RDEU (and the basic version of prospect theory) for the class of simple bets of the form $\{(x_1, x_2); (p, 1\text{-}p)\}$ where $x_1 < 0 < x_2$. They differ from RDEU in that the weighting function depends explicitly on the x_i and not merely on the ordering of the outcomes.

11.8 The Space of Outcomes

Most of the axiomatic analysis has been based on the assumption that the outcome space X is an interval of the form $[0, M]$ corresponding to monetary outcomes. This assumption may be relaxed in two ways. First, we may consider subsets of the real line that are not necessarily bounded. Wakker (1992) shows that this may be done provided that all random variables have well defined certainty equivalents[25] and that preferences satisfy truncation-continuity. That is, for any y, δ, there exist $\bar{x}$, $\underline{x}$, such that

$$min\,(y, \bar{x}) \succcurlyeq CE(y) - \delta$$

$$max\,(\underline{x}, y) \preccurlyeq CE(y) + \delta$$

where $min\,(y, \bar{x})$ is the random variable yielding $\min(y(\omega), \bar{x})$ for each $\omega \in \Omega$.

Grant, Kajii, and Polak (1992) consider the question of when RDEU preferences may be extended to cover outcomes that are bundles of goods. They employ an axiom which they describe as the axiom of 'Degenerate Independence.' This states that, for any x, x', $\in$ X, $y \in \mathcal{X}$, $\alpha \in [0, 1]$

$$x \geq x' \text{ if and only if } \alpha\delta_x \oplus (1\text{-}\alpha)y \succcurlyeq \alpha\delta_{x'} \oplus (1\text{-}\alpha)y.$$

This is closely related to the dominance axiom originally proposed by Quiggin (1982a), and encapsulates one of the main ideas of the rank-dependent model. If preferences depend only on rank, then there is no need to distinguish between outcomes that are equally preferred. Thus, we may replace any outcome in a given prospect with an equally preferred outcome and this will not affect the desirability of the prospect.

In particular this implies that it is legitimate to use a money metric, even when consumption of some goods is quantity constrained in some states of the world. Using an expenditure function approach, we may find the amount of money income that must be received to equal the utility obtained from consuming a given bundle of goods. All prospects may then be treated as if they are lotteries over these monetary equivalents.

[25] In fact, as Wakker shows, it is sufficient that each random variable should have an equivalent that is a step function.

Appendix – Notes on the Original Axiomatization of RDEU

In the notation used here, the original AU axioms proposed by Quiggin (1982a) may be stated as follows.

(AU.1) If y_1 and y_2 have the same cumulative distribution function $y_1 \sim y_2$.[26]

(AU.2) $\succcurlyeq$ is a quasi-order.

(AU.3) If $x_1 \leq x_2$, $x_1 \not\succ \{(x_1, x_2);(p, 1-p)\}$.

(AU.4) If $x_1, x_2, x_3 \in X$, $x_1 \geq x_2 \geq x_3$ there exists p^* such that

$$x_2 \sim \{(x_3, x_1);(p^*, 1-p^*)\}.$$

(AU.5) Let $y = \{\boldsymbol{x};\boldsymbol{p}\}$ and $y' = \{\boldsymbol{x}';\boldsymbol{p}\} \in \mathcal{Y}$ and let $y_c = \{\boldsymbol{c};\boldsymbol{p}\}$ be defined such that

$$c_i = \text{CE}\{(x_i, x'_i); (1/2, 1/2)\}.$$

Then

$$y_c \sim \{(\text{CE}(y), \text{CE}(y')); (1/2, 1/2)\}$$

Yaari (1987) states

> Quiggin's representation theorem is incorrect as it stands. Utility representations of the form
>
> (A.1) $$V = \sum_{i=1}^{n} x_i\, w(p_i),$$
>
> with w continuous and satisfying $w(p) + w(1-p) \leq 1$ for all p satisfy Quiggin's axioms, but they do not agree with [the RDEU functional form] unless $w(p) = p$. To fix things up, Quiggin's dominance axiom must be modified and possibly also his independence axiom.

This claim is incorrect. It will be shown here, that, except in the case $w(p) = p$, the functional form proposed by Yaari is inconsistent with the original AU axioms proposed by Quiggin (1982a). Begin by observing that the form (A.1) must satisfy $w(1/2) = 1/2$. This follows by selecting $x < x' < x''$ such that $x' = \text{CE}\{(x, x''); (1/2, 1/2)\} = w(1/2)(x + x'')$ and applying the independence axiom (AU.5) to random variables of the form:

[26] This postulate was not included in the list of axioms, but was stated as a notational convention.

$$y_1 = \{(x', x'); (1/2, 1/2)\} = \{x';1\}$$

$$y_2 = \{(x, x''); (1/2, 1/2)\}$$

Then

$$V(y_1) = x',\ V(y_2) = w(1/2)(x + x'') = x'$$

The independence axiom (AU.5) now implies that

$$x' = w(1/2)(w(1/2)(x + x') + w(1/2)\,(x + x'')) = 4\,(w(1/2))^2 x'$$

or

$$w(1/2) = 1/2$$

Now for any p, choose $x''' > x''$ and consider prospects of the form

$$y_3 = \{(x', x'', x''');(p/2, p/2, 1-p)\} = \{(x', x''');(p, 1-p)\}$$

$$y_4 = \{(x, x'', x'''); (p/2, p/2, 1-p)\}$$

Application of the independence axiom now yields

$$w(p/2)(1/2(x + x') + 1/2(x + x'')) = 1/2w(p)x' + 1/2w(p/2)(x + x''), \text{ or}$$

$$w(p) = 2w(p/2)$$

A similar argument shows that $1-w(1-p) = 2(1-w(p/2))$. These conditions can only be satisfied if $w(p) = p\ \forall\ p$, as claimed. ■

Although Yaari's counterexample is incorrect, there is a more subtle problem with the original AU axioms. The axioms do not (as is implicitly assumed by Quiggin 1982a) guarantee preservation of first stochastic dominance, since they do not exclude the possibility that q is not monotonically increasing. It is arguable that the requirement for preservation of first stochastic dominance should not be imposed axiomatically – axiom sets for EU theory often do not require that the utility function be monotonically increasing. In any case, the problem may easily be remedied by replacing the original dominance axiom with the following monotonicity axiom proposed by Chew (1989).

(AU.3*) If $x_1 \leq x_2,\ p_1 \geq p_2\ \ \{(x_1, x_2);(p_2, 1-p_2)\} \succcurlyeq \{(x_1, x_2);(p_1, 1-p_1)\}$

The original dominance axiom is equivalent to (AU.3*) restricted to the case $p_2 = 0$. Issues relating to the original axiomatic basis of RDEU are discussed in detail by Quiggin and Wakker (1992).

PART 4

GENERALIZED EXPECTED UTILITY THEORY

Introduction

The remaining chapters treat the theory of choice under uncertainty more generally. RDEU is considered along with a range of other generalizations of EU. Its relatively prominent treatment partly reflects the concern of this book and partly the ubiquity of the RDEU model in the literature.

Chapter 12 concerns the theoretical framework proposed by Machina (1982). The idea of a local utility function permits the extension of EU results concerning preferences to a wide range of generalized EU models. The RDEU model does not fit directly into Machina's framework, because it does not satisfy the smoothness assumption imposed by Machina. However, a modified form of local utility function may be defined for RDEU.

Chapter 13 shows how a range of generalized theories may be characterized by stochastic dominance, independence and betweenness rules involving different notions of the appropriate comparisons between states of the world. As its name implies, RDEU is associated with the idea that appropriate comparisons may be made when states have the same rank order in different prospects.

Finally Chapter 14 presents approaches to a range of extensions to problems beyond the scope of this book. Two kinds of extensions are considered here. The first are problems such as social choice and intertemporal choice where the tools of the theory of choice under uncertainty may be applied with an appropriate reinterpretation. The key observation is that individuals in social choice theory and time periods in intertemporal choice theory play a role similar to that of states of the world in the theory of choice under uncertainty. The final section concerns the possibility of extending the ideas developed here beyond the relatively simple problem of choice over well-defined probability distributions to tackle problems such as framing and coding.

CHAPTER 12

Generalized Smooth Utility and RDEU

The simplest response to the problems associated with the EU independence axiom is to dispense with this axiom altogether. This approach is adopted by Machina (1982).[27] Machina's central theoretical tool is the notion of a local utility function. The idea is that people will act as expected utility maximizers in a neighborhood of any distribution F, but that they will maximize the expectation of a different utility function around another distribution F^*. In particular, changes in initial wealth levels will lead, not only to decreasing absolute risk aversion effects of the kinds explored by Arrow and Pratt, but to shifts in the utility function itself.

A useful illustration is provided by Machina's proposed resolution of the Friedman–Savage paradox. As was shown in Chapter 4, people with such a utility function would display sharp changes in behavior in response to changes in initial wealth. Machina proposed a utility function that shifts with changes in initial wealth in such a way that, for any fixed level of initial wealth the individual is always at a position like C in Figure 4.1. With these preferences, small symmetric bets will always be rejected, but some long-odds bets will always be accepted.

It might seem that allowing the utility function to vary in this way would lead to a model that could encompass any possible structure of preferences, and hence from which no sharp predictions could be derived. The framework *per se* imposes very few restrictions on preferences. However, Machina shows that, in many cases, if all of the local utility functions have a given property such as concavity, this property carries over to the global preference functional. It is this result that makes his model such an attractive generalization of EU theory.

Machina's seminal work has stimulated a large number of theoretical developments, which are beyond the scope of the present work. The object of this chapter is to present a brief outline of Machina's model and to illustrate the relationship between this model and RDEU theory.

12.1 The Model

Machina considers general preference functionals $V(F)$, where $F \in \mathfrak{D}$, and the outcome space is restricted to be of the form $[0, M]$. This class includes the standard EU functional $V(F) = \int U(x)\, dF(x)$, which has the special property of being 'linear in the probabilities.'

Machina imposes the 'smoothness' requirement that V be Fréchet differentiable with respect to the norm induced by the L^1 metric on $\mathfrak{D}$. This implies the existence of a continuous functional $\varphi(\bullet;\ F)$ such that, for any $F^* \in \mathfrak{D}$

$$V(F^*) - V(F) = \varphi(F^*-F;\ F) + o\,\|F^*-F\|, \tag{12.1}$$

[27] Unless otherwise noted, references in this chapter will be to this paper.

where $\|F^*-F\| = \int_X |F^*(x)-F(x)|\, dx$. Machina demonstrates the existence of functions $\eta(\bullet;\ F)$ and $U(\bullet;\ F)$ defined on $\mathfrak{D}$, such that

$$\varphi(F^* - F; F) = \int (F^*(x) - F(x))\, \eta(x;\ F)\, dx,$$
$$= -\int (F^*(x) - F(x))\, dU(x;\ F),$$

and

$$U(x;\ F) = -\int^x \eta(s;\ F)\, ds.$$

Given the smoothness condition on V, it may be shown that U is absolutely continuous. The function $U(x;\ F)$, a linear approximation to V, which will be referred to as the local utility function at F, plays a central role in Machina's analysis. The crucial result is

$$V(F^*) - V(F) = \int U(x;\ F)(dF^*(x) - dF(x)) + o\|F^*-F\|. \tag{12.2}$$

That is, in a neighborhood of F, the individual acts as would an expected utility maximizer with utility function equal to the local utility function $U(x; F)$. It may be noted that if $U(x; F)$ does not vary with F, the model is equivalent to that of EU theory.

In an example given by Machina, the local utility function in the neighborhood of a given distribution F is given by

$$U(x; F) = x/(1+x) + 0.1 \exp(\psi(F)])\exp(x),$$

where

$$\psi(F) = \int \exp(t)\, dF(t),$$

and the global functional is

$$V(F) = \int x/(1+x)\, dF(x) - 0.1 \exp(-\,\psi(F)).$$

An additional feature of this model is that the preference functional is bounded, although all of the local utility functions are unbounded. This means that the willingness to gamble does not generate St. Petersburg paradoxes and related problems.

Machina uses a path integral approach to show that, if all the local utility functions possess certain properties (such as monotonicity), the preference functional V will exhibit the corresponding global property. This method is used to prove the following theorems:

PROPOSITION 12.1: *Let V be a Fréchet differentiable preference functional on $\mathfrak{D}$. Then $V(F^*) \geq V(F)$ whenever F^* FSD F if and only if $U(x; F)$ is non-decreasing in x for all $F \in \mathfrak{D}$.*

PROPOSITION 12.2: *Let V be a functional satisfying the conditions of Theorem 12.1. Then $V(F^*) < V(F)$ whenever F^* differs from F by a mean-preserving increase in risk if and only if $U(x; F)$ is a concave function of x for all $F \in \mathfrak{D}$.*

The reasoning behind these theorems is straightforward. If F^* first (second) stochastic dominates F, it is possible to define a path in $\mathfrak{D}$ from F to F^* along which first (second) stochastic dominance is maintained. Since the local utility functions are non-decreasing (concave) in x, it is possible to apply the envelope theorem to show that V must increase along the path. The converse parts of the theorem may be proved by considering the case of a distribution F for which $U(x; F)$ does not display the required property. In this case, it is possible to draw two paths starting at F and such that, at any given value $\alpha \in [0, 1]$, the distribution on the first path stochastically dominates that on the second, even though, in a neighborhood of F, V takes higher values on the second path. Unless all the local utility functions display the required property, V will not display it globally. From now on, it will be assumed that the conditions of Theorem 12.1 are satisfied, so that V preserves first stochastic dominance.

Unlike the case of EU theory, it is possible to obtain rational behavior in this model even when risk aversion in the sense of (12.2) is not assumed. It is possible to be risk seeking in relation to some risks, such as those characterized by a small probability of a large gain, and risk averse in relation to others.

Much of the Arrow–Pratt analysis (and the dual Diamond–Stiglitz analysis) of Chapter 2 may be taken over to Machina's more general framework. In particular, Machina proves:

PROPOSITION 12.3: *The following conditions on a pair of Fréchet differentiable functions V and V^* over $\mathfrak{D}$ with respective local utility functions $U(x; F)$ and $U^*(x; F)$ are equivalent:*

(i) *$U(x; F)$ is at least as concave a function of x as is $U^*(x; F)$ so that if these functions are twice differentiable in x, $-U''(x; F)/U'(x; F) \geq U^{*''}(x; F)/U^{*'}(x: F)$ for all $x \in X$ and $F \in \mathfrak{D}$;*

(ii) *If F^* differs from F by a simple compensated increase in risk from the point of view of V^*, $V(F) \leq V(F^*)$; and*

(iii) *If V is indifferent between a p: 1–p chance of F or F^* and a p: 1–p chance of the sure amount c or the distribution F^*, and V^* is indifferent between a p: 1–p chance of F or F^* and a p: 1–p chance of the sure amount c^* or the distribution F^*, $c \leq c^*$.*

If both individuals are 'diversifiers' and have differentiable local utility functions, the above conditions are also equivalent to

(iv) *For any $G \in \mathfrak{D}$, $p \in (0, 1]$, $r > 0$ and non–negative random variable y with mean greater than r, if α and α^* yield the most preferred distributions of the form $(1-p)G + pF_{(1-\alpha)r + \alpha y}$ for V and V^*, respectively, $\alpha \leq \alpha^*$.*

If V^* is the expectation operator, all of the above conditions yield equivalent definitions of risk aversion in the sense of Proposition 12.2. The value c in condition (iii) may be referred to as the 'conditional certainty equivalent' given F, and similarly the value α in (iv) is the conditional asset demand given G. In EU theory, the independence axiom ensures that these values are independent of F and G. However, as Proposition 12.3 shows, this axiom is not required to derive standard results on risk aversion.

Not all the standard equivalences of EU theory carry over to the more general framework, however. In particular, the most basic concept of risk aversion, namely that the certainty equivalent of any risky distribution is less than the mean, is not equivalent to the concavity condition of Proposition 12.2, nor is the corresponding definition of 'more risk averse' equivalent to the conditions of Proposition 12.3. Although the conditions of the theorems imply the corresponding conditions on certainty equivalents, the converse implication does not apply. Similarly, condition (iv) in Proposition 12.3 is strictly stronger than the requirement that the first individual, given a fixed initial wealth, will always purchase more of a risky asset than the second. It is not clear, therefore, that the characterization of risk aversion in terms of concavity yielded by Propositions 12.2 and 12.3, is the most appropriate one.

Machina (1984) considered this issue in some detail. He argues that the concavity condition and its equivalent characterizations apply in every small neighborhood in $\mathfrak{D}$, but the certainty equivalent and asset demand conditions do not. Moreover, "in the absence of additional restrictions such as linearity, neither the certainty equivalent characterization nor the asset demand characterization is strong enough to imply condition (i) or (ii), or more important still, even each other." Conditions (iii) and (iv) are generalizations of the certainty equivalent and asset demand conditions that refer to properties of every locality in $\mathfrak{D}$. Machina (1984) concluded that the theorems presented above represent the appropriate formulation of risk aversion in the general context.

Machina proposed two hypotheses on the behavior of the local utility function which, he argued, captured the central features of the observed violations of EU theory. Both are expressed in terms of the Arrow-Pratt risk aversion coefficients of the local utility function. The first was a generalization of the usual notion of decreasing absolute risk aversion.

Hypothesis I: $-U''(x;\ F)/U'(x;F)$ is non-increasing in $x\ \forall\ F \in \mathfrak{D}$.

This is not equivalent to the usual notion of decreasing absolute risk aversion, since it is necessary to take account of changes in the local utility function as F changes. In particular, it does not imply that an increase in base wealth leads to a reduction in the risk premium for a given small risk. However, it does imply that the individual will have a preference for increases in risk in the upper tail of the distribution relative to similar increases in risk in the lower tail of the distribution.

The second hypothesis has been central to the discussion of Machina's model. Indeed, most empirical tests of the Machina model have taken this hypothesis to be its defining feature

Hypothesis II: $-U''(x;\ F)/U'(x;\ F)$ is non-decreasing in $F\ \forall\ x$. That is, if F^* first stochastically dominates F, $-U''(x;\ F^*)/U'(x;F^*) \geq -U''(x;\ F)/U'(x;F)\ \forall\ x$.

Machina shows that this hypothesis is equivalent to the Generalized Common Ratio Effect ('fanning out') and to a particular characterization of the idea that individuals are more sensitive to changes in outlying probabilities.

12.2 Comparative Statics

Machina's (1982) paper showed that with smooth preferences, preferences in a neighborhood of a given cumulative distribution function F may be approximated by the local utility function $U(\bullet;\ F)$. Effects of changes in the local utility function associated with a move from $U(\bullet;\ F)$ to $U(\bullet;F^*)$ are important only when the shift, as measured by $\|F^*-F\|$, is large. Machina distinguishes between 'first order' effects of a shift (those associated with the change in evaluation using the local utility function at F) and 'second order' effects (those associated with a change in the local utility function). To preserve consistency with the terminology of Section 6.3, we shall refer to the effects associated with the utility function as second order and to those associated with a change in the local utility function as third order. In evaluating the risk premium for a small risk $k\varepsilon$ about an initial certain distribution, the effects of RDEU pessimism are $O(k)$, those of the local utility function are $o(k)$ and those of changes in the local utility function are $o(k^2)$.

Machina's path integral approach shows that results on stochastic dominance depend only on first order and second order properties of preferences. However, comparative statics normally involves third order properties of preferences. For example, EU comparative static results involving changes in initial wealth cannot be simply generalized because the change is evaluated with respect to a different local utility function. This is why Machina's Hypothesis I does not imply decreasing absolute risk aversion.

Nonetheless, Machina (1989) has shown that, for an important family of economically significant control problems, the EU analysis can be satisfactorily generalized in terms of properties of the local utility function. This class of control problems is characterized by an objective function of the form $U(\alpha, F)$, in which the control variable is separable from the random variable of economic interest. This is a fairly restrictive condition, which excludes most of the problems mentioned in the introduction. For example, in the theory of portfolio choice, the risky rate of return and the control variable (the amount allocated to the risky asset) interact to determine the distribution of total returns. The separation property does, however, apply to situations of temporal choice such as those examined in Machina (1984). It also applies to two-argument problems such as consumption–savings problems, provided these are expressed in separable form. For example, in the standard two period consumption–savings problem, it is necessary to express the objective function in the form $U(C_1, F(r))$ where C_1 is (nonstochastic) first period consumption and $F(r)$ is the distribution of the rate of return.

There are, however, important limitations to this approach. As Machina (1984) observes, problems of temporal risk are not particularly tractable even in an EU context. Similarly most studies of comparative statics using two-argument utility functions have not adopted separable representations. In the consumption–savings problem, for example, most of the available results, summarized by Dardanoni (1988), concern the objective function $U(C_1, C_2)$, which is not separable in C_1 and r.

Many EU comparative static results depend on third order properties of preferences, such as decreasing absolute risk aversion, and so cannot be carried over directly to the case of general smooth preferences. Decreasing absolute risk aversion is necessary for the extension of a number of intuitively plausible results, including positive supply response in the theory of the firm (Sandmo 1971).

Similar difficulties apply to results concerning the existence of a global optimum. A number of results have been developed on the existence of an optimal portfolio (Bertsekas 1974) and an optimal output for the firm under uncertainty (Quiggin 1982b) depending on the limiting behavior of the utility function. These results cannot be extended directly to the case of general smooth preferences.

12.3 RDEU and Generalized Smooth Preferences

Since Machina (1982) dropped the independence axiom altogether, whereas RDEU theory retains weak versions, it is natural to conjecture that RDEU theory is a special case of Machina's model. This is not so, as RDEU theory does not meet the smoothness condition (Fréchet differentiability) imposed by Machina. This was first observed by Chew, Karni and Safra (1987), who proved the result by counterexample.

A more useful interpretation of the lack of smoothness in RDEU theory comes from the discussion of the risk premium in Section 6.2. It was shown there that the risk premium for a prospect of the form $\delta_x + k\varepsilon$ is of order $O(k)$, so that individuals may display first order risk aversion. By contrast, for any EU functional, and hence for any Machina local utility functional, this difference is of order $o(k)$, and the smoothness assumption ensures that this property carries over to the global functional. That is, whereas both EU theory and Machina's theory imply that individuals are risk neutral in a neighborhood of certainty, RDEU theory does not.

To relate Machina's analysis to the RDEU case, it is necessary to derive an analog for the local utility function. For any two random variables y_1, y_2

$$V(y_1) - V(y_2) \cong \int_\Omega U'(y_1(\omega))q'(F_1(\omega))(y_1(\omega) - y_2(\omega))\, d\omega.$$

Following Machina's analysis it is natural to define the local utility function as

$$U_F(x) = \int_0^x U'(t)\, q'(F(t))\, dt, \tag{12.3}$$

which is defined whenever q is everywhere differentiable. Although this function (the Gateau derivative of V at F) does not have all of the properties of a local utility function, conditions that apply to U_F for all F will usually carry over to the preference functional V, just as in Machina's model. The first and second derivatives of the local utility function (12.3) are given by

$$U_F'(x) = U'(x)\, q'(F(x)), \tag{12.4}$$

and

$$U_F''(x) = U''(x)\, q'(F(x)) + U'(x)q''(F(x))f(x). \tag{12.5}$$

Thus, as shown in Chapter 6, concavity of U and q implies concavity of U_F for all F. The validity of this proof of the result depends on the fact that Machina's path integral method may be applied in the absence of smoothness. Chew, Karni and Safra (1987) show that this proof is valid for results concerning risk aversion. Chew and Nishimura (1989) examine the general case, and show that Machina's results may be generalized to cover any case when the Gateau derivative is defined everywhere.

Comparative static results may also be generalized. Consider the case when the distribution of returns shifts from F_0 to F_1. This shift may be regarded as a smooth path in $\mathfrak{D}$ and parametrized by a variable λ, with the image of λ in D being denoted $F(\bullet, \lambda)$ so that $F(0, \lambda) = F_0$,

$F(1, \lambda) = F_1$. Then the crucial requirement for comparative static analysis of the kind undertaken here is the legitimacy of 'differentiating under the integral' with respect to λ. Chew and Nishimura show that this is valid whenever q is everywhere differentiable. Hence, with a minor generalization of Machina's model, RDEU theory can be seen as a special case, and Machina's results may be applied.

A more complete extension of Machina's analysis is offered by Wang (1990). He observes that the weak topology employed by Machina is associated with the L^1 norm on D, and considers the implications of using the L^p norm for $p \geq 1$. He shows that an RDEU functional is L^p-Fréchet differentiable provided q' is bounded and $U' \in L^{p^*}[0, M]$ where p^* is the dual number such that $1/p + 1/p^* = 1$. The boundedness condition on q' has already been employed in Chapter 8. The condition on U' cannot be satisfied for $p=1$, $p^* = \infty$, but is unproblematic for $p > 1$.

From (12.5), the Arrow-Pratt coefficient for the local utility function is

$$U_F''(x)/U_F'(x) = -U''(x)/U'(x) \; - \; q''(F(x))f(x)/q'(F(x))$$

Because the coefficient involves a term in $f(x)$, it will not vary systematically with either x or F. Thus, neither Hypothesis I nor Hypothesis II is consistent with RDEU. On the other hand, as has been shown above, RDEU is consistent with decreasing absolute risk aversion and overweighting of outlying probabilities. These are the main stylized facts that Hypotheses I and II were designed to capture.

12.4 Risk Seeking

It is useful to consider the results of Chapter 8 in the light of Machina's general model. The local utility function concept may be used to analyze the lottery design problem in a number of ways. The first is to observe that if the local utility function at a degenerate distribution is of the basic Friedman–Savage functional form, (that is, a concave segment followed by a convex segment) utility may be increased by the purchase of an appropriately chosen lottery ticket. More generally, if the local utility function has this shape at a distribution F with support lying in the convex segment of the curve, there exists a distribution F^*, such that F^* differs from F by a mean–preserving spread, but F^* is preferred to F.

Because of the absence of smoothness in RDEU theory, the local utility function is not well behaved in a neighborhood of degenerate distributions. It is more convenient to consider the local utility function in the case of a continuous probability distribution F with most of the support lying in some small region around some wealth value x^*. The fact that the region in which the support is concentrated is small implies that U' is close to $U'(x^*)$ in this region and that the density f is large. Within this region, the second derivative of the local utility function will be dominated by the second term in (12.5), and will consist of a concave segment followed by a convex segment. Outside this region, the local utility function will be dominated by the first term in (12.5) and will therefore be concave. This implies that the local utility function will have the shape of the modified Friedman–Savage utility function.

In the context of the problem of optimal lottery design, a more interesting question relates to the shape of the local utility function at the distribution yielded by the most preferred lottery. It is useful to compare equation (12.4), the local utility function, with (8.5) giving the conditions under RDEU for the optimal prize structure, namely

$$U'(x_i) \,/\, U'(x_k) = h_k/h_i.$$

Imposing the approximation $h_k = q'(F(x_k))p_k$ implies the striking result that the optimal lottery yields a local utility function with constant marginal utility of wealth over the upper tail of the prize distribution. This condition has a natural interpretation in terms of a partition of the possible outcomes into equiprobable states, ordered by the value of the outcome. It says that for a given expected income the optimal distribution of income across states must have the property that the marginal utility of wealth is equal in all pairs of states between which actuarially fair trade is possible. Since the construction of the lottery is constrained only by the expected value of the outcome it is possible to make actuarially fair transfers between any pair of winning states.

More generally we have the following result:

PROPOSITION 12.4: Let V be a smooth preference functional and let F be a distribution such that for any F^*, $\mathrm{E}[F^*] = \mathrm{E}[F] \Rightarrow V(F^*) \leq V(F)$. Then there exists a linear function $g(x) = a + bx$ such that
(i) $U(x;\ F) = g(x)$ on the support of F; and
(ii) $U(x;\ F) \leq g(x)$ outside the support of F.

Proof: Quiggin (1991d). ■

This result raises some interesting questions concerning functionals like the example presented by Machina (1982). Given that the local utility function is everywhere convex for sufficiently large x, and $-U''(x)/U'(x)$ is everywhere decreasing, the conditions of Proposition 2 cannot be met for any F, and there is no optimal distribution having a given mean. The set $\{F\colon \mathrm{E}[F] = c\}$ is not compact and so the fact that V does not attain its maximum on the set is not surprising, though the absence of a most preferred distribution is disturbing. On the other hand, the boundedness of V implies that the supremum of V in the set $\{F\colon E[F] = c\}$ is finite and can be approached arbitrarily closely.

CHAPTER 13

Stochastic Dominance and Independence Rules

The models presented above by no means exhaust the recent literature on choice under uncertainty. The range of generalized utility theories that have been developed in the past decade often seems bewildering. In this chapter, a characterization is proposed, based on the notion of 'sure things' or, more formally, stochastic dominance and independence rules. The characterization is applied to a range of decision theories including RDEU, RLU, EU, state-dependent utility theories (Karni 1983) and regret theory (Loomes and Sugden 1982, 1983, 1987).

In the economic analysis of choice under uncertainty, the focus has been on the formulation of axiomatic rules guaranteeing that one choice is better than another. Some of these rules, such as principles of transitivity, are not specifically related to uncertainty. Stochastic dominance and independence rules are more specifically concerned with reducing choice between uncertain prospects to a sure thing. Rules of this kind have no content in the absence of uncertainty.

The primary purpose of this chapter is to show that the differences between models of choice under uncertainty may be derived primarily from different assumptions about the 'appropriate' ways in which states of the world may be compared and combined.[28] A particularly sharp contrast may be drawn between models that focus on the actual state of the world in which a given outcome occurs and those, based on cumulative distribution functions, that are primarily concerned with the ranking of the outcome. In the first case, it is natural to model an action as a mapping from the set of states of the world to an outcome space. In the second, it is more natural to identify an action with the probability distribution of outcomes it yields. Assumptions about appropriate permutations of the set of states are sufficient to characterize the first stochastic dominance and independence rules for a wide range of models of choice under uncertainty.

In essence, a stochastic dominance rule gives conditions under which a random variable taking values in an ordered set is preferred to another by all 'order preserving' evaluation functions within a given class. The idea is that, under an appropriate rearrangement of the states of the world, the first random variable yields a preferred outcome in every state. The definition of an appropriate set of rearrangements is central to the nature of a theory of choice under uncertainty.

Independence axioms take this process one stage further. Although these rules have been formulated in a number of ways, it is the 'sure thing' formulation, due to Savage (1954), which brings out most clearly their kinship with stochastic dominance rules. In this formulation, independence rules state that one random variable must be preferred to another if the states of the world may be appropriately rearranged and grouped so that the first random variable yields a

[28] The term 'appropriate' is being used in a somewhat ambiguous way, reflecting the long debate between advocates of prescriptive and descriptive approaches to the theory of choice under uncertainty. In a prescriptive model, the term 'appropriate' reflects what the theorist thinks people should do. In a descriptive model it reflects (an abstraction of) what the theorist thinks people actually do.

preferred lottery for every group of states. If each group consists of a single state, this is just the same as a stochastic dominance rule.

Throughout this discussion, rules are referred to in the plural rather than to 'the' independence axiom and 'the' dominance axiom. This is because the various models of choice under uncertainty generate different stochastic dominance and independence rules. Indeed, the type of dominance and independence rules that are imposed characterize these models fairly precisely. The differences between these models are derived largely from different assumptions about the appropriate ways in which states of the world can be rearranged, grouped and compared. To focus attention on these issues, the discussion will be kept at a relatively simple level with attention being confined to the case of discrete probability distributions, and continuity and convergence arguments presented in a non–rigorous fashion.

13.1 Notation

For ease of exposition, it will be assumed that Ω is a finite set consisting of n mutually exclusive and exhaustive states. (This assumption is imposed purely for convenience, and to make the ideas presented here more intuitively appealing. There is no difficulty, in any of the models under discussion, in extending the analysis to state spaces and the associated σ–fields). The objective in partitioning Ω into a finite set of states is to choose the partition in such a way that the states may be regarded as subjectively equiprobable. To give substance to this notion, extensive use will be made of the concept of permutations. A permutation of Ω is defined as a bijective (one–one and onto) mapping ρ: $\Omega \rightarrow \Omega$.

As usual, a prospect is defined as a mapping from Ω to X. Given the assumption that Ω consists of n states, any prospect y may be represented as a vector $(x_1, x_2 \ \dots \ x_n)$. The outcome space $\mathcal{Y}$ is thus isomorphic to X^n. Since a prospect is interpreted as a mapping from Ω to X, it may be composed with a mapping of Ω onto itself, that is, a permutation. Given a prospect y, the transformed prospect $y^\circ\rho$ yields outcome x_i in state $j = \rho^{-1}(\mathrm{i})$.

To go any further than this it is necessary to introduce notions of equivalence between states. The simplest approach is to assume known objective probabilities. Then it is natural to employ the equiprobability condition $p_i = 1/n$, $i = 1 \dots n$. In the absence of given objective probabilities, the following notion of equivalence normally proves adequate. The states $1 \dots n$ are defined as equivalent if, for any y and any permutation ρ, $\mathrm{CE}(y) = \mathrm{CE}(y\ {}^\circ\rho)$. It is straight-forward to show, that for models with given probabilities, and a sufficiently rich set of outcomes to guarantee the existence of certainty equivalents for every prospect, this condition is equivalent to the requirement of equiprobability.

The main class of models to which this definition is not applicable are state–dependent utility theories (see eg Karni 1983). It may be useful to discuss this a little further. Suppose it is assumed that there are known objective probabilities. Then a state–dependent EU theory involves a different utility function for each state. This presumably implies that there is some aspect of the state i that is not captured in the value of x_i. For example, x_i might be an indicator of wealth, and the various states might correspond to different levels of general economic prosperity. If relative wealth effects, such as those associated with 'positional goods', are important, the same level of wealth may correspond to different levels of utility in different states. More importantly, the shape of the utility function may be different in different states.

If on the other hand, an attempt is made to define a notion of equiprobability using permutations, two possibilities arise. First, y may not be a complete indicator of welfare, as in the case of positional goods. In this case, there will not, in general, exist a partition of Ω into n equiprobable states. Alternatively y may be completely specified, but may include elements that are strictly state–specific. In this case the idea of composing a prospect with a permutation becomes a contradiction in terms.

13.2 Dominance Rules

For the sake of completeness, it is useful to begin with a notion of 'zero order dominance.'

Rule 0. Let $x^0, x^1 \in X$. Then if $x^0 \geq x^1$, $\delta_{x^0} \succcurlyeq \delta_{x^1}$.

This is just a restatement of preferences over X, and is not even a non–satiation principle, since there is nothing to prevent the existence of a bliss point in X. However, the zero order dominance rule is sufficient to motivate the notion of certainty equivalence. Let y be an arbitrary prospect. Define

$$\mathrm{CE}_1(y) = \inf \{x \in X, y \sim \delta_x\}$$
$$\mathrm{CE}_2(y) = \sup \{x \in X, y \sim \delta_x\}.$$

An individual has well defined certainty equivalents if, for any y, $\mathrm{CE}_1(y) = \mathrm{CE}_2(y)$. In this case, the certainty equivalent will be denoted $\mathrm{CE}(y)$. It is straightforward to show that each of the models presented above yields well defined certainty equivalents, provided X is sufficiently rich. It is natural to suggest the hypothesis that $y^0 \succcurlyeq y^1$ if and only if $\mathrm{CE}(y^0) \geq \mathrm{CE}(y^1)$. This is true for each of the models that assigns a single value to each prospect, but not for those (regret theory and SSB) based on pairwise comparisons between prospects.

The concept of first order stochastic dominance relies only on pairwise comparisons between states. The idea is to match states so that one prospect leaves the individual better off in every state than in the corresponding state under the other prospect. The simplest interpretation of this idea is

Rule 1.A: Let $x_i^0 \geq x_i^1 \; \forall \; i$. Then $y^0 \succcurlyeq y^1$.

Under Rule 1.A, the individual is better off in every state of the world. This is a true sure thing principle. It guarantees that the individual is better off with probability 1.

Rule 1.A has nearly universal acceptance both as a normative rule and as a descriptive statement about behavior. It has, however, been criticized by Pope (1990) and Grant (1991). Pope offers examples of behavior (eg mountaineering) where danger *per se* is claimed to add to the enjoyment of the activity. Related to this is the normative claim that a prospect dominated under Rule 1.A might rationally be chosen in order to enjoy the relief which arises when low probability bad outcomes do not occur. Grant considers the case of multi-dimensional outcome spaces and argues that decision-makers might be averse to risk over outcome bundles, even though the bundles themselves were indifferent. This would imply violation of the monotonicity required by Rule 1.A.

Rule 1.A is the natural stochastic dominance concept for state-dependent utility.

PROPOSITION 13.1: *The following conditions are equivalent*

(i) $x_i^0 \geq x_i^1 \; \forall \, i$; *and*

(ii) *For every state–dependent utility function V that is order preserving in X,* $V(y^0) \geq V(y^1)$.

Proof: Trivial. ■

Rule 1.A and the state–dependent utility theories do not admit any rearrangement of the states. At the other extreme, EU theory permits a direct comparison between any two equiprobable states. There are a number of interesting intermediate stages. Suppose that the outcomes in prospect y^1 are rearranged by a permutation ρ such that $\rho(i) = j$ and $\rho(j) = i$, in such a way that each pair *i, j* satisfies

$$x_j^1 < x_i^0, \; x_i^1 < x_j^0. \tag{13.1}$$

Then comparing y^0 with the permuted prospect $y^1 \circ \rho$, it is apparent that y^0 is a 'sure thing', yielding a better outcome in every state of the world. This may be stated more formally as

Rule 1.B *Suppose there exists a permutation* ρ *such that*

(a) $\rho^{-1} = \rho$

(b) $x_i^0 \geq x_{\rho(i)}^1 \; \forall \, i.$

Then $y^0 \succcurlyeq y^1$.

Quiggin (1989a) shows that this rule precisely characterizes the stochastic dominance properties of regret theory (Loomes and Sugden 1982). In regret theory, preferences are determined by a *regret–rejoice function* Ψ that expresses the expected regret (or rejoicing) from receiving an outcome x, given that, had an alternative choice been made, a better (worse) outcome x′ would have been received. The idea of the stochastic dominance rule for regret theory is that any regret associated with a state *i* where the dominating prospect has a lower outcome is more than offset by the rejoicing associated with the state *ρ(i)*. For this reason, if y^0 and y^1 satisfy the conditions of Rule 1.B, y^0 will be said to regret–dominate y^1.

PROPOSITION 13.2: *Given two prospects* y^0 *and* y^1, *the following conditions are equivalent:*

(i) For any order preserving regret–rejoice function Ψ, $E[\Psi(x_i^0, x_i^1)] \geq 0$,

(ii) Let $\{[a_r, b_r] : r = 1 \ldots s\}$ *be any collection of intervals in W. Then the number of states i such that*

(a) $\exists \, r, \; x_i^0 \leq a_r < b_r \leq x_i^1$

is less than or equal to the number of states j such that

(b) $\exists \, r, \; x_j^1 \leq a_r < b_r \leq x_j^0$

(iii) y^0 *regret–dominates* y^1.

Proof: Quiggin (1989a). ■

Although regret theory permits some comparisons between outcomes in different states of the world to enter into stochastic dominance rules, its essential rationale is concern with the difference between the observed outcome and what might have been obtained with a different decision *for a given state of the world.* An alternative approach is to ignore the information as to which state of the world occurs and consider a prospect as a collection of outcomes with associated probabilities (in the special case considered here, n outcomes with probability $1/n$). It may then be asked, in comparing two or more prospects, what is the natural arrangement of the outcomes. An obvious answer is that the best outcome under y^0 should be compared with the best outcome under y^1 and similarly for the worst outcome. This approach is adopted, for example, by maximin and maximax rules. However, rules of this kind give exclusive attention to one or two outcomes, whereas it would seem more reasonable to give some weight to all outcomes. This may be done by rearranging the states in each prospect in order of desirability.

Rule 1.C *Suppose there exist permutations* ρ_0, ρ_1 *such that*

(a) $i \geq j \Rightarrow x_{\rho_0(i)}{}^0 \geq x_{\rho_0(j)}{}^0$, $x_{\rho_1(i)}{}^1 \geq x_{\rho_1(j)}{}^1 \; \forall \; i, \; j$

(b) $x_{\rho_0(i)}{}^0 \geq x_{\rho_1(i)}{}^1 \; \forall \; i.$

Then $y^0 \succcurlyeq y^1$.

If rearrangement in order is permitted, preferences can be expressed in terms of the cumulative probability distribution. It is straightforward to observe that Rule 1.C is equivalent to the usual definition of first stochastic dominance, presented by Quirk and Saposnik (1962). Rule 1.C is, therefore, equivalent to the requirement that $V(y^0) \geq V(y^1)$ for all order preserving EU functionals V. Similar results have been proved to apply for Machina's Generalized EU model (Machina 1982) and for RDEU theory (Quiggin 1982a), and can easily be extended to the RLU model.

As far as stochastic dominance is concerned, the rearrangement of states in order of desirability is the natural choice and there is no need to go any further. However, much analysis is undertaken on the assumption that any two equiprobable states may be compared, and this becomes very important in the analysis of independence rules. Hence it is useful to define:

Rule 1.D *Suppose there exist arbitrary permutations* ρ_0, ρ_1 *such that*

(a) $x_{\rho_0(i)}{}^0 \geq x_{\rho_0(i)}{}^0 \; \forall \; i.$

Then $y^0 \succcurlyeq y^1$.

Although rules 1.C and 1.D are equivalent in terms of their implications for stochastic dominance the intuition behind them is rather different. Rule 1.D is very much in line with the spirit behind the development of EU theory, which takes probabilities for granted. By contrast, rule 1.C is closer to the idea of statewise dominance. The difference is that in state–dependent utility theories, outcomes are compared on the basis of the state that gives rise to them, under rule 1.C they are compared on the basis of their ranking in the set of possible outcomes under a given prospect. Rule 1.C has a natural affinity with the RDEU and RLU models. This affinity will be developed further in the context of independence rules.

As has been shown above, different conditions on permissible comparisons between states imply different dominance conditions. It is useful to examine the relationships between these conditions. It is easy to show that statewise dominance implies regret dominance but not the reverse (for the latter result, consider the case when $n = 2$ and $x_2^1 < x_1^0 < x_1^1 < x_2^0$). Similarly, it may be shown that regret dominance implies first stochastic dominance, but not the reverse.

There are, however, conditions under which two or more of these conditions are equivalent. One of the most useful conditions is that of comonotonicity. If prospects are comonotonic, statewise dominance is equivalent to first stochastic dominance, and hence both are equivalent to regret dominance. Conditions under which regret dominance is equivalent to first stochastic dominance are given by Quiggin (1989a).

13.3 Independence

The EU independence rule has been one of the main targets for critics of the EU model. Many of the alternatives to and generalizations of EU theory have been based on modified independence rules. Machina (1982) cut the Gordian knot by dispensing with independence rules altogether.

Assumptions as to the appropriate comparisons to be made between states are crucial in determining the intuitive appeal of independence rules just as they are in the case of dominance rules. This parallel may be taken further. Stochastic dominance rules derive preferences in choices between risky prospects from preferences over the set of possible outcomes. Independence rules take the process a stage further, deriving preferences over particular pairs of prospects from known preferences over other pairs. Their 'sure thing' interpretation may be derived from their close relationship to stochastic dominance rules. The difference is that whereas stochastic dominance rules require comparisons between states, independence rules require comparisons between groups of states.

A number of different stochastic dominance rules have been advanced in this chapter. Each of them may be extended to generate an independence rule. Each of the rules 1.A to 1.D is based on a notion of appropriate permutations of the state space. Under rule 1.A, the only appropriate permutation is the identity mapping. Rule 1.B is specific to a comparison between two prospects, one of which may be composed with a transformation ρ such that $\rho = \rho^{-1}$. Under Rule 1.C, there is a single appropriate permutation for each prospect, namely that which results in the outcomes $x_1 \dots x_n$ being in order of preference. Under Rule 1.D any permutation is appropriate.

Now consider the following formulation for an independence rule.

Rule 2.A Let $y^1, y^2, y^3, y^4 \in \mathcal{Y}$ and let $\rho_1, \rho_2, \rho_3, \rho_4$ be appropriate permutations. Suppose

(i) $y^1 \succcurlyeq y^2$;

(ii) for $j \in S$, $y^1 \circ \rho_1 = y^3 \circ \rho_3$ and $y^2 \circ \rho_2 = y^4 \circ \rho_4$; and

(iii) for $j \notin S$, $y^3 \circ \rho_3 = y^4 \circ \rho_4$ and $y^1 \circ \rho_1 = y^2 \circ \rho_2$

Then $y^3 \succcurlyeq y^4$.

The implications of this rule depend on the interpretation of the term 'appropriate permutations.' Each of the interpretations given in Rules 1.A, 1.C and 1.D corresponds to one or more of the models of choice under uncertainty presented above.

PROPOSITION 13.3.

(a) *All state–dependent utility functionals and regret–theoretic functionals satisfy Rule* 2.A *with the only appropriate permutations being the identity mapping.*

(b) *All RLU functionals (including RDEU functionals) satisfy Rule* 2.A *with the appropriate permutations defined as in Rule* 1.C(a)

(d) *All EU functionals satisfy Rule* 2.A *with all permutations defined as appropriate, as in Rule* 1.D

Proof: Since all the proofs are similar, only the proof for the case of the state–dependent utility model will be given in detail

Since the only permissible permutations are those given by the identity mapping, conditions (i) – (iv) apply to y^1, y^2, y^3, y^4 themselves.

$$
\begin{aligned}
V(y^1) - V(y^2) &= \sum_{i=1}^{n} p_i\, U_i(x_i^1) - \sum_{i=1}^{n} p_i\, U_i(x_i^2) \\
&= \sum_{i \in S} p_i\, (U_i(x_i^1) - U_i(x_i^2)) \\
&= \sum_{i \in S} p_i\, (U_i(x_i^3) - U_i(x_i^4)) \\
&= V(y^3) - V(y^4)
\end{aligned}
$$

The proof for the regret–theoretic and EU cases is similar. For the RLU case, it is only necessary to observe in equation (10) that, under appropriate transformations, the rank $r(j,\ y^{i\circ}p_i)$ is equal to j for all j, i . The proof then follows the lines above. ■

13.4 Independence in RDEU

From the discussion in Chapter 10, the extension from RLU to RDEU requires an additivity condition such as the projection consistency axiom of Segal or the trade-off consistency requirement of Wakker. Quiggin (1989b) proposed a condition based on the notion of RDEU-equivalent segments. In essence, intervals (p_1, p_2) and (p_3, p_4) are RDEU-equivalent if and only if $q(p_1) - q(p_2) = q(p_3) - q(p_4)$. Chew and Epstein (1989) propose a related condition, which they refer to as multiplicative separability.

The idea of RDEU-equivalent segments may be developed as follows. As has been shown above, the class of RLU models corresponds to a permutation of the (equiprobable) states so that they are ranked in order of outcomes. Because RDEU theory is based on probability weights, it implies the existence of a separate equivalence concept on the ordered set of states. Roughly, two states i and j (or sets of states S_1, S_2) are equivalent if they have the same weight; that is $q(r(i,\ \mathbf{x})) = q(r(j,\ \mathbf{x}))$ or, more generally,

$$\sum_{i \in S_1} q(r(i, \mathbf{x})) = \sum_{i \in S_2} q(r(i, \mathbf{x})) \tag{13.2}$$

For convenience, attention will be confined to sets of states which are contiguous after the application of the ranking permutation. For convenience, from this point on in the analysis of the RDEU case, prospects will be assumed to be comonotonic and states numbered in order of desirability. Thus the set $\{i., \ldots i+k\}$ corresponds to the section of the cumulative distribution function ranging from the point where $F(x) = (i\text{-}1)/N$ to the point where $F(x) = (i+k)/N$. Since N and k may be chosen arbitrarily large, the probability associated with this segment may take any rational value between 0 and 1, and may approximate any real value arbitrarily closely.

Assume that preferences can be characterized by an RLU model, and consider a partition of the set of states into segments $S_1, S_2 \ldots S_m$ (assumed to be disjoint and ordered by outcome rank). Then Proposition 13.3 indicates that, if prospects differ only on segments $S_{i_1}, S_{i_2}, \ldots S_{i_k}$, their ranking will be determined only by the values they take on those segments. Now consider the set of vectors $\{(x_1, \ldots x_k): x_1 \leq x_2 \ldots x_k\}$. For any given group of segments $S_{i_1}, S_{i_2}, \ldots S_{i_k}$, this set inherits an ordering from the preference ranking on X^N, namely that associated with all those prospects that differ only on $S_{i_1}, S_{i_2}, \ldots S_{i_k}$ and take the value x_j on segment S_{ij}.

Two segments S_a, S_b with $a \leq b$ will be defined as RDEU-equivalent if, for any c such that $a \leq b \leq c$ or $c \leq a \leq b$, the ordering induced by S_a and S_c on the set $\{(x_1, x_2): x_1 \leq x_2\}$ is the same as the ordering induced by S_b and S_c. Given RDEU preferences, two segments are RDEU-equivalent if and only if they have the same weight.

We may now define the following independence rule

Rule 2.*C* Let S_a, S_b, S_c, S_d be RDEU-equivalent segments and let $\mathbf{x}^1, \mathbf{x}^2, \mathbf{x}^3, \mathbf{x}^4 \in X^N$ such that:

(i) $\mathbf{x}^1 = \mathbf{x}^2$ except on S_a, S_b

(ii) $\mathbf{x}^1$ and $\mathbf{x}^2$ are both constant on S_a and on S_b

(iii) $\mathbf{x}^1 \succcurlyeq \mathbf{x}^2$.

(iv) The values of $\mathbf{x}^1$ on S_a and $\mathbf{x}^3$ on S_c and of $\mathbf{x}^1$ on S_b and $\mathbf{x}^3$ on S_d are the same and similarly for $\mathbf{x}^2$ and $\mathbf{x}^4$

(v) Except on S_c, S_d, $\mathbf{x}^3 = \mathbf{x}^4$

Then $\mathbf{x}^3 \succcurlyeq \mathbf{x}^4$.

The proof of Proposition 13.3 may be used to show that all RDEU functionals satisfy Rule 2.C. It may be noted that in more general models, there can be no presumption that there exist any pairs of distinct segments which are RDEU-equivalent. Indeed, as will be shown below, the existence of a sufficiently rich set of RDEU-equivalent segments is a defining characteristic of RDEU theory.

The principal remaining task is to show that these independence properties give an exact characterization of the corresponding models. To do this in full would be equivalent to the provision of an axiomatic derivation of each of the models. As this task has already been undertaken for each of the models analyzed above, it will not be duplicated here. An alternative procedure will be sketched in outline. The EU model is a special case of RDEU which is in turn a special case of RLU. Given slight adjustments to Machina's smoothness assumptions and the associated definitions of convergence, RLU may be regarded as a special case of the generalized EU model. It will be shown that any generalized EU functional satisfying the relevant independence rule must be an RLU model, and so on.

Define the space Ω^* as the image of Ω under the class of permutations described in Rule 1.*C*(a). That is, Ω^* is the subspace of $\Omega \approx \Re^N$ satisfying the condition $x_1 \leq x_2 \ldots \leq x_N$, $\forall$ $\mathbf{x} \in \Omega^*$. Let V^* be a mapping from Ω^* to $\Re$ such that $V(x_1, x_2, \ldots x_N)$ is increasing and continuously differentiable in each of its arguments (note that this condition is weaker than the smoothness condition imposed by Machina.). Then V^* represents a preference ordering on Ω^*. It is useful to consider the marginal rate of substitution between states *i* and *j*, which is given by $(\partial V^*/\partial x_i)/(\partial V^*/\partial x_j)$. For the RLU functional, this will be given by $(\partial U_i/\partial x_i)/(\partial U_j/\partial x_j)$ and will depend only on x_i and x_j. The converse is also true. If the marginal rate of substitution between states *i* and *j* depends only on x_i and x_j, then preferences may be represented by an RLU functional. If the preferences represented by V^* satisfy the natural version of the independence condition 2.A, then :

PROPOSITION 13.4: *Let V^* be as above. Suppose that an individual's preferences can be represented by V^* and that preferences satisfy Rule 2.A with the appropriate set of permutations being those having images in Ω^*. Then V^* is a monotonic transformation of an RLU functional.*

Proof: It is sufficient to show for any *i, j* that $(\partial V^*/\partial x_i) / (\partial V^*/\partial x_j)$ is independent of x_k, $k \neq j$, *i*. Suppose this condition is not satisfied for some pair of values of $\boldsymbol{x}$, say $\boldsymbol{x}^1$ and $\boldsymbol{x}^3$. Suppose without loss of generality that $\partial V^*/\partial x_i \,/\, \partial V^*/\partial x_j$ is greater at $\boldsymbol{x}^1$ than at $\boldsymbol{x}^3$ and that $\boldsymbol{x}^1$ and $\boldsymbol{x}^3$ are in the interior of Ω^* i.e. they satisfy the condition $x_1 < x_2 \ldots < x_N$. Then there must exist δ_i , δ_j and $\boldsymbol{x}^2$, $\boldsymbol{x}^4$ such that

$$\text{(i) } x_k^1 - x_k^2 = x_k^3 - x_k^4 = \begin{cases} \delta_i & k=i \\ -\delta_j & k=j \\ 0 & \text{otherwise} \end{cases}$$

(ii) $\boldsymbol{x}^1 \succcurlyeq \boldsymbol{x}^2$, $\boldsymbol{x}^4 \succcurlyeq \boldsymbol{x}^3$.

But this contradicts Rule 2.A. ■

Thus, the RLU functionals are precisely characterized by the independence Rule 2.A with the class of permutations being those with images in Ω^*. The next stage is to consider the conditions under which an RLU functional will be an RDEU functional. All that is required is that the set of RDEU-equivalent segments should be sufficiently rich. In particular, suppose that there exists a partition of the set of states into segments S_1, S_2 ... S_m (disjoint and ordered by rank) such that the S_i are RDEU-equivalent. Now consider the subspace X^M consisting of prospects taking a fixed value on each S_i. For any functional V on X^N there exists a natural restriction V^* on X^M.

PROPOSITION 13.5: *Let S_1, S_2 ... S_m be a partition of the set of states into RDEU-equivalent segments and let V, V^* be defined as above. Then if V is an RLU functional, V^* is equivalent to an RDEU functional.*

Proof: We may define

$$V^* = \sum_{i=1}^{m} U_i(x_i)$$

It is necessary to show that for each i, j, x

$$U_i'(x) = U_j'(x) \ \forall \ x$$

Assume without loss of generality $m = 3$. For given x_1^0, x_2^0, x_3^0 there exists a set of pairs (x_a, x_b) such that

$$V^*(x_1^0, x_a, x_b) = V^*(x_1^0, x_2^0, x_3^0). \tag{13.3}$$

By the definition of RDEU-equivalence and the independence property 2.A, it is also true that for any x_a, x_b satisfying (13.3),

$$V^*(x_a, x_2^0, x_b) = V^*(x_1^0, x_2^0, x_3^0).$$

But this is only possible if $(\partial V^*/\partial x_1)/(\partial V^*/\partial x_3) = (\partial V^*/\partial x_2)/(\partial V^*/\partial x_3) \ \forall \ x_1, \ x_2, x_3$. That is, $U_1'(x) = U_2'(x) \ \forall \ x$, as required. ■

13.5 Betweenness Rules

The notion of betweenness, discussed in Chapter 9, may be represented as a weakening of the independence rules discussed in the previous section. The critical modification is that substitutions are permitted only between indifferent prospects

Rule 3.A Let y^1, y^2, y^3, $y^4 \in \mathcal{Y}$ and let ρ_1, ρ_2, ρ_3, ρ_4 be appropriate permutatations. Suppose

(i) $y^1 \circ \rho_1 = y^2 \circ \rho_2$ except on a set of states S;
(ii) $y^1 \sim y^2 \sim y^3$;
(iii) for $j \in S$, $y^1 \circ \rho_1 = y^3 \circ \rho_3$ and $y^2 \circ \rho_2 = y^4 \circ \rho_4$; and
(iv) for $j \notin S$, $y^3 \circ \rho_3 = y^4 \circ \rho_4$.

Then $y^3 \sim y^4$.

Dekel (1986) shows that the class of preference functionals satisfying betweenness may be represented implicitly by the requirement that the certainty equivalent $c = \text{CE}(y)$ is given by the unique implicit solution to the equation

$$\sum_{i=1}^{n} p_i \tau(x_i, c) = 0. \qquad (13.2)$$

An important special case is the weighted utility model of Chew (1983), which arises when

$$\tau(x, c) = w(x)(v(x) - v(y)),$$

permitting the explicit representation

$$V(y) = \sum_{i=1}^{n} p_i\, w(x_i)v(x_i) \Big/ \sum_{j=1}^{n} p_j\, w(x_j).$$

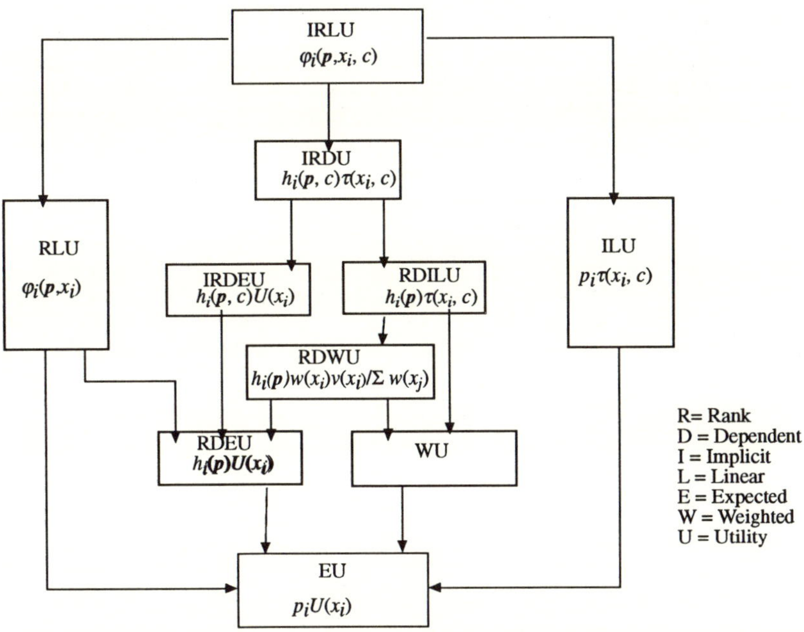

Figure 13.1: A taxonomy of generalized models
(after Chew and Epstein 1989)

Any preferences that may be represented by a functional of the form (13.2) satisfy Rule 3.A with arbitrary permutations permitted. Chew and Epstein (1989) show that, in combination with the usual axioms (EU.1-4) Rule 3.A is sufficient for the existence of a representation of this kind, which they refer to as implicit linear utility (ILU). They go further to consider a general class of implicit rank-linear utility (IRLU) functionals incorporating both ILU and RLU. These are simply the functionals satisfying Rule 3.A with the appropriate permutations defined as in Rule 1.C(a).

Using multiplicative separability and related requirements, Chew and Epstein define a wide range of intermediate functional forms resulting in the taxonomy illustrated in Figure 13.1, and examine their implications for preferences in Machina's triangle diagram.

Concluding Comments

The notion of 'appropriate' rearrangements and combinations of states is a powerful tool in understanding the relationships between alternative theories of choice under uncertainty, and their stochastic dominance properties. 'Sure thing' arguments with the same formal structure yield stochastic dominance rules characteristic of a range of alternative models when they are combined with the corresponding assumptions about appropriate rearrangements of the set of states of the world. Savage's 'sure thing' principle may be seen as a similar argument with the same formal structure, applied to pairwise combinations of states instead of individual states. Once again, the independence properties of a range of models may be derived by applying such arguments in combination with assumptions about appropriate permutations and combinations of states. A promising area for future research is the examination of higher degrees of stochastic dominance and more general consideration of the conditions under which one distribution may be regarded as 'more risky' than another.

CHAPTER 14

Extensions

Although the previous chapters have covered a wide range of topics, the discussion has been confined to the theory of choice under uncertainty. The object of this chapter is to give a brief indication of the ways in which the ideas developed above, and particularly the rank-dependent model, may be extended to a range of contexts beyond the theory of choice under uncertainty with known probabilities.

The first class of extensions may be obtained by exploiting the formal similarities between random probability distributions, income distributions, and distributions of income and consumption over time. These similarities lead to analogies between the problems of choice under uncertainty, constitutional design, optimal taxation and intertemporal optimization.

The final section deals with issues arising from the psychological literature on framing and coding of decision problems. It is argued that the techniques used to analyze the RDEU model may be applied to problems of coding and framing.

None of these topics is treated in depth. Nevertheless the discussion is sufficient to indicate that there is significant potential for extending many of the results obtained above for the theory of uncertainty to other fields of interest in economics. There are also some useful insights into the theory of choice under uncertainty to be obtained by considering these alternative interpretations.

14.1 Social Welfare Functions

There is a natural relationship between models of individual choice under uncertainty and models of social choice. A random variable allocating outcomes to potential states of the world has the same formal properties as a constitution allocating outcomes to people in different social positions, and a preference functional over probability distributions has the same formal properties as a social welfare functional over income distributions.

This in turn implies a natural relationship between expected utility theory as a model for choice under uncertainty and utilitarianism as a social choice rule. If evaluations of social welfare are expressed as preference functionals over cumulative wealth distributions, the additive case of classical utilitarianism has the same formal properties as does expected utility theory.

Machina (1982) was the first to draw the link between generalized theories of choice under uncertainty and modifications of classical utilitarianism. After developing his model of generalized smooth preferences over cumulative probability distributions, he observed that there is an analogous extension to arbitrary smooth social welfare functionals, each of which is locally utilitarian.

The same link was not initially made in the literature on rank-dependent models, where developments in the theory of choice under uncertainty and the theory of social choice proceeded independently for a number of years. At the same time as the RDEU functional was first proposed by Quiggin (1981, 1982a) as a theory of choice under uncertainty, a similar model with a linear utility function was advanced by Weymark (1981) as a generalization of the Gini measure of income inequality. The relationship between concepts of income inequality and concepts of choice under uncertainty was discussed by Chew (1983, 1989) and the presentation here draws on his work.

Consider a social welfare functional $V(x_1, \ldots x_n)$. This income distribution may be treated like a random variable over n equiprobable states. The representative income is defined as the level of income x^* which, if received by all members of society, would give rise to the same level of social welfare as the existing income distribution. The representative income plays the same rôle in the theory of income distribution as a certainty equivalent in the theory of choice under uncertainty. Indexes of income inequality (Kolm 1969, Atkinson 1970) are defined by taking the difference between, or the ratio of, the representative income and the arithmetic mean income. These indexes are analogous to absolute and relative risk premiums under uncertainty.

Rank dependent functionals provide a class of representative incomes which include as a special case the Gini mean, obtained by taking a linear U and letting $q(p) = 1 - (1-p)^2$. The well known Gini coefficient is equal to one minus the ratio of the Gini mean to the arithmetic mean. It attains the minimum value, zero, in the case where income is distributed equally.

A central requirement in the theory of income distribution is the *principle of transfer* (Dalton, 1920) which states that transferring a small amount from a richer to a poorer individual should increase (or at least, not reduce) the representative income. It is easily seen that this principle is related to the Rothschild-Stiglitz definition of a simple mean preserving spread (one satisfying the single crossing property). Indeed, any simple mean preserving spread may be built up from a series of transfers from worse to better states. A large literature, centered on the concept of Schur concavity, developed to analyze the conditions under which the principle of transfer would apply (see Marshall and Olkin 1979 for a summary). Many of the results of the literature on second stochastic dominance and increasing risk were developed independently (and earlier) in the literature on income distribution.

It follows from the relationship between the transfer principle and the concept of simple mean preserving spreads that a rank-dependent social welfare functional will satisfy the transfer principle if and only if the corresponding functional on random variables preserves second stochastic dominance, that is, if and only if U and q are both concave.

There are many other results which may usefully be transferred from the rank-dependent model of choice under uncertainty to the theory of income distribution. Most notably, the economic control problem analyzed in Chapters 3 and 7 may be modified to yield results in the theory of optimal taxation and income redistribution. Writing the control problem once again as

$$\mathrm{Max}_{\alpha} E[V(\phi(\theta, \alpha, W_0))],$$

let W_0 denote the level of per capita GDP in the absence of redistribution, α the level of some costly redistributive activity and θ the distribution of pre-tax income. With a slight modification of the arguments given in Chapters 3 and 7, it is possible to obtain the following results for the case when U satisfies DARA and $q(p) \geq p \ \forall \ p$.

- A fixed increase (reduction) in pre-tax income for all members of society leads to a reduction (increase) in the optimal level of redistribution.
- A monotone spread (contraction) in the distribution of pre-tax income leads to an increase (reduction) in the optimal level of redistribution.
- An increase (reduction) in the deadweight cost of redistribution leads to a reduction (increase) in the optimal level of redistribution.

It seems likely that a number of other results in the theory of uncertainty would have interesting implications in terms of income distribution, and conversely that results in the theory of optimal taxation might usefully be transferred to the theory of choice under uncertainty.

It is also of interest to consider the implications of replacing the requirement that q be concave with the weaker requirement that $q(p) \geq p \ \forall \ p$. The weaker condition is not sufficient for the transfer principle to hold. This is reasonable if income is not an exact measure of welfare. It may be, for example, that some low income earners, such as teenagers, are actually better off than some people earning higher incomes. The requirement that $q(p) \geq p \ \forall \ p$ admits this possibility. The condition may be interpreted as saying that for any level of income, a uniform transfer from everyone above the cut-off to everyone below the cut-off will make society better off. As shown above, a number of results in the theory of income distribution follow from this weak condition.

14.2 Constitutional Choice

In the previous section, the formal similarity between social choice and choice under uncertainty was considered as a method for extending analytical results from one field to the other. A number of writers have gone beyond this formal similarity to derive prescriptions for social choice from normative ideas about choice under uncertainty. This idea is most popular in relation to issues of constitutional choice and is best exemplified by the work of Rawls (1971).

The contractarian approach advocated by Rawls is based on the following thought experiment. Imagine a group of people who understand what a human society is, but do not know what position they will occupy in society. That is, they do not know whether they will be rich or poor, male or female, or any other such characteristics. A group of people in such circumstances are referred to as being in the *original position.* Rawls argued that, if people in the original position were asked to choose rules for society, the rules which they would choose would be the fair rules. This is because under these conditions people would have no incentive to choose rules which favor any particular group in society.

Rawls argued for a maximin choice rule under uncertainty and hence derives as a central rule of fairness the *difference principle*, that any change should be such as to improve the position of the worst off members of society. However, a similar style of argument combined with a different normative theory of choice under uncertainty leads to quite different conclusions.

Harsanyi (1953, 1955) argued that utilitarianism could be justified provided that people in the original position satisfy the von Neumann–Morgenstern axioms. It is assumed that every person could occupy any position in society with equal (known) probability. Then people will choose rules which will maximize their expected utility. This implies maximizing the sum total of utilities across society. This analysis has the implication that if individuals become more (less) risk averse they will choose a society with less (more) inequality.

The use of the original position to justify utilitarianism is helped by assuming that the decision is made under conditions of risk rather than uncertainty. Rawls justified his critique of utilitarianism by postulating ambiguity rather than risk in the original position. People do not know the probability with which they will occupy any given position in society, nor do they know what their risk attitudes will be.[29] With this description, the original position is not unlike the conditions postulated by models of choice under ambiguity. In general, this literature has justified procedures, like Rawls' difference principle, which place special emphasis on the worst outcome.

The distinction between Rawls' difference principle and utilitarianism turns partly on whether the decision in the original position should be made under conditions of risk, or of ambiguity. However, even under ambiguity the maximin criterion is unsatisfactory. As has been suggested by Ebert (1988), the rank-dependent/non-additive probability approach could be adapted to provide a range of criteria including EU and the Rawls criterion as special cases.

The separability between decision weights and utilities is central to this argument. One of the fundamental issues in Rawls' (1970) critique of utilitarianism is that the aggregation process involved 'does not take individuals seriously'. Because Machina's approach to social welfare functionals, based on a non-separable choice functional, necessarily refers to preferences in terms of the entire income distribution, it seems open to Rawls' charge that it does not 'take individuals seriously.'

A central problem with the whole framework is now raised by the fact that in both Rawls' and Harsanyi's arguments egalitarianism is derived from some form of risk aversion. Yet the rank-dependent model is quite consistent with some degree of risk preference. A direct analogy from choice under uncertainty would suggest that extreme outcomes at both ends of the scale tend to be overweighted. Use of the rank-dependent model would place a high weight on the welfare of the worst-off groups, but also on that of the best-off groups.

The possibility that choice under uncertainty would imply overweighting of extreme outcomes at both ends of the scale raises difficulties for Rawls' contractarian approach. One possibility is to accept the implications of the model and support policies which benefit the very well off as well as the very poor. The anti-egalitarian implications of this approach would be softened, but not necessarily eliminated, by the effects of decreasing marginal utility of wealth. Given a weighting function q displaying sufficiently strong overweighting of extreme outcomes, and a moderately concave utility function U, the very poor would have a higher weight than the very well off, but both would have a higher weight than middle income groups.

This approach has some plausibility. It certainly appears that some people are quite favorably disposed to the existence of very wealthy people, especially those who may be regarded, literally or metaphorically, as winners in a lottery (for example, people who succeed in notably risky professions such as acting). Arguments of this kind have been put forward by Hayek (1960) among others.

It is unlikely, however, that Rawls, or egalitarians generally, would want to follow this approach. The rank-dependent model yields the alternative interpretation that risk attitudes associated with probability weighting are separable from the marginal utility of wealth, and unrelated to the question of weights to be placed on individuals in income distributions. Thus,

[29] It might be suggested that the requirement that individuals do not know their own risk attitudes permits Rawls to impose his risk attitudes on them.

there is no reason why the weighting function which would be adopted in choosing between risky prospects should be the same one which would be used in social choice. However, this argument leaves unresolved the question of how such a social choice weighting function might be arrived at.

A final option would be to fall back on classical utilitarianism and accept a defence of egalitarianism arising solely from declining marginal utility of wealth. If social choice is considered as being made in a current real world situation, rather than an *ex ante* constitutional framework, then utilitarianism in social choice is compatible with non-expected utility preferences under risk and uncertainty.

14.3 Choice over Time

As with social choice, choice over time has obvious formal similarities with choice under uncertainty. Any analysis of the problem of choice under uncertainty may be reinterpreted as an analysis of intertemporal choice, with states of the world interpreted as time periods and random variables interpreted as consumption streams. It follows that results on preferences over random variables, for example those derived from stochastic dominance analysis, have an interpretation in terms of preferences over consumption streams, and *vice versa*.

The simplest case of intertemporal preferences is that of additive separability. For a consumption stream $C(t)$

$$V = \int_0^T \delta(t)\, U(C(t))\, dt\,, \tag{14.1}$$

where V is lifetime utility over an interval $[0, T]$, U is a 'short term' utility function and δ is a general specification for a pattern of discounting. For the discrete case, which will be presented

$$V = \sum_{i=1}^{n} \delta(t)\, U(C(t))\, dt\,. \tag{14.2}$$

Thus, V may be interpreted as an Expected Utility functional, with $\delta(t)$ being treated as a probability measure, or in the discrete case, a probability distribution. Hence, the usual stochastic dominance results apply. For example, the first stochastic dominance results of Chapter 2 may be applied by defining, for any level of consumption x, the cumulative function

$$G(x) = \int_{\{t:t \le x\}} \delta(t)\, dt. \tag{14.3}$$

A consumption stream $C^*(t)$ will be preferred to an alternative $C(t)$ for arbitrary monotonic U, if and only if $G^*(t) \le G(t)\ \forall\ t$. The corresponding results for second and higher degree stochastic dominance also carry over.

This translation of results may be regarded as unsatisfactory, because it is confined to a specific $\delta(t)$. In the random variables setting, this requires all individuals to have the same subjective probability distribution, an assumption which, although heroic, is usually made. In the intertemporal choice setting, the requirement is that all individuals should be equally impatient, and this assumption is not standard.

For an important sub-class of problems, the RDEU analysis presented here overcomes this difficulty. The class concerned is that for which $C(t)$ is non-decreasing in t. Consumption paths of this kind will emerge under perfect capital market conditions whenever the rate of return on capital is greater than the discount rate implicit in the function $\delta(t)$. This result is robust to the usual violations of perfect capital market assumptions, such as credit constraints, since these constraints normally affect the ability to bring consumption forward, but not the ability to postpone it. In this case we may define, for any consumption path $C(t)$, an inverse function $F_C(x) = C^{-1}(t)$.

For consumption paths increasing over time, temporal order and rank order coincide. It is now possible to treat the natural time measure F as the 'true' measure, and regard the discounted time measure G as a 'transformed' measure $q^\circ F$. As long as δ is a decreasing function of t, the associated transformation function q will be concave. Hence, Lemma 6.2 may be translated to yield

PROPOSITION 14.1: *The following conditions on two increasing consumption streams $C(t)$, $C^*(t)$ are equivalent.*
(i) *For all concave U and decreasing δ, $V(C^*(t)) \geq V(C(t))$*
(ii) $\int^x F_{C^*}(x)\,dx \leq \int^x F_C(x)\,dx \;\; \forall\, x$

By the Rothschild-Stiglitz analysis of simple mean-preserving spreads, condition (ii) will be satisfied whenever F_{C^*} is derived from F_C by changes which move consumption forward in time. Horowitz and Quiggin (1991) refer to this as a *mean-preserving advancement in consumption* and derive a number of results relating the theory of intertemporal choice to the theory of choice under uncertainty.

Stronger results can be obtained by imposing restrictions on U. In particular, it is common to confine attention to functions of the form

$$U(C) = \alpha/(1-\alpha)\, C^{1-1/\alpha} \quad \alpha \neq 1$$
$$= \log(C) \quad \alpha = 1,$$

corresponding to constant relative risk aversion for choice under uncertainty. The parameter α is interpreted as a measure of intertemporal substitution. Since all functions of this kind satisfy DARA, the results of Whitmore (1970) may be applied.

It is also possible to derive inferences for the theory of choice under uncertainty from consideration over time. In Chapter 6, the Allais approach to the RDEU model, based on the assumption of known cardinal utility of wealth, was discussed. Choices between known flows of income over time potentially provide a basis for inferring cardinal utility independent of choice under uncertainty. Suppose that these are additively separable, as in (14.2). Then, given a range of choices between known consumption streams, it is, in principle, possible to infer U and δ. Thus, sharp predictions could be made concerning the relationship between risk attitudes relating to outcomes and those relating to probabilities.

While this formal correspondence between choice over time and choice under uncertainty yields useful analytic results, more fundamental issues arise with the interaction between choice over uncertainty and choice over time. Machina (1984) has observed the difficulties associated with modelling temporal choice even when the underlying preference structure is that of Expected Utility. Pope (1990) has stressed the rôle of the waiting period between making a decision and the resolution of the associated uncertainty. An adequate account must incorporate both the sequential aspect of decision making, central to the debate over dynamic consistency, and the more properly dynamic aspect of choices made in real time. The closest approach so far is the work of Chew and Epstein, discussed in the following section.

14.4 Time and Uncertainty

The analysis of choice under uncertainty (including that presented in this book) is typically concerned with choices over lottery-type prospects which are assumed to be resolved instantly. An RDEU approach has been used by Chew and Epstein (1990) to model intertemporal choices under uncertainty. This work is the most important example of RDEU preferences where the outcome space is not an interval. Instead, Chew and Epstein consider outcomes that are infinite sequences of consumption levels $\boldsymbol{c}$. For given $\delta < 1$, they define the space $\ell_{++}(\delta)$ to consist of all strictly positive sequences such that $\sum_{t=1} \delta^t c_t < \infty$. They consider the space P of random variables of the form $(c_0, \boldsymbol{p})$ where c_0 is an initial level of consumption (known with certainty) and $\boldsymbol{p}$ is a probability measure over $\ell_{++}(\delta)$. Elements of P are referred to as consumption programs. A deterministic consumption program is given when $(c_0, \boldsymbol{c})$ is received with probability 1.

For a given deterministic consumption program $(c_0, \boldsymbol{c})$, utility is assumed to be given by an additively separable function of the form

$$U(c_0, \boldsymbol{c}) = u(c_o) + \textstyle\sum_t \beta^t u(c_t), \tag{14.4}$$

where β is a discount factor and U is a concave utility function. The RHS is well defined[30] whenever $\beta \leq \delta$. A given random variable (c_0, p) is associated with a cumulative distribution function

$$F_{(c_0, p)}(u; U) = Pr\{U(c_0, \boldsymbol{c}) \leq u. \tag{14.5}$$

The main difference between this problem setting and the usual problem with random variables taking values in $[0, M]$ is that the space of outcomes is no longer strictly ordered. For any given U, and program $(c_0, \boldsymbol{c})$ there will be a large class of programs

$$\{(c_0', \boldsymbol{c}'): U(c_0', \boldsymbol{c}') = U(c_0, \boldsymbol{c})\}.$$

To permit the use of a rank-dependent approach, it is necessary that only the rank ordering of outcomes matters. That is preferences must depend only on the cumulative distribution function of utility and not on the marginal distribution over programs yielding a given utility level.

---

[30] Chew and Epstein consider the case where U may take on the values $\pm\infty$. This exposition here will be confined to the case where U is finite.

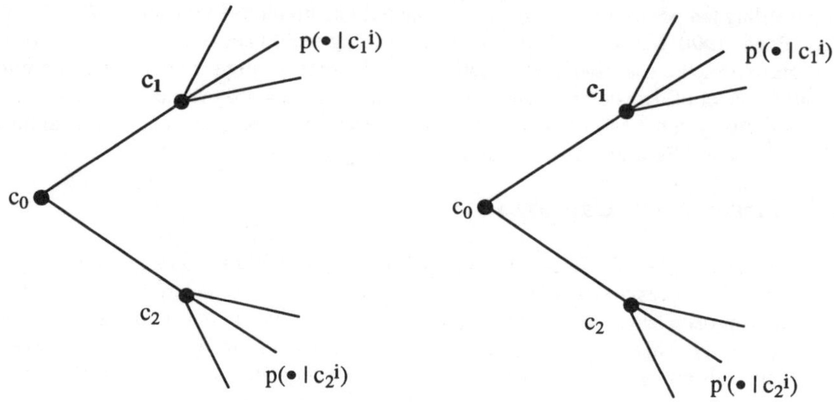

Figure 14.1: Recursivity

This is equivalent to axiom (EU.1), and incorporates the reduction of compound lotteries axiom. It is possible to select a representative program for each utility level. The natural choice is the set of stable consumption programs, satisfying $c_t = c_0, \; \forall \, t.$ Chew and Epstein also impose continuity and stochastic dominance axioms, which play a similar role to (EU.3) and (EU.4).

The final requirement is some form of independence axiom. Since preferences are given over paths of the form (c_0, p), the usual definition of a probability mixture is inappropriate. This would yield a probability distribution in which initial consumption was probabilistic. Instead, Chew and Epstein, in effect, identify the decision tree with the consumption path. The critical idea is that after the decision-maker has consumed c_0 and the uncertainty about consumption at $t = 1$ has been resolved, the structure of the problem remains unchanged. The decision maker now faces known consumption c_1 and a probability distribution p over the path $(c_2, c_3 \ldots)$. This pair is (isomorphic to) a member of P, with the obvious renumbering of time indexes.

Thus, we have the situation illustrated in Figure 14.1, where $p(\bullet \mid c_1^{\,i})$ is the probability distribution over $(c_2, c_3 \; \ldots\ldots)$ conditional on the realization c_1 for period 1 consumption. The equivalent to (EU.5) is the requirement that, in this situation, whenever

$$(c_1^{\,1}, p'(\bullet \mid c_1^{\,i})) \succcurlyeq (c_1^{\,1}, p'(\bullet \mid c_1^{\,i}))\; i = 1, 2, \tag{14.6}$$

it is also true that $(c_0, p') \succcurlyeq (c_0, p)$.

This requirement is usually referred to as *dynamic consistency*, and obviously corresponds to the notions of dynamic consistency discussed in Section 9.3. Chew and Epstein prefer the more neutral term *recursivity*. Given this assumption, preferences over P are represented by the usual additively separable EU functional

$$V = E_p[U(c_0, \mathbf{c})] = \int u \, dF_{(c_0, p)}(u; U). \tag{14.7}$$

There are a number of problems with this functional. In particular, the concavity of the utility function U is required to capture both aversion to risk and aversion to intertemporal variations in consumption. Chew and Epstein propose the following criterion of comparative risk aversion for preferences over P. They say that $\succcurlyeq^*$ is more risk averse than $\succcurlyeq$ if for all $(c_0, p) \in P$ and $\mathbf{c} \in \ell_{++}(\delta)$,

$$(c_0, \mathbf{c}) \succcurlyeq (c_0, p) \Rightarrow (c_0, \mathbf{c}) \succcurlyeq^* (c_0, p). \tag{14.8}$$

EU functionals derived from different utility functions cannot be compared in this way. The problem is that if the utility functions are different so are preferences over deterministic consumption paths. Hence, in particular there must exist deterministic paths $(c_0, \mathbf{c})$, $(c_0, \mathbf{c}')$ that violate (14.8).

Chew and Epstein propose to replace the recursivity requirement (14.6) with a weaker requirement, referred to as *stationarity*. This is the requirement that preferences be unchanged by the move from period 0 to period 1 whenever consumption in both periods is known in period 0. More formally, for all c_0, c_1, p, p', $(c_0, c_1, p') \succcurlyeq (c_0, c_1, p) \Leftrightarrow (c_1, p') \succcurlyeq (c_1, p)$. From (14.7), stationarity implies a requirement equivalent to Allais' postulate of cardinal isovariation, since a change in c_0 corresponds to an addition of utility to every state. It follows therefore that preferences may be represented by an RDEU functional

$$V = \int u \, dq^\circ F_{(c_0, p)}(u; U). \tag{14.9}$$

Consider preferences $\succcurlyeq^0$ and $\succcurlyeq^1$ representable by a common utility function U and transformation functions q and q^*. From the results of Chapter 6, $\succcurlyeq^1$ is more risk averse than $\succcurlyeq^0$ if and only if $q^1(p) \geq q^0(p) \; \forall \, p$. Chew and Epstein apply this notion to a study of consumption-savings behavior.

14.5 Framing and Coding

The problem of ambiguity, discussed in previous sections, may be put in a more general framework by the observation that, even when presented with explicit probability information, people do not necessarily choose solely on the basis of the relevant probability distribution. Rather they may code probability information in a manner that depends on the frame in which information is presented.

The classic example of framing is a problem posed by Kahneman and Tversky, concerning a choice of medical treatment for 600 patients. Treatment A will result (with probability 1) in 400 patients living and 200 dying. Treatment B is uncertain. With 1/3 probability all 600 patients will die. With 2/3 probability all 600 patients will live. Kahneman and Tversky present this information in two different ways. One group of respondents is told

Under treatment A, 400 patients will live with probability 1;

Under treatment B, there is a 2/3 probability that 600 patients will live and a 1/3 probability that none will live.

A second group of respondents is told

Under treatment A, 200 patients will die with probability 1;

Under treatment B, there is a 2/3 probability that no patients will die and a 1/3 probability that 600 will die.

With the first presentation, the majority of subjects choose treatment A, but with the second presentation a majority choose treatment B.

Kahneman and Tversky use the terms *framing* and *coding* to describe the processes by which people distil the information available to them into a form which can be used for decision-making. Although it does not coincide exactly with the usage of Kahneman and Tversky, the following distinction between framing and coding will be adopted. Framing will be used to refer to aspects of the problem setting, distinct from the probability distribution of the prospect under consideration, which affect the way in which the prospect is evaluated. Coding will be used to model the process by which information on the probability distribution is transformed so that it can be used for decision-making.

Although Kahneman and Tversky (1979) emphasized the importance of framing and coding effects, their prospect theory does not incorporate a formal representation of framing and coding, with the partial exception of reference point effects. Kahneman and Tversky argue that behavior will differ between problems which are treated as lying in the domain of losses and problems which are treated as lying in the domain of gains even if the associated probability distribution over final wealth is the same. Prospect theory incorporates this idea by using deviations from a reference wealth level, rather than levels of final wealth, as the carriers of value. However, the reference wealth level is not formally derived within the model. When initial wealth is certain, then the reference level is presumably equal to initial wealth, but this provides little guidance in the case when initial wealth is uncertain.

A number of other models of choice under uncertainty may be interpreted in terms of framing and coding. One is the reference prospect theory of Viscusi (1989). Despite its name, this model is not closely related to that of Kahneman and Tversky. Reference prospect theory may be regarded as a coding model. The idea is that probability information is combined, in a Bayesian fashion, with a diffuse prior, yielding a posterior distribution which is normally a probability mixture between the given probability distribution and a uniform distribution. Although this model has some unappealing features, notably an appeal to the principle of insufficient reason to produce the diffuse prior, the Bayesian updating process is of interest particularly for work on perception of hazards from pesticide residues in food and similar environmental problems.

There are a number of models of choice under uncertainty which do not rely on an evaluation functional defined over probability distributions. With a little more effort, these models may be interpreted in the context of framing and coding. For example, regret effects may be regarded as providing a frame which determines the coding of outcomes in different states on the basis of the alternative which might have been obtained by a different choice for that state. Changes in the choice set imply a change of frame which will alter the evaluation of a prospect. As with regret theory models in which frame changes are relevant will not, in general, preserve first stochastic dominance, since the same probability distribution may be evaluated differently (that is, have a different certainty equivalent) in different frames. However, as the example of regret theory illustrates, framing models may preserve weaker notions of stochastic dominance, such as statewise dominance.

The RDEU model may be interpreted as a coding model. Given an independently known cardinal utility function and information on a probability distribution, a number of simple coding systems could be considered. Individuals might take account of only the minimum and maximum outcomes, as in the focus loss and gain models advocated by Shackle (1952, 1968). They might code these values and the median into the associated triangular distribution. These, and other coding processes, may be interpreted as replacing the given probability distribution with a transformed distribution. As has already been noted, the RDEU model may be given precisely the same interpretation. The extension to framing may be made by supposing that the coding process depends on information extraneous to the derivation of probabilities.

It is now possible to present an analysis of the Kahneman-Tversky example in terms of the approach suggested here. Begin with three equiprobable states of nature, and denote outcomes by pairs (x_1, x_2) where x_1 is the number dying and x_2 is the number living. Treatment *A* yields the same outcome (200,400) in all states. Treatment *B* yields (0,600) in states 1 and 2 and (600,0) in state 3. Because zero is an origin for the natural numbers, there is a tendency to focus more on zero outcomes than other outcomes. The problem above illustrates this phenomenon. In this case, there is no natural zero. The first presentation leads respondents to regard the outcome when no patients survive as the zero outcome, leading to a high weight on state 3, and a consequent preference for treatment *A*. The second presentation leads respondents to regard the outcome when no patients die as the zero outcome, leading to a high weight on states 1 and 2, and preference for treatment *B*. A broadly similar, though more complex, account may be given of the more general phenomenon of risk preference in the domain of losses.

The Correspondence Principle derived in Section 7.2 is the principle tool that has been used to extend EU comparative static results to the RDEU case. This principle does not depend on the specific features of the RDEU model, but only on the fact that RDEU may be interpreted as EU applied to a transformed cumulative distribution function. The discussion here indicates that *any* coding process may be interpreted in this way, and hence that a version of the Correspondence Principle will apply for all coding processes. Of course the Correspondence Principle is empty in the absence of appropriate restrictions on the coding processes which guarantee the preservation of relevant relations between distributions, such as stochastic dominance and monotone spreads. Its role is to indicate a research agenda, namely the determination of these restrictions, which will yield the comparative static results for general coding processes.

A rather similar approach may be used for framing. For a given coding process, a change in frame may be treated as a change from one distribution to another. Hence, given knowledge on the type of change of distribution engendered by a given change in frame, the results of EU comparative static analysis may be applied to determine the effects of a change of frame.

This section has provided little more than a sketch of the treatment of framing and coding. Nevertheless, it appears that this seemingly intractable class of problems could be analyzed and incorporated within the standard framework of economic analysis.

References

Akerlof, G. (1970), 'The market for "lemons": Qualitiative uncertainty and the market mechanism', *Quarterly Journal of Economics* 84, 488-500.

Ali, M. M. (1977), 'Probability and utility estimates for racetrack betting', *Journal of Political Economy* 85(4), 803–15.

Allais, M. (1953), 'Le comportement de l'homme rationel devant le risque: critique des axioms et postulates de l'école Americaine', *Econometrica* 21(4), 503–46.

Allais, M. (1987), The general theory of random choices in relation to the invariant cardinal utility function and the specific probability function: The (U, θ) model – A general overview, Paris, Centre National de la Recherche Scientifique.

Allais, M. (1988), The general theory of random choices in relation to the invariant cardinal utility function and the specific probability function, pp. 233–289in Munier, B.(ed.), *Risk, Decision and Rationality*, Dordrecht, Reidel.

Allais, M. and Hagen, O. (eds). (1979), *Expected Utility Hypotheses and the Allais Paradox*, Reidel, Dordrecht, Holland.

Anderson, J., Dillon, J. and Hardaker, B. (1977), *Agricultural Decision Analysis*, Iowa State University Press, Ames, Iowa.

Anscombe, F. and Aumann, R. (1963), 'A definition of subjective probability', *Annals of Mathematical Statistic* 49, 453–67.

Arrow, K. (1951), 'Alternative approaches to the theory of choice in risk-taking situations', *Econometrica* 19, 404–437.

Arrow, K. (1963), 'Uncertainty and the welfare economics of medical care', *American Economic Review* 53(5), 941–73.

Arrow, K. (1965), *Aspects of the theory of risk-bearing*, Yrjo Jahnsson Lecture, Helsinki.

Arrow, K. (1974), *Essays in the Theory of Risk-Bearing*, North-Holland, Amsterdam.

Arrow, K. and Lind, R. (1970), 'Uncertainty and the evaluation of public investment decisions', *American Economic Review* 60(2), 364–78.

Asch, P. and Quandt, R. (1987), 'Efficiency and productivity in exotic bets', *Economica* 54(215), 289–98.

Atkinson, A. (1970), 'On the measurement of inequality', *Journal of Economic Theory* 2, 244–63.

Bailey, M., Olson, M. and Wonnacott, P. (1980), 'The marginal utility of income does not increase: Borrowing, lending and Friedman-Savage gambles', *American Economic Review* 70, 372–79.

Battaglio, R., Kagel, J. and Jiranyakul, R. (1990), 'Testing between alternative models of choice under uncertainty: Some initial results', *Journal of Risk and Uncertainty* 3(1), 25–50.

Bawa, V. (1975), 'Optimal rules for ordering uncertain prospects', *Journal of Financial Economics* 2(1), 95–121.

Bawa, V. (1982), 'Stochastic dominance: A research bibliography', *Management Science* 28, 698–712.

Becker, G., DeGroot, M. and Marschak, J. (1964), 'Measuring utility by a single-response sequential method', *Behavioral Science* 9, 226–32.

Bernoulli, D. (1954, first published 1738), 'Exposition of a new theory of the measurement of risk', *Econometrica* 22(1), 23–36.

Bertsekas, D. (1974), 'Necessary and sufficient conditions for the existence of an optimal portfolio', *Journal of Economic Theory* 8, 235–47.

Binswanger, H. (1981), 'Attitudes towards risk: Theoretical implications of an experiment in rural India', *Economic Journal* 91(4), 867–90.

Bird, R. and McCrae (1984), Gambling markets: A survey of empirical evidence, pp 114-122 in Caldwell, G., Haig, B. D.,Dickerson, M. and Sylvan, L.(eds.), *Gambling in Australia*, Sydney, Croom Helm.

Bond, G. and Wonder, B. (1980), 'Risk attitudes amongst Australian farmers', *Australian Journal of Agricultural Economics* 24(1), 16–34.

Borch, K. (1969), 'A note on uncertainty and indifference curves', *Review of Economic Studies* 36(1), 1–4.

Camerer, C. (1989), 'An experimental test of several generalized utility theories', *Journal of Risk and Uncertainty* 2(1), 61–104.

Camerer, C. and Ho, T. (1991), Nonlinear weighting of probabilities and violations of the betweenness axiom, Working Paper, Dept. of Decision Sciences, University of Pennsylvania.

Chateauneuf, A. and Cohen, M. (1991), Risk-seeking with diminishing marginal utility in a non-expected utility model, Working Paper, Université de Paris I.

Chew, S. (1983), 'A generalisation of the quasilinear mean with applications to the measurement of income inequality and decision theory resolving the Allais paradox', *Econometrica* 51(4), 1065–92.

Chew, S. (1989), An axiomatic generalization of the quasilinear mean and Gini mean with application to decision theory, Working Paper, Johns Hopkins University.

Chew, S. and Epstein, L. (1989), 'A unifying approach to axiomatic non-expected utility theories', *Journal of Economic Theory* 49(2), 207-40.

Chew, S. and Epstein, L. (1990), 'Nonexpected utility preferences in a temporal framework with an application to consumption-savings behavior', *Journal of Economic Theory* 50(1), 54–81.

Chew, S. and Nishimura, N. (1989), Differentiability, comparative statics and non-expected utility preferences, Working Paper, Johns Hopkins University.

Chew, S. and Waller, W. (1986), 'Empirical tests of weighted utility theory', *Journal of Mathematical Psychology* 30(1), 55–72.

Chew, S., Karni, E. and Safra, Z. (1987), 'Risk aversion in the theory of expected utility with rank-dependent preferences', *Journal of Economic Theory* 42(2), 370–81.

Choquet, G. (1953-4), 'Theory of capacities', *Annales Institut Fourier* 5, 131–295.

Coes, D. (1977), 'Firm output and changes in uncertainty', *American Economic Review* 67(2), 249–51.

Conlisk, J. (1987), 'Verifying the betweenness axiom or not: Take your pick', *Economics Letters* 25, 319–322.

Conlisk, J. (1989), 'Three variants on the Allais example', *American Economic Review* 79(2), 392–407.

Crawford, V. (1990), 'Equilibrium without independence', *Journal of Economic Theory* 50(1), 127–54.

Dardanoni, V. (1988), 'Optimal choice under uncertainty: The case of two-argument utility functions', *Economic Journal* 98(2), 429–50.

de Finetti, B. (1963), Foresight: Its logical laws, its subjective sources, in Kyburg, H. and Smokler, H.(ed.), *Studies in Subjective Probability*, New York, Wiley.

Debreu, G. (1952), 'A social equilibrium existence theorem', *Proceedings of the National Academy of Sciences* 38, 886–893.

Dekel, E. (1986), 'An axiomatic characterization of preferences under uncertainty: Weakening the independence axiom', *Journal of Economic Theory* 40, 304–18.

Dekel, E. (1989), 'Asset demands without the independence axiom', *Econometrica* 57(1), 163–9.

Diamond, P. and Stiglitz, J. (1974), 'Increases in risk and in risk aversion', *Journal of Economic Theory* 8(3), 337–60.

Drèze, J. (1982), The marginal utility of income does not increase:Comment, CORE Discussion paper 8231, Louvain.

Drynan, R. (1981), 'Risk attitudes amongst Australian farmers; Comment', *Australian Journal of Agricultural Economics* 25(1), 73–76.

Ebert, U. (1988), 'Rawls and Bentham reconciled', *Theory and Decision* 24, 215–223.

Edwards, W. (1953), 'Probability preferences in gambling', *American Journal of Psychology* 66, 349–64.

Edwards, W. (1954), 'Probability preferences among bets with differing expected values', *American Journal of Psychology* 67(1), 56–67.

Edwards, W. (1962), 'Subjective probabilities inferred from decisions', *Psychological Review* 69(1), 109–35.

Eeckhoudt, L. and Hansen, P. (1980), 'Minimum and maximum prices, uncertainty and the theory of the competitive firm', *American Economic Review* 70, 1064–68.

Ellsberg, D. (1961), 'Risk, ambiguity and the Savage axioms', *Quarterly Journal of Economics*

75(4), 643–69.

Feder, G. (1977), 'The impact of uncertainty in a class of objective functions', *Journal of Economic Theory* 16, 504–12.

Feldstein, M. (1969), 'Mean-variance analysis in the theory of liquidity preference and portfolio selection', *Review of Economic Studies* 36(1), 5–12.

Fishburn, P. (1978), 'On Handa's "New Theory of Cardinal Utility" and the maximisation of expected return', *Journal of Political Economy* 86(2), 321–4.

Fishburn, P. (1982), *The Foundations of Expected Utility*, Reidel, Dordrecht, Holland.

Fishburn, P. (1983), 'Nontransitive measurable utility', *Journal of Mathematical Psychology* 26(1), 31–67.

Fishburn, P. (1988), *Nonlinear Preference and Utility Theory*, Johns Hopkins, Baltimore.

Fishburn, P. (1989), 'Retrospective on the utility theory of von Neumann and Morgenstern', *Journal of Risk and Uncertainty* 2(2), 127–58.

Friedman, M. and Savage, L. J. (1948), 'The utility analysis of choices involving risk', *Journal of Political Economy* 56(4), 279–304.

Gallagher, P. (1978), 'The effectiveness of price support policy – some evidence of US corn acreage response', *Agricultural Economics Research* 30(4), 8–14.

Gilboa, I. (1987), 'Expected Utility with purely subjective non-additive probabilities', *Journal of Mathematical Economics* 16(1), 65–88.

Grant, S. (1991), Subjective probability without monotonicity:Or How Machina's Mom may also be probabilistically sophisticated, University of Melbourne.

Grant, S., Kajii, A. and Polak, B. (1992), 'Many good risks: An interpretation of multivariate risk and risk aversion without the independence axiom', *Journal of Economic Theory* forthcoming.

Green, J. (1987), '"Making book against oneself," the independence axiom and non-linear utility theory', *Quarterly Journal of Economics* 102(4), 785–796.

Green, J. and Jullien, B. (1988), 'Ordinal independence in non-linear utility theory', *Journal of Risk and Uncertainty* 1(4), 355–88.

Grether, D. and Plott, C. (1979), 'Economic theory of choice and the preference reversal phenomenon', *American Economic Review* 69, 623–38.

Griffith, R. M. (1949), 'Odds adjustments by American horse race bettors', *American Journal of Psychology* 62(2), 290–4.

Gul, F. (1991), 'A theory of disappointment aversion', *Econometrica* 59(3), 667–686.

Hadar, J. and Russell, W. (1969), 'Rules for ordering uncertain prospects', *American Economic Review* 59(1), 25–34.

Handa, J. (1977), 'Risk, probabilities and a new theory of cardinal utility', *Journal of Political Economy* 85(1), 97–122.

Hardy, G., Littlewood, J. and Polya, G. (1952), *Inequalities*, Cambridge University Press, Cambridge.

Harless, D. (1990), Predictions about unit triangle indifference curves inside the unit triangle: A test of competing decision theories, Drexel University.

Harsanyi, J. (1953), 'Cardinal utility in welfare economics and in the theory of risk taking', *Journal of Political Economy* 61, 434–435.

Harsanyi, J. (1955), 'Cardinal welfare, individualistic ethics and interpersonal comparisons of utility', *Journal of Political Economy* 63, 309–321.

Hayek, F. (1960), *The Constitution of Liberty*, Routledge and Kegan Paul, London.

Heisenberg, W. (1930), *The Physical Principles of the Quantum Theory*, (translated C.Eckart &F. Hoyt) Dover, , N.Y.

Herstein, I. and Milnor, J. (1953), 'An axiomatic approach to measurable utility theory', *Econometrica* 21, 291–97.

Hildreth, K. (1974), Ventures,bets and initial prospects, in Balch, M. M. D.(ed.), *Essays on Economic Behaviour under Uncertainty*, Amsterdam, North-Holland.

Hilton, R. (1988), 'Risk attitude under two alternative theories of choice under risk', *Journal of Economic Behavior and Organisation* 9(2), 119–36.

Just, R. (1974), 'An investigation of the importance of risk in farmers decisions', *American Journal of Agricultural Economics* 56(1), 14–25.

Just, R. (1975), 'Risk response models and their use in agricultural policy evaluation', *American*

Journal of Agricultural Economics 57(5), 836–43.

Kahneman, D. and Tversky, A. (1979), 'Prospect theory: an analysis of decision under risk', *Econometrica* 47(2), 263–91.

Karmarkar, U. (1974), The effect of probabilities on the subjective evaluation of lotteries, Working Paper No 698-74, MIT.

Karmarkar, U. (1978), 'Subjectively Weighted Utility: A descriptive extension of the expected utility model', *Organisational Behavior and Human Performance* 21(1), 61–72.

Karmarkar, U. (1979), 'Subjectively Weighted utility and the Allais paradox', *Organisational Behavior and Human Performance* 24(1), 67–72.

Karni, E. (1983), 'Risk aversion for state-dependent preferences: Measurement and applications', *International Economic Review* 24(3), 637–647.

Karni, E. and Safra, Z. (1987), '"Preference Reversal" and the observability of preferences by experimental methods', *Econometrica* 55(3), 675–85.

Karni, E. and Safra, Z. (1989), 'Ascending bid auctions with behaviorally consistent bidders', *Annals of Operations Research* 19, 435–46.

Karni, E. and Safra, Z. (1989), 'Dynamic consistency, revelations in auctions and the structure of preferences', *Review of Economic Studies* 56, 421–34.

Karni, E. and Safra, Z. (1990), 'Rank-dependent probabilities', *Economic Journal* 100(401), 487–95.

Kelsey, D. (1990), Dutch Book arguments and learning in a non-expected utility context, Australian National University.

Knight, F. (1921), *Risk, Uncertainty and Profit*, Houghton Mifflin, New York.

Koestler, A. (1965), *The Roots of Coincidence*, Picador, London.

Krantz, D., Luce, R., Suppes, P., Tversky and A. (1971), *Foundations of measurement, Volume I*, Academic Press, New York.

Lakatos, I. (1970), Falsification and the methodology of scientific research programmes, in Lakatos, I. M. and A.(ed.), *Criticism and the Growth of Knowledge*, Cambridge, Cambridge University Press.

LaValle, I. (1991), Small worlds and sure things: Consequentialism by the back door, in Edwards, W.(ed.), *Utility:Measurement, Theory and Applications*, Amsterdam, Kluwer, Nijhoff.

LaValle, I. and Wapman, K. (1986), 'Rolling back decision trees requires the independence axiom!', *Management Science* 32(3), 382–5.

Leland, H. (1972), 'Theory of the firm facing uncertain demand', *American Economic Review* 62(3), 278–91.

Lichtenstein, S. and Slovic, P. (1971), 'Reversals of preferences between bids and choices in gambling decisions', *Journal of Experimental Psychology* 89, 46–55.

Lichtenstein, S. and Slovic, P. (1973), 'Response-induced reversals of preferences in gambling: an extended replication in Las Vegas', *Journal of Experimental Psychology* 101, 16–20.

Lintner, J. (1965), 'The valuation of risky assets and the selection of risky investments in stock portfolios and capital budgets', *Review of Economics and Statistics* 47(1), 13–37.

Loomes, G. and Sugden, R. (1982), 'Regret theory: An alternative theory of rational choice under uncertainty', *Economic Journal* 92(4), 805–24.

Loomes, G. and Sugden, R. (1983), 'Regret theory and measurable utility theory', *Economics Letters* 12, 19–22.

Loomes, G. and Sugden, R. (1987), 'Testing for regret and disappointment in choice under uncertainty', *Economic Journal* 97(S), 118–29.

Luce, R. D. (1991), 'Rank- and sign-dependent linear utility models for binary gambles', *Journal of Economic Theory* 53(1), 75–100.

Luce, R. D. and Fishburn, P. (1991), ' Rank- and sign-dependent linear utility models in finite utility first order gambles', *Journal of Risk and Uncertainty* 4(1), 29-59.

Luce, R. D. and Narens, L. (1985), 'Classification of concatenation measurement structures according to scale type', *Journal of Mathematical Psychology* 29 (1), 1-72.

Luce, R. D. and Raiffa, H. (1957), *Games And Decisions*, John Wiley & Sons, New York.

MacCrimmon, K. and Larsson, S. (1979), Utility theory: Axioms versus paradoxes, in Allais, M. H. and O.(ed.), *Expected Utility Hypotheses and the Allais Paradox*, Dordrecht, Holland, Reidel.

Machina, M. (1982), '"Expected Utility" analysis without the independence axiom',

Econometrica 50(2), 277–323.
Machina, M. (1983a), The economic theory of individual behavior toward risk: Theory, evidence and new directions, Technical Report No. 433, Centre for Research on Organisational Efficiency, Stanford.
Machina, M. (1983b), Generalised expected utility analysis and the nature of observed violations of the independence axiom, in Stigum, B., and Wenstøp F.(eds.), *Foundations of Utility and Risk with Applications*, Reidel, Dordrecht, Holland.
Machina, M. (1984), 'Temporal risk and the nature of induced preferences', *Journal of Economic Theory* 33, 199–231.
Machina, M. (1987), 'Choice under uncertainty: Problems solved and unsolved', *Journal of Economic Perspectives* 1(1), 121–54.
Machina, M. (1989a), 'Comparative statics and non-expected utility preferences', *Journal of Economic Theory* 47(2), 393–405.
Machina, M. (1989b), 'Dynamic consistency and non-expected utility models of choice under uncertainty', *Journal of Economic Literature* 27(4), 1622–1688.
Machina, M. and Neilson, W. (1987), 'The Ross characterization of risk aversion: Strengthening and extension', *Econometrica* 55, 1139–49.
Markowitz, H. (1959), *Portfolio Selection: The Efficient Diversification of Investments*, Yale University Press, New Haven.
Marschak, J. (1950), 'Rational behavior, uncertain prospects and measurable utility', *Econometrica* 18, 111–141.
McCord, M. and de Neufville, R. (1983), Empirical demonstration that expected utility analysis is not operational, in Stigum, B., and Wenstøp, F.(ed.), *Foundations of Utility and Risk with Applications*, Dordrecht, Holland, Reidel.
Merton, R. (1973), *The Sociology of Science*, University of Chicago Press, Chicago.
Meyer, J. (1975), 'Increasing risk', *Journal of Economic Theory* 11(1), 119–32.
Meyer, J. (1977a), 'Choice among distributions', *Journal of Economic Theory* 14(2), 326–36.
Meyer, J. (1977b), 'Second degree stochastic dominance with respect to a function', *International Economic Review* 18(2), 477–87.
Meyer, J. (1987), 'Two-moment decision models and expected utility maximization', *American Economic Review* 77(3), 421–30.
Meyer, J. and Ormiston, M. (1983), 'Comparative statics of cumulative distribution changes for the class of risk-averse agents', *Journal of Economic Theory* 31(1), 153–69.
Meyer, J. and Ormiston, M. (1989), 'Deterministic transformation of random variables and the comparative statics of risk', *Journal of Risk and Uncertainty* 2(2), 179–88.
Mitchell, R. and Carson, R. (1989), *Using Surveys to Value Public Goods: The Contingent Valuation Method*, Resources for the Future, Washington D.C.
Miyamoto, J. M. (1988), 'Generic utility theory: measurement foundations and applications in multiattribute utility theory', *Journal of Mathematical Psychology* 32, 357–404.
Mosteller, F. and Nogee, P. (1951), 'An experimental measurement of utility', *Journal of Political Economy* 59, 371–404.
Nakamura, Y. (1992), 'Multi-symmetric structures and non-expected utility', *Journal of Mathematical Psychology* , forthcoming.
Newbery, D. (1970), 'A theorem on the measurement of inequality', *Journal of Economic Theory* 2, 264–66.
Newbery, D. and Stiglitz, J. (1981), *The Theory of Commodity Price Stabilisation – A Study in the Economics of Risk*, Oxford University Press, Oxford.
Ng, Y. K. (1965), 'Why do people buy lottery tickets?: Choices involving risk and the indivisibility of expenditure', *Journal of Political Economy* 73, 530–35.
Officer, R. and Halter, A. (1968), 'Utility analysis in a practical setting', *American Journal of Agricultural Economics* 50(2), 257–77.
Pommerehne, W., Schneider, F. and Zweifel, P. (1982), 'Economic theory of choice and the preference reversal phenomenon: A re-examination', *American Economic Review* 72, 569–74.
Pope, R. (1990), Rational people do not always prefer stochastically dominant prospects, Duke University.
Pope, R. D. and Just, R. (1977), 'On the competitive firm under production uncertainty',

Australian Journal of Agricultural Economics 21(2), 111–8.

Pratt, J. (1964), 'Risk aversion in the small and in the large', *Econometrica* 32(1), 122–36.

Prelec, D. (1990), 'A "pseudo-endowment" effect and its implications for some recent nonexpected utility models', *Journal of Risk and Uncertainty* 3(3), 247–60.

Puppe, C. (1990), 'Preference functionals with prize-dependent distortion of probabilities', *Economics Letters* 13(2), 127–31.

Quiggin, J. (1979), The theory of the multiproduct firm under uncertainty, Australian National University, B. Ec. Honors thesis.

Quiggin, J. (1981), 'Risk perception and risk aversion among Australian farmers', *Australian Journal of Agricultural Economics* 25(2), 160–9.

Quiggin, J. (1982a), 'A theory of anticipated utility', *Journal of Economic Behavior and Organisation* 3(4), 323–43.

Quiggin, J. (1982b), 'A note on the existence of a competitive optimum', *Economic Record* 55(161), 174–6.

Quiggin, J. (1985), 'Anticipated utility, subjectively weighted utility and the Allais paradox', *Organisational Behavior and Human Performance* 35(1), 94–101.

Quiggin, J. (1986), Anticipated Utility: Some developments in the economic theory of uncertainty, Ph. D. thesis, University of New England.

Quiggin, J. (1987), 'On the nature of probability weighting: Response to Segal', *Journal of Economic Behavior and Organisation* 8(4), 641–5.

Quiggin, J. (1989a), 'Sure things – Dominance and independence rules for choice under uncertainty ', *Annals of Operations Research* 19, 335–57.

Quiggin, J. (1989b), 'Stochastic dominance in regret theory', *Review of Economic Studies* 57(2), 503–11.

Quiggin, J. (1991a), 'Comparative statics for Rank-Dependent Expected Utility theory', *Journal of Risk and Uncertainty* 4(4), 339–50.

Quiggin, J. (1991b), Increasing risk: another definition, in Chikan, A.(ed.), *Progress in Decision, Utility and Risk Theory,* Amsterdam, Kluwer.

Quiggin, J. (1991c), 'On the optimal design of lotteries', *Economica* 58(1), 1–16.

Quiggin, J. (1991d), Uncontrolled gambling as a dynamic consistency problem, Working paper, Australian National University.

Quiggin, J. (1992), Regret theory – the general case, Australian National University, Working paper, Australian National University.

Quiggin, J. (1993), 'Testing between alternative models of choice under uncertainty – comment', *Journal of Risk and Uncertainty* , forthcoming.

Quiggin, J. and Anderson, J. (1981), 'Price bands and buffer funds', *Economic Record* 57(156), 67–73.

Quiggin, J., and Wakker, P. (1992), The axiomatic basis of anticipated utility theory, NICI, Nijmegen, Working paper.

Quirk, J. and Saposnik, R. (1962), 'Admissibility and measurable utility functions', *Review of Economic Studies* 29, 140–46.

Quizon, J., Binswanger, H. and Machina, M. (1984), 'Attitudes towards risk: further remarks', *Economic Journal* 94(1), 144–8.

Raiffa, H. (1961), 'Risk, uncertainty and the Savage axioms: Comment', *Quarterly Journal of Economics* 5(4), 690–5.

Rawls, J. (1971), *A Theory of Justice*, Clarendon, Oxford.

Reilly, R. (1982), 'Preference reversal: Further evidence and some suggested modifications in experimental design', *American Economic Review* 72, 576–84.

Robbins, L. (1938), 'Interpersonal comparisons of utility: a comment', *Economic Journal* 48(4), 635–41.

Roell, A. (1987), 'Risk-aversion in Quiggin and Yaari's rank-order model of choice under uncertainty', *Economic Journal* 97, 143–59.

Ross, S. (1981), 'Some stronger measures of risk aversion in the small and in the large with applications', *Econometrica* 49(3), 621–38.

Rothschild, M. and Stiglitz, J. (1970), 'Increasing risk: I. A definition', *Journal of Economic Theory* 2(4), 225–243.

Rothschild, M. and Stiglitz, J. (1971), 'Increasing risk: II. Its economic consequences', *Journal of*

Economic Theory 3(1), 66–84.
Safra, Z., Segal, U. and Spivak, A. (1990), 'Preference reversals and non-expected utility behavior', *American Economic Review* 80, 922–30.
Safra, Z., Segal, U. and Spivak, A. (1990), 'The Becker-DeGroot-Marschak mechanism and non-expected utility', *Journal of Risk and Uncertainty* 3(2), 177–190.
Samuelson, P. (1975), *Foundations of Economic Analysis (2nd ed)*, Harvard University Press, Cambridge, Massachusetts.
Sandmo, A. (1970), 'The effect of uncertainty on savings decisions', *Review of Economic Studies* 37, 353–60.
Sandmo, A. (1971), 'The competitive firm under output price uncertainty', *American Economic Review* 61(1), 65–73.
Savage, L. J. (1954), *Foundations of Statistics*, Wiley, N.Y.
Schlee, E. (1990), 'The value of information in anticipated utility theory', *Journal of Risk and Uncertainty* 3(1), 83–92.
Schmeidler, D. (1989), 'Subjective probability and expected utility without additivity', *Econometrica* 57, 571–87.
Segal, U. (1987a), 'Some remarks on Quiggin's Anticipated Utility', *Journal of Economic Behavior and Organisation* 8(1), 145–54.
Segal, U. (1987b), 'The Ellsberg paradox and risk aversion: An anticipated utility approach', *International Economic Review* 28(1), 175–202.
Segal, U. (1988), 'Does the preference reversal phenomenon necessarily contradict the independence axiom', *American Economic Review* 78, 233–36.
Segal, U. (1989), 'Anticipated utility: A measure representation approach', *Annals of Operations Research* 19, 359–74.
Segal, U. (1990), 'Two-stage lotteries without the independence axiom', *Econometrica* 58(2), 349–377.
Segal, U. and Spivak, A. (1987), 'Non-Expected Utility risk premiums: The cases of probability ambiguity and outcome uncertainty', *Journal of Risk and Uncertainty* 1(3), 333–347.
Segal, U. and Spivak, A. (1990), 'First-order versus second-order risk-aversion', *Journal of Economic Theory* 51(1), 111–25.
Segal, U., Spivak, A. and Zeira, J. (1988), 'Precautionary saving and risk aversion: An anticipated utility approach', *Economics Letters* 27, 223–27.
Shackle, G. (1952), *Expectations in Economics*, Cambridge University Press, Cambridge.
Shackle, G. (1968), *Expectations, Investment and Income (2nd ed)*, Oxford University Press, Oxford.
Sharpe, W. (1964), 'Capital asset prices: A theory of market equilibrium under conditions of risk', *Journal of Finance* 19, 425–442.
Sinn, H. (1983), *Economic decisions under uncertainty*, North Holland, Amsterdam.
Skinner, B. F. (1971), *Beyond Freedom and Dignity*, Knopf, N.Y.
Slovic, P. and Lichtenstein, S. (1968), 'The relative importance of probabilities and payoffs in risk taking', *Journal of Experimental Psychology* 78, 1–18.
Slovic, P., Fischoff, P., Lichtenstein, S., Corrigan, B. and Coombs, B. (1977), 'Preference for insuring against probable small losses: Insurance implications', *Journal of Risk and Insurance* 44(4), 237-58.
Smith, A. (1776, 1976), *The Wealth of Nations* , Clarendon, Oxford.
Starmer, C. and Sugden, R. (1987), Testing prospect theory, Economics Research Centre,School of Economic and Social Studies, University of East Anglia.
Stigler, G. (1982), Merton on multiples, denied and affirmed, in Stigler, G.(ed.), *The Economist as Preacher and other Essays*, Chicago, University of Chicago Press.
Stigum, B. and Wenstøp, F. (1983), *Foundations of utility and risk with applications*, Reidel, Dordrecht, Holland.
Tobin, J. (1958), 'Liquidity preference as behavior toward risk', *Review of Economic Studies* 25(1), 65–86.
Tversky, A. (1969), 'Intransitivity of preferences', *Psychological Review* 76(1), 31–48.
Tversky, A. and Kahneman, D. (1990), Cumulative prospect theory: an analysis of attitudes towards uncertainty and value, paper presented at FUR Conference, Duke University.
Viscusi, K. (1989), 'Prospective reference theory: Toward an explanation of the paradoxes',

Journal of Risk and Uncertainty 2(3), 235–64.
von Neumann, J. and Morgenstern, O. (1944), *Theory of Games and Economic Behavior*, Princeton University Press.
Wakker, P. (1988), 'Nonexpected utility as aversion of information', *Journal of Behavioral Decision Making* 1(1), 169–75.
Wakker, P. (1989a), *Additive Representations of Preferences, A New Foundation of Decision Analysis*, Kluwer Academic Publishers, Dordrecht.
Wakker, P. (1989b), Transforming probabilities without violating stochastic dominance, pp. 29–47 in E.E.Ch.I. Roskam (ed.), *Mathematical Psychology in Progress*, Berlin, Springer.
Wakker, P. (1990a), 'Under stochastic dominance Choquet- expected utility and anticipated utility are identical', *Theory and Decision* 29, 119–132.
Wakker, P. (1990b), 'Characterizing optimism and pessimism directly through comonotonicity', *Journal of Economic Theory* 52(2), 453–463.
Wakker, P. (1991a), Separating marginal utility and probabilistic risk aversion, Nijmegen.
Wakker, P. (1991b), A Criticism of Segal (1989) 'Anticipated Utility: A Measure Representation Approach', Nijmegen, The Netherlands.
Wakker, P. (1992), 'From finite- to infinite-dimensional integral representations; unbounded utility for Savage (1954) and others', *Mathematics of Operations Research* , forthcoming.
Wakker, P. and Tversky, A. (1991), An axiomatization of cumulative prospect theory, Nijmegen, The Netherlands.
Walker, M. (1984), Explanations for gambling, in Caldwell, G., Haig, B. D.,Dickerson, M. and Sylvan, L.(eds.), *Gambling in Australia*, Sydney, Croom Helm.
Wang, T. (1991), L^p Frechet differentiable preference and "local utility" analysis, University of Toronto.
Weymark, J. (1981), 'Generalized Gini inequality indices', *Mathematical Social Sciences* 1, 409–30.
Whitmore, G. (1970), 'Third order stochastic dominance', *American Economic Review* 50, 457–59.
Yaari, M. (1969), 'Some remarks on measures of risk aversion and their uses', *Journal of Economic Theory* 1(3), 315-29.
Yaari, M. (1984), Risk aversion without diminishing marginal utility, London School of Economics.
Yaari, M. (1986), Univariate and multivariate comparisons of risk aversion: a new approach, in Heller, W., Starr, R. and Starrett, D.(ed.), *Essays in Honor of Kenneth J. Arrow*, Cambridge, Cambridge University Press.
Yaari, M. (1987), 'The dual theory of choice under risk', *Econometrica* 55(1), 95–115.
Zeckhauser, R. and Keeler, E. (1970), 'Another type of risk aversion', *Econometrica* 38(5), 661–5.

Index of Names

Index of Topics